Running the Granite City

Local Government in Aberdeen
1975–1996

Kirsteen Davidson
John Fairley

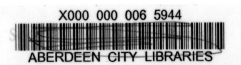

First Published 2000 by
SCOTTISH CULTURAL PRESS
Unit 13d, Newbattle Abbey Business Annexe
Newbattle Road
Dalkeith EH22 3LJ
Tel: 0131 660 6366 • Fax: 0131 660 6414
e-mail: scp@sol.co.uk • web: www.scottishbooks.com

BRITISH LIBRARY CATALOGUING IN PUBLICATION DATA
A catalogue record for this book is available from the British Library

ISBN: 1 84017 032 8

LO
352·041235

Printed and bound by First Impression, Edinburgh

Contents

Foreword

Lord Provost, Councillor Margaret Farquhar, JP

This book was commissioned by the former City of Aberdeen District Council. I am pleased now to welcome its publication on behalf of the new Aberdeen City Council.

The book was commissioned for two reasons. The first was to mark the end of a very important period for the City and its local government. The 1975–96 period was the only one when Aberdeen developed under two tiers of local government, the City district and the Grampian Regional Council. And this was of course the period when the oil industry had such a major impact on the City and its people, requiring the local authorities to respond to new pressures and to work in new ways. It was important that this period be marked in some way, and the writing of a book by two academics who were not directly involved, and therefore who were able to be more objective, seemed to be ideal.

However, the second reason may be even more important, and it is this which gives this book its very unusual and unique style. The council asked John Fairley and Kirsteen Davidson to try to make the complex business of local government as simple to understand as they could and to make their book as interesting as possible. Local authorities now face a great challenge to help their citizens to know and understand local government and to get involved in its workings. This book is a unique contribution to meeting that challenge in Scotland. I believe that it will help people to understand how local government has developed in the City, how it makes its decisions, and its impact on the community. This book fits in very well with the Council's determination to improve access for Aberdeen's citizens.

I would like to commend this book to you. Interested citizens, school and college pupils will find a lot of information in it, much of which was not previously available. Many senior officials and councillors will learn from it. People elsewhere in Scotland may find interest in how we've done things in the 'Granite City'.

Introduction

The idea for this book came from a discussion between John Fairley and the then Lord Provost of the City of Aberdeen District Council, Councillor James Wyness. We felt that it was important to mark the passing of the Wheatley era in a way which provided a record and which was also open and accessible to interested citizens.

The project became one of producing a short book which would offer an account of local government in Aberdeen in the 1975–96 period focusing on the role of the City District Council. The book would outline the evolution of local government in the city, place modern local government in the context of economic and social change, set out the breadth and complexity which local government had achieved by the mid-1990s, and do all of these things in a style which was as open and jargon-free as possible.

We relied on a number of sources to produce this book. The few pages which cover the history of the City up to 1850 draw on Alexander Keith's *A Thousand Years of Aberdeen* (Aberdeen University Press, 1987). We worked from District Council archives, departmental records and minutes. The first major difficulty was that of selecting from the mountain of available information. This book is certainly not the last word on local government in the City!

We interviewed a large number of elected politicians and officials (some retired). These interviews gave us a range of insights into the evolution of the District Council, and the key events of the 20 year period. We were fortunate in that for every chapter appropriate senior officials volunteered to read our drafts. This helped to confirm our analyses, and as a check on the factual information presented in the book.

Most important of all was our volunteer 'Reading Committee'. This consisted of Frank Donnelly, Denis Sangster and Fay Robinson. They read our drafts trying to take the perspective of the 'interested citizen' who did not have specialist inside knowledge of local government. Their comments were invaluable to the project and influenced many parts of the book. Jacqueline Beattie's work on the preparation of the manuscript was invaluable. We were grateful to Jill Dick of Scottish Cultural Press for helping to knock the manuscript into shape.

The selection and presentation of material, the analyses and the views expressed in this book are the responsibility of the authors.

The Authors

Kirsteen Davidson is a lecturer in the School of Public Administration and Law at the Robert Gordon University in Aberdeen. John Fairley is Professor in the Department of Environmental Planning at the University of Strathclyde in Glasgow.

Abbreviations used in the text

The worlds of local and central government are full of acronyms. We tried wherever possible to avoid their use; however the following appear in the text:

AET	Aberdeen Enterprise Trust
CCDA	City Centre Development Area
CCT	Compulsory Competitive Tendering
DSM	Devolved School Management
EU	The European Union
GEL	Grampian Enterprise Limited
GRC	Grampian Regional Council
MSC	Manpower Services Commission
NESDA	North East Scotland Development Agency
NESJPAC	North East Scotland Joint Planning Advisory Committee
NESTA	North East Scotland Tourist Association
NHS	National Health Service
RGIT	The Robert Gordon Institute of Technology
RGU	The Robert Gordon University
SDA	Scottish Development Agency
SE	Scottish Enterprise
SEPA	Scottish Environmental Protection Agency
SH	Scottish Homes
SNH	Scottish National Heritage
SSC	Scottish Sports Council
STUC	Scottish Trades Union Congress
UN	United Nations
UNICEF	United Nations Children's Fund

Acknowledgements to the following interviewees and people who gave
assistance:

Councillor Brian Adam, ADC
Councillor Gordon Adams, ADC
Norman Adams, ADC
Councillor Yvonne Allan, ADC
Councillor Robert Anderson, ADC
Bert Allen, ADC
Lesley Bale, Aberdeen Airport
Jacqueline Beattie, Robert Gordon University
Barclay Braithwaite, Aberdeen Harbour Board
Councillor Rita Buchan, ADC
Leslie Brown, ADC
Councillor John Brown, GRC
Alan Campbell, GRC
Bill Chalmers, formerly ADC
Councillor Cecil Clevitt, ADC
David Cockburn, GRC
Peter Cockhead, GRC
Judith Cripps, ADC
Frank Donnelly, ADC
Councillor James Donnelly, ADC
George Duffus, ADC
Councillor Margaret Farquar, ADC
Bob Findlay, ADC
Dr Howard Fisher, GRC
Councillor William Fraser, ADC
Hance Fullerton, Grampian Enterprise Limited
Alan Fulton, ADC
Councillor Richard Gallacher, ADC
Fiona Gardiner, ADC,
Ian Gerrie, ADC
Ray Gibson, ADC
William Glennie (B control), ADC
Jimmy Graham, formerly GRC
Peter Grant, formerly ADC
Frank Hartnett, Grampian Health Board
Bill Howie, Voluntary Services Aberdeen
Councillor Sheila Henderson, ADC
Gordon Henry, Grampian, Highlands and Aberdeen Tourism Marketing
   Company

Councillor Maureen Irons, ADC
Councillor June Lamond, ADC
Firemaster Sandy Lobban, Grampian Fire Brigade
Councillor John Logan, ADC
Robert Loughridge, ADC
Alexander McConnachie, ADC
Donald McDonald, ADC
Councillor Pamela MacDonald, ADC
Ian McAdam, GRC
Ian McKay, GRC
Roger McKechnie, ADC
Bob Mann, ADC
Derek Marnoch, Aberdeen Chamber of Commerce
Councillor Tom Mason, GRC
Councillor Charles Massie, ADC
Anne Mearns, ADC
Eric Melrose, GRC
Councillor Robert Middleton, GRC
Councillor Nanette Milne, ADC
Alan Morrice, ADC
Walter Murray, Aberdeen City Centre Partnership
Jim Pratt, ADC
Councillor John Porter, GRC
Councillor Henry E Rae, ADC
Elizabeth Reinach, ADC
Councillor Shauna Reith, ADC
Archie Robb, GRC
Fay Robinson, ADC
Denis Sangster, ADC
Councillor Malcolm Savidge, ADC
Mike Scott, ADC
Murray Scott, ADC
Bert Smith, ADC
Councillor Margaret Smith, ADC
Tom Steele, ADC
Jeremy Taylor, Grampian Health Care
Alan Towns, ADC
Councillor George Urquart, ADC
Lynn Warren, ADC
Councillor Maureen Watt,
Nikki Webster, GRC
Chief Superintendent Wilkie, Grampian Police
Councillor James Wyness, ADC

1: The Development of Local Government

Introduction

This book is concerned with the very recent history of the City of Aberdeen, in particular the two decades between the reorganisations of local government in 1975 and 1996. In this period the city experienced rapid and fundamental change. Local government had to respond to these changes and provide the community with leadership and vision.

The local government structures which were created by the reforms of 1975 were placed on very deep foundations. The available records of local government in Aberdeen stretch back to the thirteenth century. These records provide a fascinating account of the development of Aberdeen from its humble beginnings to its present day position as one of Scotland's foremost cities with a unique place on the world stage as 'The Oil Capital of Europe'. And they also show how the city has been governed during the different stages of its development. Throughout most of this history the government of the city was in the hands of small and generally self-perpetuating elites. This was the pattern of the Scottish burghs. Democratic pressures grew in the eighteenth century and made their first significant impression in the reforms of the 1830s. Modern local government, providing local services within a democratic framework, really emerged in the twentieth century.

A number of factors helped to shape local government in the city. Some of these affected all of Scotland's cities whilst some were unique to Aberdeen. Among these were the emergence of the burgh as a key local government unit, industrial growth and urbanisation, the extension of the franchise, growing demands for services such as education, health and housing, the creation of the Scottish Office, the growth of party politics at local level, and the discovery and commercial exploitation of oil.

The Evolution of the Burgh

At the beginning of the twelfth century, Aberdeen was little more than a village with fewer than two thousand inhabitants. Around 1179, a Charter granted by William the Lyon to the Burgesses of 'Abedeon' confirmed the right of trading 'when and where they pleased'. By this time Aberdeen was already a trading community of some importance and, as a Royal Burgh, had a corporate existence and power to manage its own affairs subject only to the Burgh Laws. The town

11

received two other Charters around 1196, and these are still in existence. They granted immunity from all tolls and customs in markets and fairs throughout Scotland. But the most important change was the establishment of a Merchant Guild which was to control the Burgh for the next few centuries.

The establishment of the Burghs was a very significant event in the development of local government. The Burghs' particular responsibilities lay in providing law and order and overseeing trade. As trade grew in the sixteenth and seventeenth centuries, so did the number of Burghs and by the beginning of the eighteenth century over three hundred had been established in Scotland. As a Royal Burgh, Aberdeen enjoyed a relatively powerful and prosperous position in Scotland and was able to send a representative to the Scottish Parliament. The Burghs remained a core unit of local administration until the reforms of 1975.

Merchant Guild and Craft Guild

Aberdeen was divided into four 'Quarters' – Futty, The Green, Even and Crooked – with a Baillie responsible for each Quarter. In addition to Alderman and Baillies, a Common Council was drawn from the Burgesses of the Guild whose responsibility it was to guard the laws and customs of the Burgh. These twelve Burgesses were known as 'Dusane' and are generally considered to be the origin of the modern Town Council.

Aberdeen was governed by a few families who, by virtue of their status as Burgesses and members of the Merchant Guild, were able to preserve for themselves the function of electing Aldermen, Baillies, Deans of Guild and Common Council. It wasn't just that the Craftsmen Burgesses were excluded but also that the vast majority of the population had no say in either local or national affairs.

The distinction between Merchant and Craft Guilds was as important in Aberdeen's development as it was throughout Scotland. Only Burgesses of the merchant class could exercise real power within the Burgh; all others were 'Unfreemen' with no say in the affairs of the town. The distinction between Merchant and Craft Burgesses provided a source of deep division. On the one hand, Craftsmen had all the financial burdens of being a member of the Burgess class. On the other hand they had none of the political influence that the Merchant class exercised. In Aberdeen the Craftsmen were allowed to elect representatives to vote at the election of Provost and Baillies, although they could not themselves become members of the Council.

Towards the end of the fourteenth century, reforms took place in the government of the town, including the introduction of elections for Alderman, Baillies and Common Council. A new code of conduct was formulated to govern municipal conduct and procedure. New financial rules were introduced which provided controls on the handling of the Burgh's finances, confined the handling of the rents to the Baillies, limited the term of office of Alderman, Baillies and

Office bearers to one year, and tightened up on the council's supervision of markets and food shops. In addition to the Alderman and Baillies, other Burgh officials in medieval Aberdeen included the Dean of Guild, whose responsibility it was to maintain and enforce trade regulations and standards; a Master of Works, who was responsible for building works and repairs, care of the Burgh tools and supervision of the burgh workmen; the Burgh Clerk, who kept the town's records; a Fiscal, with responsibility for legal prosecutions, assisted by 'Officers' who maintained peace and provided the guard for the Tolbooth; Burgh inspectors of various sorts, for example ale-testers, fish and flesh prisers (an early form of meat or fish inspector); and Lineators, who checked the Burgh boundaries to ensure that they provided adequate protection. The burgh also employed the Hospital Master, Kirk Master and Master of Shoreworks, an executioner, a drummer, and numerous other minor officials. Local government was becoming a complex business.

The Burgh was dependent on taxes levied on property and on trade tolls and customs paid by incomers to the town's markets. Royal Burghs were required to pay the Crown in return for their trading privileges. The first measure of financial independence for Aberdeen came in 1319, when Robert the Bruce gave to the Burgesses and community ownership of the Burgh itself together with the Forest of Stocket. The Common Good Fund had its origins in these early developments.

The most important duty of any town council was the protection of the burgh. Aberdeen was geographically isolated and relied on the good graces of neighbouring landlords for its protection. The city also took its own measures making each Burgess responsible for 'watch and ward' under pain of banishment. Every citizen had to keep two weapons ready at all times in readiness for the alarm being rung on the Tolbooth bell. The unsettled years following the accession of the Stewarts to the Scottish Crown, served to strengthen the authority of the burgh rulers and the importance of defence.

The Struggle for a Voice in Local Affairs

The most important group demanding change were the Craftsmen. They had growing economic power but were unable to gain entrance to local administrative power. The Craftsmen were able to obtain a few concessions which gave them a voice, albeit a faint one, in local affairs. In 1469 an Act described as 'the most damning Act of the Scottish Parliament', made Burgh Councils self-electing, effectively denying the Craftsmen a say in local affairs. But the struggle for a say in local affairs continued and eventually in 1560, the Crafts were able to send a representative to vote in the election of the town's office bearers. Matters came to a head once again in 1587, resulting in a conference in Aberdeen to try and resolve the position. Agreement was finally reached in August. The Crafts were permitted annually to choose six of their members for the leet from which members of the Council were elected, and two had to be on the board of auditors chosen by the Council to examine the burgh accounts. However, they were not eligible for election to the offices of Provost, Baillie, Dean of Guild or Treasurer, until they had been admitted as a Burgess of Guild and in order to achieve that they had to renounce their Craft.

In 1596 the Convention of Royal Burghs introduced further changes. Two craftsmen of the old council, two of the new and six deacons formed the 'Set' which governed the election of municipal office bearers until the Burgh Reform Act two and a half centuries later in 1833.

Industrialisation

At the beginning of the seventeenth century, the population of the town was around eight thousand, and the town had changed little in appearance since its early development as a Burgh. There was little in the way of sanitation, and famine and plague were common problems. Apart from the use of the Common Good Fund to purchase supplies for the poor in times of famine, and draconian measures to isolate the town in time of plague, there was little in the way of municipal intervention to relieve suffering. This was a situation which prevailed until the rapid growth in industry in the eighteenth and early nineteenth centuries required more radical reforms.

By the beginning of the nineteenth century, Aberdeen had a thriving textile industry with the emergence of such notable local firms as Alexander Hadden and Sons and Crombie Knowles and Co. (later J and E Crombie) employing around two thousand people in mills and factories. Other industries such as paper making, brewing, and comb manufacturing flourished. At the heart of the city lay the harbour, which had remained largely unaltered until the Aberdeen Harbour Act of 1770 allowed for the construction of a new pier and other improvements. This led to the transformation of the harbour into a thriving commercial and fishing port employing over two thousand seamen by the 1820s. They were employed in a variety of enterprises including fishing and trade with England and Europe. When the first Register of Shipping was introduced in 1820, Aberdeen was the principle shipbuilding centre in Scotland. Growth in industry led to a dramatic increase in business and commercial activity within the city.

Political Reform

Change in local administration was slow and tended to lag behind economic progress. In the last decades of the eighteenth century there was growing discontent at the handling of the town's affairs by the Provost and Magistrates, and suspicion about the handling of public funds. This was not peculiar to Aberdeen as corruption was widespread in the burghs and economic growth put the essentially medieval structure of local government under considerable strain. The Town Council, which had previously been preoccupied with law and order and trade, was required to respond to complex challenges of urban development which were industrial, political, social, scientific and technical in nature.

In the 1780s the town's Burgesses discussed the reform of civil administration. The Aberdeen Police Act of 1795 provided the first significant reform of the administrative process. It provided for 'the better paving, lighting, cleansing and otherwise improving the Streets, Lanes, and other Publick Passages of the City of Aberdeen...for the better supplying of the Inhabitants with fresh water, and for the removing and preventing of all obstructions and annoyances within the said City and Royalty'. The Act resulted in some improvements to the administration of the Burgh and in the range and level of services provided in the city.

The Burgh Reform Acts of 1833 and 1834 were the first serious attempts to alter the administrative structure of local government in Scotland. They began the process of democratising local government. Householders who paid a rateable value of £10 gained the right to elect Town Councils. In Aberdeen only 3.5% of the population were enfranchised but the idea that more people could be given the right to vote was established.

The reforms authorised the adoption of a 'police system' and the election of 'Commissioners of Police', extending Aberdeen's Police Act of 1795. Commissioners levied rates for the purpose of watching, lighting, paving and cleansing the streets, improvement of water and gas supplies, and the prevention of infectious diseases. They regulated slaughterhouses, apprehended vagrants, and named and numbered streets and houses.

In 1862 the Burgh Police Act allowed for new police burghs to be set up. The reform increased burgh autonomy, but the approach was essentially pessimistic. It was rooted in the view that the elitist ancient town councils were so corrupt as to be beyond reform. New structures were needed to bypass them. This parallel system of local administration lasted until the end of the nineteenth century, eventually giving way as democracy was extended.

As local administration grew and was modernised, and as the franchise was extended, the power of the burghs grew. Their responsibilities changed as Parliament gave them new roles. They were seen as a fourth estate after the law, the churches and the boards which ran the poor law system. The Convention of Royal Burghs rivalled the churches providing a national voice for Scotland. It was the Convention's campaign which led to the setting up of the Scottish Office and the establishment of the position of Scottish Secretary in 1885.

In 1868, the franchise was further extended. The Scottish universities were put on the same footing as those in England and two parliamentary seats were allocated to them. Edinburgh and St Andrew's shared one seat and Aberdeen and Glasgow the other. Campaigns for democratic reform led to a gradual process which increased the electorate.

In 1869, women householders obtained the vote for local elections. In 1884, the franchise was extended to all adult males. The 1918 Representation of the People Act gave the vote to women over the age of thirty. In 1928, adults over twenty-one years of age were allowed to vote and women were fully enfranchised. In the late 1960s the voting age was lowered to 18, which is the current position. Generally the extension of democracy at local level followed similar reforms to Westminster.

In order to cope with the additional demands that were being placed on local government by industrial expansion and growth in population, Parliament created a number of new authorities to run some local services. By the end of the nineteenth century, the system of local government in Scotland consisted of 200 Burgh Councils, 33 County Councils, and 869 Parish Councils. There were also a number of other authorities delivering local services including County Roads Boards and Burgh and Parochial School Boards.

In 1918, a rationalisation of local government took place with around 1,000 School Boards being replaced by 38 directly elected Education Authorities. In 1929, the Local Government (Scotland) Act abolished Parish Councils, District Committees, Standing Joint Committees and the old Royal, Parliamentary and Police Burghs. They were replaced by four Counties of Cities, including Aberdeen, 33 County Councils, 21 Large Burghs, 176 Small Burghs and 196 District Councils. Each level had responsibilities set out in statute.

In the new structure, Aberdeen, Glasgow, Edinburgh and Dundee became all-purpose councils. The view in the main cities was that a simple and effective system of local government had been put in place. However in much of Scotland the reform left a complex system in place. There were fewer councils but many of those left proved too small. As communities demanded better services and better local government these weaknesses were increasingly exposed.

In 1975, Aberdeen and the rest of mainland Scotland was given a two-tier system of local government. The City of Aberdeen District Council was responsible for a number of important local services including housing, environmental services and local planning. The Grampian Regional Council was responsible for the more costly education, social work and roads programmes and for strategic planning over a very large area which stretched from the river North Esk to the Moray coast.

The 'Granite City'

The dramatic increase in the population of Aberdeen by the beginning of the nineteenth century made expansion outwith the old medieval boundaries of the burgh imperative. New housing was built on what had been the outskirts of the town and new streets were constructed within the city boundary. Thriving suburbs sprang up around the town on land which had been feued by the town council to private developers. Within the town, it became clear that the old medieval streetscape could no longer cope with the rising level of traffic into the town and to the developing outlying areas.

The response to this problem was the Aberdeen New Streets Act of 1800, which led to the construction of the city centre as it largely exists today. The scheme which was intended to open up the city centre was conceived by Charles Abercrombie, a road engineer and surveyor. Central to the plan was the creation of Union Street. This began in 1801, the city's main street being named after the Union of the British and Irish Parliaments.

The construction of Union Street was a major feat of civil engineering. It entailed the removal of St Katharine's Hill and the erection of a series of arcades and viaducts stretching from Adelphi in the east to Diamond Street further west. The old medieval heart of the city rapidly disappeared under the new construction and today very little remains.

The reconstruction of the town centre was an ambitious project for the city's council. Between 1817 and 1825 the Burgh could not meet the interest charges on the huge loans raised to finance the project and was brought to the brink of bankruptcy. A delegation of the city's councillors was called before a special committee of the House of Commons in order to explain their handling of the city's finances. The unexpected and fortuitous boom in trade that followed the Napoleonic Wars helped to rescue Aberdeen from financial ruin.

A new straight exit from the town centre to the north, ultimately linked to the Ellon turnpike road was built with the completion of King Street in 1830. Access to the Inverurie turnpike and to the west was achieved through the construction of George Street. Each year from 1800 onwards, new streets were constructed and new public buildings completed – the city itself was gradually being opened up.

In 1850 the first train reached Ferryhill station, the terminus for the city until 1854 when Guild Street came into use. Railways brought a revolution in communications and great economic benefits to the city by improving access to the hinterland and to other parts of the country. Two railway companies operated between London and Aberdeen, and in August 1895 they held a race: The Caledonian Railway Company won completing the 541 miles between London Euston and Aberdeen in 8 hours 32 minutes. The arrival in Aberdeen of horse drawn trams in 1874 provided access to the developing areas of the town and the tramway system was taken over by the Corporation in 1898. The last tram completed its journey to Woodside in 1958. The omnibus which had first appeared in Aberdeen in 1921, and an increase in the use of the car, opened up all areas of the city.

New buildings often required new sites. In the newly opened up areas of the city, this was not a problem but, in the city centre, sites had to be cleared. Aberdeen's Town House was opened in 1872. The magnificent building was built on land gained by clearing the homes of the poor and other buildings on the site. When eviction notices were served on the tenants of Huxter Row, one petitioned the Council to allow him to remove 'the almost indispensable commodit, my water closet' which 'would be of very little use to the said gentlemen, but might be very useful to me'.

A number of other equally splendid buildings were built including an Art

Gallery in 1883, a Public Library in 1892 and His Majesty's Theatre in 1902. Granite from the city quarries of Loanhead, Dancing Cairns, Sclattie and Rubislaw was used in the construction of the new town and in the creation of the 'Granite City'.

Many outlying areas of the city had originally been outwith the burgh boundary, but hey were annexed as the need grew for new land for housing, industry and commerce. In the early 1860s the population of the burgh was around 74,000, straining the old boundaries, and boundary extensions in 1871 added some areas to the south around the Dee estuary. In 1883 the area of the burgh was more than doubled by incorporating Woodside, Old Aberdeen and Torry.

By 1881, a direct route to Torry was opened with the building of Market Street and the Victoria Bridge. Two years later access to the north-west of the town was improved with the completion of Rosemount Viaduct. Affluent suburbs grew up along Queen's Road, Great Western Road, King's Gate and Rubislaw. Tenement buildings were erected in Rosemount and Union Grove. The development of the city was towards the north and west, a trend which continued until the second half of the twentieth century.

The growing population, the modernisation of the city, the needs of industry and other factors created needs for new types of service. Health, infrastructure, housing and education became priorities, and these came to shape the modern role of local government in service provision.

Public Health

The benefits of a clean and sufficient water supply were recognised by the Police Commissioners in 1794 when improvements were made to the city's water supply. After 1854, when it was acknowledged that contaminated water was a key factor in the spread of cholera, the first major step was taken to modernise the water supply. In 1862 a Private Bill was passed which enabled the Town Council to tap the River Dee upstream of the town at Cairnton and convey the water via a nineteen mile long aqueduct from Cairnton to Springbank. The same Act gave the Council power to make all houseowners whose homes were within ten yards of a water pipe introduce water for a sink and water closet. Additions and alterations were made to the water supply in the following years to keep up with the ever increasing demands of the city.

The creation of a modern sewerage system in the 1860s was vital to the improvement in the public health. In the early nineteenth century, the sewerage system of Aberdeen comprised a number of sewers running eastwards along Union Street and down into the Denburn together with a number of other privately-owned sewers. In 1862 parliamentary authority was obtained to make provision for a proper sewerage system, but it was not until the completion of the Cairnton water scheme that it became possible to undertake the project. In 1871 control passed to the Town Council. In 1899 major changes were made to the system which enabled discharge into Nigg Bay. Further powers were sought in 1935 in order to add to the sewerage network.

The first infirmary in Aberdeen opened in 1742 at Woolmanhill. It was extended within eight years, and received a Royal Charter in 1773. A new building was erected on the site in 1840, and extended in 1887. A mental hospital opened at the beginning of the nineteenth century, a vaccine institution in 1803, and a blind asylum in 1843. The Public Health (Scotland) Act of 1867 gave local authorities powers to deal with infectious diseases and in 1877 a fever hospital was established on the site of what is now the City Hospital in Urquhart Road. Five years later a separate Sanitary Department was set up within the Council under a Medical Officer of Health.

Other improvements in medical care came with the opening of the Eye Institute in 1835, a maternity hospital in 1874, and the Sick Children's Hospital in 1877, the last two of these were both originally located in Castle Terrace. These and a number of other institutions provided the core of medical provision in the city until the end of the nineteenth century. The idea that the state and local government should be involved in the provision of a free and comprehensive medical service was somewhat slower to develop. Free medical treatment was viewed as only necessary for the poor. Hospital provision for those who could not afford to pay for treatment was often administered within the Poorhouse.

Social Welfare

Each parish was responsible for its own poor, but it became clear that the system could no longer cope with the increasing demands being placed upon it. Various organisations attempted to alleviate poverty including Friendly Societies, the Co-operative Society and some trade unions, all of which offered assistance to those in need. Local philanthropy played a role. The Aberdeen Sick Man's Friendly Society, a public soup kitchen and local coal funds were available in Aberdeen. The Poor Law Act of 1845 brought social welfare partly within the remit of local government. A central Board of Supervision was set up in Edinburgh for the administration of the poor law in Scotland and there were inspectors of the poor in each parish. The Act also recommended that poorhouses should be built in all large cities and that poor relief should be paid from local rates. There were two main aims of the Poor Law: to enable local authorities to administer to the needs of the aged and infirm, and to furnish a test for poverty. It was in its second aim that the Act achieved most success, as the poorhouse was seen as a deterrent and a place to be feared – very much a last resort for those in need. Charitable organisations provided most of the few social services available.

A sense of history – the entrance to the Town House

Housing

In nineteenth-century Aberdeen, as in the other Scottish cities, housing was the most acute social problem. In Scotland in the 1870s over 70% of families lived in two rooms or less. The failure of the market to meet housing need led directly to the local authority role.

Aberdeen built its first council houses during the 1890s, but the housing role really began to develop after 1919 when Lloyd George's coalition government passed legislation which conceded the principle of state subsidies to local authority housing to provide servicemen returning from the First World War with 'Homes Fit for Heroes'. Aberdeen Corporation was able to provide over six thousand new homes in a ring of estates around the city in Torry, Ruthrieston, Middlefield, Woodside, Hilton and Seaton, as well as improving almost two thousand older properties in the city centre.

By the late 1940s over eight thousand houses were built. By the mid-1950s, the worst of the post-war housing problems seemed to have been overcome, and the corporation's attention turned to dealing with the poorest of its housing stock. In the following two decades the emphasis shifted to the clearance of slum areas and the rehousing of the inhabitants in new estates and developments around the city. In its most successful house-building period, the Corporation took pride in building more than 1,000 new homes each year. This era established housing as the local government service which mattered most to people and which dominated the enquiries made to councillors.

After 1979, Conservative governments changed the emphasis of housing policy. Tenants were enabled to buy their properties at substantial discounts – a policy which proved popular with those in the better houses – and the local authority landlord role declined. However, in 1995, ADC still remained the largest landlord with 32,000 properties – about a third of the entire city stock – although as its landlord role declined a new one emerged for it as strategic leader by trying to bring together all housing providers to ensure that the city's needs were met.

Planning

Modern active town planning emerged from legislation of 1909, and burghs began to control the use of land and buildings. In 1933 the Aberdeen and District Joint Planning Scheme was set up. The Corporation, and Aberdeen and Kincardine County Councils came together to exercise control over the area surrounding Aberdeen. A Plans and Town Planning Committee was appointed by the Town Council in order to plan the central area of the City. Great advances were made in road improvements, in urban amenity with the establishment and preservation of public and private open spaces, in the planned development of new buildings and in the preservation of buildings of special historic or architectural interest.

The Town and Country Planning (Scotland) Act 1947 extended these powers and placed on the local planning authorities an obligation to prepare development plans for their areas. The Corporation was ahead of the field already preparing a comprehensive planning survey and development plan. 'Granite City' was published in 1952 and it strongly influenced planning in Aberdeen for the next four decades.

In 1975, the strategic planning role passed to the Regional Councils. The District Councils provided local plans within this wider framework. The oil industry brought intense development pressures with it and the new planning system was far from ideal. There was some friction between ADC and Grampian Regional Council (GRC), but also a lot of co-operation. Within the two-tier system, ADC was able to see through major developments including three modern shopping centres, industrial estates, and the preservation of historic buildings.

Education

Aberdeen had a long and rich tradition with two universities, a Grammar School, Robert Gordon's Hospital and a number of other minor schools. The local authorities built a close relationship with the education sector. Industrialisation and urbanisation led to education being seen as essential social investment rather than simply moral or religious instruction. The need to modernise education led to schooling becoming a local government responsibility.

The Education Act of 1872 brought most schools into the state system. School Boards were established and compulsory education was introduced for five to twelve year olds. Secondary education still had to rely on fees and endowments and remained the preserve of the middle classes who could afford to educate their children. The Education Act of 1908 provided some state grants which helped to open up secondary education to the working classes. In 1929 School Boards and separate Education Authorities were abolished. Responsibility for the provision of education passed to County Councils and the four Counties of Cities including Aberdeen.

In the 1960s schools were reorganised on comprehensive lines in a reform which had consensus support in Scotland. By the mid-1970s almost all public sector schools were comprehensive. Local authorities were extremely important in the successful implementation of this major reform. Education became the most costly council service, accounting for more than 45% of local authority expenditure. In 1975 education was made a regional responsibility, with the GRC the education authority for Aberdeen. The local authority role was focused on schools and further education colleges, the latter being removed from council control in 1992. Community education, adult education, nurseries and a range of other services were also provided.

Libraries

Several reading rooms and libraries were established, the most notable of which was the Athenaeum. In 1884 following public demand, plans were put in place for the establishment of a public library. In 1885 Aberdeen had its first public library when the Mechanics' Institute in Market Street was handed over to the town council, to be replaced a few years later by a purpose built public library on Rosemount Viaduct.

In 1975, libraries were made a district responsibility. There were seventeen branch libraries and some mobile services. ADC invested in the service and modernised the Central library – Aberdeen's library service came to be recognised as one of the best in Scotland.

Leisure and Recreation

Improvements in urban amenity began with the opening of Victoria Park in 1871, Union Terrace Gardens a year later and the Duthie Park in 1883. At the same time community provision of recreational facilities was expanded with the opening of the art gallery in 1883, a new public library in 1892, and His Majesty's Theatre in 1906. Early recreational facilities were provided by the donations of local benefactors or by the Town Council.

The local government role developed after the Second World War but was not firmly grounded in legislation until the 1980s. ADC developed a range of facilities including His Majesty's Theatre, the Music Hall and the Lemon Tree; Aberdeen established a reputation as a 'festival city', regularly hosting music, youth and football festivals. Leisure and recreation were developed to help the tourist industry and the local economy. A range of indoor and outdoor sports facilities was provided, and ADC developed its twinning links with cities in Europe and Africa to promote cultural exchanges

Towards a Welfare State

Legislation in the opening years of the twentieth century laid the foundation of the welfare state by introducing social services outside the Poor Law to help those in need. Old age pensions and national insurance, which had been introduced in 1911, were extended following the First World War as the newly enfranchised electorate began to make it known that they were not prepared to return to their pre-war standard of living. In 1929 local government took over responsibility for the administration of the poor law and a more constructive approach to social welfare. Widespread unemployment and poverty resulting from the economic recession of the 1930s put considerable strains on the services provided by local government.

The Second World War heightened the determination not to return to the appalling unemployment and poverty of the 1930s. In 1942 the Beveridge Report laid the groundwork for a planned welfare state to tackle the social problems of 'ignorance, squalor, disease, idleness and want'. The report recommended that the poor law be replaced by a more humane system of national assistance, as a 'safety net' in times of hardship. There was a commitment to full employment and a belief that unemployment would become a very minor problem. The National Assistance Act of 1948 transferred welfare services for the elderly, homeless and handicapped to local authority welfare departments. A National Health Service was established to provide free health care to all citizens. Scottish Office control of this service was established in 1948 and this led to some reduction in the local authority role. In child welfare, the Children's Act of 1948 created new children's departments to care for those who were 'deprived of a normal home life'. A third arm of the social services, the probation service, developed independently.

In the 1950s a more comprehensive approach was taken with the introduction of generic social work qualifications. In 1968, the Social Work (Scotland) Act brought together the range of social services. Local authorities set up social work departments. An innovative children's hearing system followed in 1971. In 1975 social work responsibilities passed from the corporation to the GRC.

Local Government Reform

The structure of local government which had been set up in 1929 had barely had a chance to settle down when the depression of the 1930s put considerable strains on the social services. Following the Second World War, the basis of the modern welfare state was laid. The post-war government decided that some local authorities were too small to run basic services. Some of these were transferred to non-elected agencies and Government departments – for example National Assistance, hospitals, electricity and gas – whilst education, child welfare, the police and fire services were given to local authorities. The role and functions of local government had changed dramatically since 1929, but the structure was largely unaltered.

In the 1960s the need for change seemed clear. It was generally believed that larger administrative units would provide more efficient local government but concern was also expressed at the effect this might have on local democracy. In 1966 the government commissioned a major review of local government under the chairmanship of Lord Wheatley. This was the most thorough enquiry ever carried out into the structure and operation of local government.

The Wheatley Report was published in 1969. It concluded that local government was not working efficiently. Its structure was fragmented and old fashioned, and out of step with society's changing needs. Some services had grown to such an extent that they could no longer be accommodated within small local authorities. Society needed local government to increase its scope and powers and new structures were needed to accommodate this change.

The Commission identified four general aims:

Power – Local Government should be able to play a more important, responsible and positive part in the running of the country, in order to bring the reality of government nearer to the people.

Effectiveness – Local Government should be equipped to provide services in the most satisfactory manner, particularly from the point of view of the people receiving the service,

Local Democracy – Local Government should constitute a system in which power should be exercised through the elected representatives of the people and in which those representatives are locally accountable for its exercise.

Local Involvement – Local Government should bring the people into the process of reaching decisions as much as possible, to enable those decisions to be made intelligible to the people.

The Wheatley Commission supported the concept of the 'city region', arguing that 'the distinction between town and country cannot be maintained'. It took the view that the city and its surrounding area were dependent on each other. It recommended a major restructuring of local government with the introduction of a two tier system on mainland Scotland. The report also recommended that community councils be established to act as a voice for local people.

The reforms came into force on 16 May 1975. Nine regional councils were set up to provide 'strategic services' such as education and social work, fire, police, water and industrial development on a larger and more efficient scale. The GRC provided strategic services for Aberdeen. Fifty-three district Councils were set up to provide a range of local services – in particular, housing, local planning, leisure and recreation, environmental services and the provision of public libraries and museums. The City of Aberdeen District Council was one of these. In Orkney, Shetland and the Western Isles single councils provided all services. The small, all-purpose island councils were to provide the model for the next shake-up twenty years later.

For the first time in its history Aberdeen was administered by two local authorities: the GRC (which also covered the new district areas of Moray, Banff and Buchan, Kincardine and Deeside and Gordon) and the City of Aberdeen District Council. The City district covered the area of the outgoing Corporation of the City of Aberdeen, together with the electoral divisions of Bucksburn, Newhills landward, Old Machar, Stoneywood and the parishes of Dyce and Peterculter (all formerly within the county of Aberdeen) and the electoral division of Nigg (formerly within the county of Kincardine).

Aberdeen vigorously opposed these changes in the consultation period before the Act. The corporation repeatedly argued for all-purpose status for Scotland's four main cities. It argued that the cities had a large enough population and financial base to deliver the full range of local government functions themselves. However, the case for all-purpose status was not accepted and Scotland's four cities were made responsible for the same limited range of functions as the other districts. In Aberdeen the new council continued to use its traditional coat of arms.

The two-tier system was never an easy one to operate, though the effectiveness of councillors and officials made it successful in very many ways. Local government became much more professional under the Wheatley system. Each tier successfully managed service innovations and improvements. Problems sometimes emerged in areas where responsibilities were shared and where partnership was required. The regional councils, with control of 'strategic services' and the lion's share of the budget, always tended to see themselves as more important than the districts. The cities and the other districts with long traditions of local government resented this. The first council elections in the new system produced a Labour administration in ADC and a Conservative GRC, which perhaps didn't help a good partnership to get off the ground. However, elsewhere in Scotland, where the same political party controlled both tiers, relations between districts and regions were not always good.

The public never fully understood the system which was not helpful to its effectiveness or to local democracy. Twenty years after the change, regional councillors found that they were still receiving lots of letters and phone calls about housing, even though that was made a district responsibility in 1975!

The Wheatley Era

The Corporation of the City of Aberdeen, when it closed for business on 15 May 1975, served a population of 181,000 and covered an area of approximately 19.77 square miles. The next day the new City of Aberdeen District Council started up, serving a population of around 208,000 in an area extending to 71 square miles. For the majority of the population within the city little or no difference could be seen in the services they received. Yet the new council was a vastly different organisation from the Corporation with fewer functions, a larger administrative area and an entirely new local government system. The twelve months of planning and preparation carried out by ADC over 1974/75 produced a new committee and departmental structure, based on the new range of functions and duties.

Governments continued to monitor and redefine the role of local government. Numerous pieces of legislation were introduced to alter powers, management and structures. The Stodart Committee reported in 1981 that the two tier system was generally working well. Once again it rejected calls for single tier local government in the cities. It recommended that recreation and leisure, countryside matters and nature conservation, tourism and the supporting of community councils be made the sole responsibility of the districts.

Not all public services were provided by local authorities. Some were defined and delivered as national services and others were delivered by local non-elected bodies. Health services were provided by the National Health Service through Grampian Health Board and then by two autonomous Trusts. A range of social and personal services was delivered by voluntary organisations. In 1991 Grampian Enterprise Limited became the local economic development and training provider for Scottish Enterprise. The Chamber of Commerce was also very active in these areas. Scottish Homes was set up as the government's housing agency; housing associations provided some low cost housing and tenant's co-operatives emerged to manage housing estates. The local authorities serving Aberdeen worked in close co-operation with these bodies to ensure the provision of an adequate public services and to influence their plans.

In the 1960s, Aberdeen, along with the rest of Scotland, was suffering from economic decline. The discovery of oil in the North Sea in the late 1960s dramatically altered the city's economic fortunes. Within a few years the city became known as 'The Texas of the North' and 'The Oil Capital of Europe' and a new phase in Aberdeen's development began. During the 1970s and '80s, the city had to respond to the demands placed upon it by a rapidly growing industry. There was an unprecedented demand for the provision of land and infrastructure and substantial growth in the use made of the city's harbour and airport. The impact on planning and housing was particularly severe, but great pressure was placed on all the services provided by ADC and GRC.

During the Wheatley era a revolution took place in information and communication technologies. This had not been foreseen by the architects of the local government system yet it affected every aspect of local government activity. It affected people's expectations and created new opportunities for the design, delivery and consumption of services. It also provided new opportunities for the involvement of citizens.

2: Local Democracy and Leadership

The concept of local democracy is relatively recent in the history of local government. Most of that history is one of local administration overseen by small and usually self-perpetuating elites. Pressures for democratic change were expressed by reformers particularly from the late eighteenth and early nineteenth centuries. In the 1830s the gradual process of extending the franchise began. Generally the democratic reform of local government followed similar changes to the system at Westminster. Eventually all adults over eighteen were 'given the vote' in local, national and European elections, and in occasional referenda.

Democratisation provided a second set of pressures to local government. On the one hand it had to respond to changing social needs in the services which it provided and the ways in which these were managed. On the other it had to make itself function more democratically. The two sets of pressures concerned reformers and ensured that the world of local government became one of change. While local government was generally successful in achieving high service standards in the 1975–95 period, the 'democratic agenda' proved more difficult.

The extension of the right to vote meant that local government became democratically as well as financially accountable through these processes. Citizens elected a group of local people to oversee the delivery of services and the government of their community. The number of elected councillors for the city grew from 48 in 1974 to 52 in 1992. In principle this group could be removed from office by the electorate if they failed to live up to expectations or keep pre-election promises. In practice democratic accountability was often weak. A combination of low voter turnout and strong local identification with particular political parties made many seats effectively impregnable. At local level though, councils were the only institutions which had this democratic link with communities and could lay claim to this modern form of accountability.

Frequently the electorate did change things. Seats on the council changed hands and sometimes the political colour of the administration changed. Aberdeen was run by Labour administrations throughout the 1975–1995 period, with the exception of a short period in 1987–88 when a Conservative and Liberal–Democrat coalition took over the reins. The Labour Party won the six district elections held in the city between 1974 and 1992. In a sense Aberdeen fitted in with the Scottish pattern in this respect. In 1984 Edinburgh was taken by Labour and from then urban local government in Scotland was dominated by that party in Scotland's four main cities.

In north east Scotland the GRC provided an interesting contrast. It was won initially by the Conservatives who formed the 1975 administration. In the period up to 1995, Labour, the Liberal–Democrats and the Scottish Nationalists each took their turn, singly or with a coalition partner, in running the council. Similarly the north east's seat in the European Parliament passed through the hands of the parties. The Conservatives won the seat in 1979 and 1984 with James Provan as their candidate. In 1989, the seat was won by the Labour candidate, Henry McCubbin, who then lost it to the SNP's Dr Alan McCartney in 1994.

The Structure of the Wheatley System

The Wheatley reform reduced the number of Scottish councils from 430 to 65. It also substantially reduced the number of councillors across Scotland. In 1975, ADC had 48 councillors and there were twenty city divisions of the GRC. By 1992, it had 52 councillors, while the number of regional councillors representing city divisions remained at twenty. From 1975 onwards, councillors had to represent constituencies which were generally a little smaller than before but which had only one councillor in each. The representational workload increased considerably. The creation of the new unitary Aberdeen City Council in 1995 saw a further reduction in the number of local elected politicians. The new council had fifty members, of which thirty were Labour, ten Liberal Democrat, nine Conservative and one Scottish National Party.

The fundamental belief of the Wheatley system was that fewer, larger councils would be more rational and effective in their planning, and more economical and efficient in their activities. In other countries similar debates on how to balance efficiency and democracy led to very different local government systems. In countries throughout Europe, in North America and in Japan, local government units were typically smaller than in Scotland. For example, in Denmark, Norway, Italy and France, the average population size of local authorities was 18,000, 9,000, 7,000 and 1,500 respectively. The idea that a city the size of Aberdeen should have only one level of elected local government would not find favour in many other advanced countries.

Local Elections

Prior to 1975 there were two local electoral systems in operation. Elections to burgh councils, including the Corporation of the City of Aberdeen, took place annually, with one third of the elected representatives of the council retiring each year. In the counties, elections took place every third year with the entire council retiring at once. Each system had its supporters.

The Wheatley Commission was keen to strengthen local democracy. It looked at the issue of local elections and found that 67% of seats were not contested. The turnout of voters averaged 47%. The Commission viewed this state of affairs as 'inconsistent with a healthy democratic system'. The research seemed to show that when elections were held annually, as in the burghs, voter turnout tended to be low. The Commission took the view that elected local authorities required time to formulate a programme and to carry it out, and that electors required time in order to judge whether a council's policies were satisfactory. Democratic accountability had an appropriate time-frame which annual elections would not serve well.

The new regional and district councillors were given a four year term of office. Regional/island and district elections alternated with an election taking place every two years. It was believed that this would give local authorities sufficient time to formulate and implement their policies. It would also keep local government firmly in the minds of the electorate without the potential for confusion that simultaneous regional and district elections would bring. Democratic accountability would be strengthened.

The Wheatley recommendations provided the basis for elections to local government in Scotland until the 'shadow elections' for the current set-up in 1995. The first elections to the Wheatley councils were held in 1974, and after 1980 elections were held every four years. Elections to the City of Aberdeen District Council were held in 1974, 1977, 1980, 1984, 1988 and 1992, and elections to the GRC were held in 1974, 1978, 1982, 1986, 1990 and 1994. A shadow election for the new, unitary Aberdeen City Council was held in 1995.

The Wheatley Commission wanted a local government system which would interest and even excite the electorate to the point where people would seek to become involved in some way. In this area it did not succeed. Local elections in Scotland did not capture the public's imagination to the same extent as General Elections and voter turnout was generally low. Neither the Wheatley reforms nor the 'take-over' of local politics by the big parties fundamentally changed levels of voter participation.

The emergence of party politics in local elections during the latter half of the twentieth century certainly resulted in more wards being contested but it did not significantly improve overall electoral turnout. The number of candidates contesting city council elections grew unevenly during the period. In 1977, 113 candidates contested 48 seats. By 1988, boundary adjustments and population change had increased the council to 52, and these seats were contested by 192 candidates.

Initially it appeared that the Wheatley reform might have made local politics more popular. Around 50% of the electorate voted in the 1974 elections, but the improvement was short lived. In 1977 the overall turnout for the City of Aberdeen District Council elections was only 36%. There was a slight increase to 38% in 1980 but generally voter participation was poor. High turnouts seemed to be associated with local controversies, high-profile candidates, or particular contests between candidates. These were the exceptions rather than the rule.

In this Aberdeen was no better and no worse than other parts of Scotland or Britain, and the problem of low voter turnout was shared in North America and in Japan. The contrast appeared to be provided by Europe where in many countries turnout was considerably better. The growing interest taken in Europe by Scottish local authorities was much more focused on accessing funds and influencing decisions than on learning how other countries manage their democratic systems.

There are probably many reasons for low voter turnout. Within the Wheatley system it quickly became clear to voters that while the district councils were closer to their communities than the larger regions, it was the regions which controlled the bulk of the expenditure and the larger services. This meant that the regions were more visible to the public and that they got more media attention. In elections in the 1990s voter turnout was generally a little higher in some regional elections than in urban districts.

Throughout Scotland many instances of poor relationships between district and regional councils emerged, even where the same political party controlled both levels! The consequent lack of co-operation and the occasional bickering between councils may have been a 'turn off' for some voters. Sometimes the media seemed to take it upon themselves to attack local government, though this was perhaps less true in Scotland than in the south of England. Certainly local authorities at times provided 'easy targets'.

It was difficult to make local government exciting when it was so much the creature of central government. Wheatley envisaged local authorities growing in power and scope. However, in the 1975–96 period local government was considerably reduced in power and discretion. By the end of the Wheatley system local government income and expenditure were tightly controlled by the Scottish Office. On average Scottish councils raised less than 15% of their costs through the Council Tax. It was easy to blame low turnout on voter apathy, but why should people vote in elections for councils which lacked power and autonomy? Some critics argued that voter interest and accountability were both undermined by the high level of financial dependence on central government.

In the context of weakened local government it was hardly surprising that the electorate took much more interest in national issues. This perspective was perhaps strengthened by the growth of local control by the major political parties which worked to national programmes and priorities. The press and media tended to focus on the national issues. Local government issues made the front pages only when there seemed to be a whiff of scandal.

The Wheatley system may inadvertently have weakened aspects of local accountability, in so far as the device of alternating elections sometimes created a situation where voters expressed their views about a district council in elections at regional level, and vice versa. In 1994, for example, some Aberdeen Labour councillors believed that their party lost control of GRC because of the bad publicity received by ADC when its Chief Executive left under a cloud.

The statutory basis, growing professionalism amongst the officials, and changing service technologies all tended to make local government complex. The division of labour between regions and districts was never fully grasped by the public. The language in which council business was conducted and recorded was often obscure and old-fashioned. Generally the Wheatley councils saw it as their job to get on and do rather than to simplify and explain. In 1981, somewhat ahead of the field, ADC adopted a 'plain English' policy. The council records showed a marked improvement from about that time, but it proved a difficult policy to monitor. Some departments did better than others and those which were required, like planning or housing, to consult the public, did best. And while 'plain English' brought improvements, 'plain' was not always 'simple'!

Public Participation

The Wheatley Commission wanted to improve elective democracy and also to encourage citizens to participate in the working of local government. However attempts to involve voters in the life of the councils were piecemeal. Councils generally did not approach this part of the Wheatley reform in a comprehensive or strategic way. Here and there, now and again, citizens as service users would be brought into contact with officials and councillors through consultation processes, advisory procedures and management arrangements. However, involving citizens was not seen as a general council issue, and its potential for improving local democracy was not widely recognised.

In the 1970s and 1980s the principle of 'representative' democracy was widely accepted but this was not the case for emerging ideas of 'participative democracy'. In the former elected representatives take decisions and oversee policy implementation on behalf of the electorate. In participative models these processes take place and in addition ways are sought to involve people in the processes of government in between elections. The main political parties in Britain were more comfortable with traditional concepts of representation. At local level many councillors thought that too much involvement might be a bad thing because it could undermine their representative role. In 1969 the Wheatley Commission observed that 'success in increasing public participation is almost always the result of hard work and imaginative enterprise.' But most of the councils in the two-tier system neither worked hard nor showed enterprise in this area.

Nevertheless useful experiments were made and valuable experience was gained. There were housing initiatives where tenants and council architects worked together on plans. Aberdeen City's 'Planning for Real' initiative involved hundreds of people in discussing the future of the Bridge of Don area. Special mechanisms were set up to consult with disabled people so that their particular needs could be taken into account, but progress in involving people was patchy and piecemeal. In the mid-1990s, as the Wheatley system was nearing its end, there was much more acceptance that democracy would be improved by involving citizens in the work of councils, and that this needed to be addressed by councils as a strategic priority.

In addition to district and regional council elections, there were some other limited opportunities for the local community to vote or to be represented. The 1973 Act required district and islands councils to establish community councils in their areas. Community councils were not given clear responsibilities and they were not set up in every area. By 1995, twelve community councils had been set up in Aberdeen, but generally they did not excite much public interest.

Representatives of religious interests and teachers served as members of the regional council education committees alongside elected councillors. In 1988 the School Boards Act introduced the election of boards consisting of parents, teachers and co-opted members. The boards were advisory with only a very limited responsibility for certain aspects of school management. The arrangements for school board elections were made by the regional councils as education authorities. These too failed to excite the community. Not all schools wanted boards, and often the willing volunteer was 'elected' without any opposition. In Aberdeen, in 1996, 52% of primary schools and 77% of secondary schools had their own board. Between them these boards did permit 419 citizens to play a role in the education service.

In other services user groups were set up. A number of sports facilities user groups, and tenant participation groups were established. Planning and housing had statutory consultation procedures. From time to time the public would be asked its views about the council and its services. In 1993/4, ADC carried out a fairly extensive survey of the level of satisfaction with council services. These devices helped citizens and service users to voice concerns and hopes about local services. They helped to keep the council in touch with the public in between elections, and to identify real ways in which services could be improved.

Equal Opportunities

On 8 May 1984, the ADC took a historic decision to create a new standing committee to be known as the Women's Committee and became the third Scottish council to take this step. Councillor Nikodem was the committee's first convener.

The development of local authority women's committees was controversial. It reflected a growing view that government structures did not adequately involve women or meet their needs. Ensuring greater equality for women was considered to be central to the project of modernising democracy itself.

The formation of the committee reflected the Labour administration's concern to promote equality and its feeling that new, more focused structures were required. The committee's broad objectives were to promote the welfare and interests of women in the city; to implement policies which would promote equal opportunities for women in the council's employment and elsewhere in the city; and to work towards the abolition of discrimination against women.

The great majority of councillors across the political parties supported these aims in some way. However, the decision to set up a separate and relatively high profile committee proved controversial. A number of attempts were made to change the committee's name to the 'Equal Opportunities Committee' on the grounds that this would better demonstrate the breadth of the council's commitment to equality. The supporters of the original concept successfully resisted this attempt. They felt that a dedicated and high profile committee was needed to give some impetus to the campaign for equality for women and that decades of a 'softly softly' approach hadn't achieved much. And they considered that some of those who would change the name were actually trying to undermine the policy.

The council budget was finalised by the time the Women's Committee was formed. The budget planning process had made no provisions for the new committee and in its first year it had no resources. In 1985/86 its first budget was £98,100, a small sum compared with traditional and established committees, but enough to get the new programme started.

One of the committee's first tasks was to decide how Aberdeen should mark the UN Decade for Women which was to be celebrated in June 1985. A series of events were held, and an Aberdeen Woman of the Year Award was launched. Women's achievements and contributions to society often went unnoticed, and the award was a small contribution towards redressing that balance. Each year councillors were asked to suggest a theme for which an outstanding woman could be identified. Sometimes the chosen theme produced more than one winner. On its tenth anniversary in 1995, a record number of six women shared the award in recognition of their outstanding contributions to community life. Three of the winners – Pat Spanswick, Ena Dickson and Pearl Corstophine – were honoured for their contribution to the Torry 500 Festival, an event which celebrated the 500th Anniversary of the grant of a Royal Charter to Torry. The remaining three winners – Chrissie Bruce, Pam Gallant and Bertha Yakuba – received the award for their tireless efforts in helping local communities.

The committee carried out an audit of women employees, focusing on the numbers and on their grades. It found that, as in most public organisations, the council's women employees were concentrated in the low-paid grades and under-represented nearer the top. It created a register of women's organisations and interests and it campaigned for better child care in the city.

In 1986, the first staff were appointed to a Women's and Equal Opportunities Unit. This enabled the committee to achieve more by implementing its decisions: the unit provided advice on the council's equality policies to other departments, and worked with the personnel department to establish good employment practices; a free shoppers' crèche was set up, helping women and the retail trade; a working party was established to look into the problem of domestic violence;

Town and Gown: Sir Kenneth Alexander, Chancellor of the University of Aberdeen, receiving the Freedom of the City on behalf of the University (see page 157)

and a biennial Women's Festival was started (providing a week of events at which women could meet for discussions, entertainment and information). Support was offered to the Aberdeen Women's Centre, Rape Crisis and the Grampian Racial Equality Council.

In 1994, the high profile 'Zero Tolerance' campaign against the problem of the violent abuse of women by men was launched. Edinburgh City Council had run the campaign the previous year and it was felt to have been a very effective way to highlight the issues. Local posters, leaflets and discussions, and a campaign on national television made the 'No Man has the Right!' slogan very well known indeed. The convener of the committee, Councillor Smith, said that the campaign had been effective because it 'caught people's imagination through its eye-catching posters, blunt advertising messages and media coverage'.

3: The Organisation and Leadership of Aberdeen District Council

The council changed considerably as an organisation during the 1975–96 period. It changed in response to a range of pressures – legislation, Scottish Office controls, new ideas about management, the EU, and information technology (IT) all had an impact.

Citizens all want more from their local services, and some wanted more say over how the council worked. The city's professional staff worked to improve services and to ensure that local services conformed with the best practices elsewhere. And the elected politicians brought their ideas about how the council should be shaped and led to meet the needs of the people.

The Statutory Framework

Local government was a Scottish Office responsibility. Scottish local authorities were responsible to the Scottish Office and the Secretary of State for Scotland. Traditionally most major legislation for Scotland was framed in Edinburgh then passed in the Westminster parliament. However in the 1980s a busy government took to 'tagging on' some clauses about Scotland to UK legislation, a practice which was much resented. Some very important legislation was widely perceived in Scotland to have been a response to particular problems in London, but it was imposed on Scottish councils just the same! The 1988 Local Government Act and its bureaucratic paraphernalia of CCT was a case in point.

Parliament set out most of what councils could and could not do. Any other actions were ruled out as ultra vires in the quaint old fashioned language of government. This was not the case in many other advanced countries where local councils enjoyed their own defined constitutional role and greater discretion over local taxes. Councils in some countries enjoyed a 'power of general competence'; that is, the power to do almost anything provided it was for the general good of the area and wasn't the specific responsibility of some other body.

In Britain the discretion available to democratically elected councils was heavily and increasingly constrained by central government during the 1975–96 period. This was particularly true of local government finance, but was also true of the detail of many services. Some critics felt that in Scotland, where a relatively small number of councils reported to the Scottish Office, there was even greater centralisation than existed south of the border. The Layfield Committee concluded in 1976 that 'the drift towards centralisation has been even more marked' in Scotland than in England. In a system where such a high level of centralisation existed, the relationship between central and local government was crucial.

The Wheatley Commission warned that its proposals would probably fail if central government did not take steps to improve its relationship with local councils. In particular it wanted to see more trust in local government on the part of central government, and the replacement of the traditional restrictive set-up with the more modern power of general competence. It concluded that the strict controls exercised by central government had an overall damaging effect on the independence and initiative of local government and argued that the working relationship between central and local government required a radical rethink to ensure the future viability of local government.

> It is really a question of confidence. Is a reorganised local government to be trusted to get on with the job? If it is, then there is reason to hope that a sense of responsibility will develop and that the constitutional position of local government will be vindicated. If it is not, then there is little chance that a sense of responsibility will develop: local government will become little more than a facade, and might be better dismantled and replaced by something else.

In the event this new relationship of trust did not fully emerge. The 1973 Act ushered in a modern two-tier system of local government but left it shackled by the restrictive traditions of the ultra vires system. The new councils did have some areas of discretion but these tended to be minor or to be additions to statutory requirements set down by Parliament. More importantly the restrictions of the old fashioned approach tended to discourage innovation and experiment. Where most activities were defined and governed by statute, one result was a culture of compliance. In some areas innovation was discouraged because the consequences of being challenged could be very serious, particularly for elected councillors who could face surcharge or disqualification. The nearest the councils had to 'general competence' was section 83 of the 1973 Act which allowed a wide range of actions provided these benefited the local community. However, section 83 was cash-limited to the product of a 2p rate, which in turn was 'frozen' to the value of that product in 1989 when the rates were abolished. Aberdeen District Council also had available very wide discretion in the use of its Common Good Fund. And because of this, it was perhaps a little less restricted than most of the district councils.

The permitted range of action for the new councils was set out in the 1973 Act. Some services, in particular the large regional services of education and social work, and the district responsibility of housing, tended to be driven by their own unique legislation. Similarly, the major management changes of the 1980s were generally driven by specific legislation or by 'enabling' Acts which empowered the Scottish Secretary to issue directives.

Increasingly during the 1980s and early '90s the legal framework originated in Europe. The European Parliament's 'directive' would form the basis of EU law and the UK government's response would, along with the directive, form the legal framework for local authorities. Recognising this, Scottish councils set about trying to influence the EU by working with MEPs, through international links between professional bodies, through a special office in Brussels known as Scotland Europa, and through the European Committee of the regions.

The Scottish Office

The high level of control and oversight exercised by the Scottish Office over local government did not pass without criticism. Many local authorities in Scotland found it hard to accept that the Scottish Office really 'knew best' and resented what they saw as interference by central government in local affairs. The greater professionalism which resulted from the Wheatley reform increased the self-confidence of local authorities. On many issues councils came to have much more in-house expertise than was available to the Scottish Office. The good partnership between central and local government, which Lord Wheatley saw as central to the viability of effective local government, was at times placed under considerable strain. Given the strong Labour dominance in Scottish local government and society and the contrast with Conservative control of central government since 1979, it is perhaps remarkable that the partnership worked as well as it did.

Within the Scottish Office a number of separate departments dealt with the affairs of local government. Following Scottish Office reorganisation in October 1995, the two most important departments were the Scottish Development Department and the Scottish Office Education and Industry Department. In a very few cases, specialist local authority services reported to Whitehall rather than Edinburgh. An example of this was Regional Council Trading Standards which was overseen by the Department of Trade and Industry in London. In general it was the professional relationships between senior council officials and their civil service counterparts which made the Scottish Office–local government relationship work.

Local Government Finance

It was an unfortunate aspect of the local government reforms of 1975 and 1995/96 that finance was not considered in detail along with appropriate structures. Wheatley noted the importance of the issues but left an in-depth analysis to a separate and later enquiry. In 1995 the government simply assumed that its reforms would save money though little was offered in the way of proof or convincing argument.

By the mid-1990s local councils were spending some £7bn annually, about half of the Scottish Office total. Much of this expenditure was highly visible because of its importance to communities. Government routinely criticised councils for their alleged 'profligacy'. The reality was that local authorities generally spent money carrying out central government instructions which were often quite detailed and that they provided services to meet growing local needs. The more important issue of whether or not councils secured value for money was given much less attention.

It was misleading to compare council budgets in different periods because changes reflected gains and losses of statutory responsibilities, as much as changing levels of activity. Similarly comparing different councils tended to overlook real differences in the needs of local communities. Much of the change between 1975 and 1995 could be attributed to two decades of inflation. The ADC also acquired new responsibilities and their associated costs: the expansion of leisure and recreation after 1983, the housing role in community care, and complying with compulsory competitive tendering were examples. The combined effects of inflation, changes to statutory responsibilities, and the improving quality of services meant that local government became a multi-million pound enterprise. In its last year of operation, 1995/96, Aberdeen District Council spent over £145m on its services. Once income was set against this, the net expenditure was £48.8m.

In 1967–68 government grant financed 57% of local government spending. In some local areas the proportion was much higher and in the crofting counties it was 80%. The 'rates', a property-based tax, was the main device available to local authorities to raise money. Charges for some services also contributed to income. Money raised locally through the rates and spent by councils was not viewed by the government in the same way as normal public expenditure and so it avoided some of the tight controls which were introduced elsewhere in the public sector in the 1980s.

As a property tax, rates were easy to collect and their yield was predictable. These were both big advantages from the local authority point of view. The rates though were not related to a person's ability to pay. The pensioner with a small fixed income had the same tax liability as the household next door which had three working adults. The system seemed unfair, and regular property revaluation led to large and very visible increases in the rates. Every time this happened the small business lobby complained about the impact on costs, particularly given that re-valuations were sometimes avoided south of the border because of their unpopularity!

In 1989, the rates were abolished and replaced by the Community Charge. The same change took place in England and Wales a year later. The new tax was a personal levy: it was quickly dubbed the 'poll tax' and this name stuck throughout its short, troubled life. As a personal tax it was highly 'regressive', as the lower an eligible person's income the higher the proportion he or she had to pay to meet the poll tax. The millionaire and the low paid office cleaner had identical poll tax bills.

People were harder to keep track of than buildings and the tax proved much harder to collect, as the local authorities had predicted. There was some evasion of the tax, and there was a political protest against it in the form of a 'non payment' campaign. Local authority income from the tax was hard to predict, and this made financial planning more difficult. The introduction of the tax to England and Wales proved very unpopular. Widespread protests made further change inevitable.

In April 1993, the Council Tax replaced the poll tax, which was property-based, with a personal element. The GRC described it as 'a 50% property tax and a 50% personal tax'. While it remained largely unrelated to a person's ability to pay, it proved an easy tax to collect and a predictable if insufficient instrument. Properties were put in one of eight bands according to their estimated market value. Properties with an estimated value between £45,000 and £58,000 were placed in band D, and this band provided the basis for working out the tax liability in all the other bands.

Under the poll tax each taxpayer received a bill. With the council tax, paperwork and bureaucracy were reduced as each household received only one bill. The 'band D' bill in Aberdeen in 1994/95 was £657, the lowest of Scotland's four main cities. This figure had three elements: the GRC tax of £389, the ADC tax of £179 and the GRC water charge of £89. In 1995/96 Aberdeen's income from the council tax was £14.8m, a sum equal to about 10% of the council's gross revenue expenditure.

Two major fiscal changes in six years imposed enormous pressures on local authorities. Finance departments had to cope with the huge bureaucratic task of setting up new systems for the poll tax and then quickly scrapping these to plan for the council tax; and with each change there was a drop in the proportion of expenditure which councils raised locally. In Scotland in the mid-1990s the council tax financed only 15% of local authority spending, the remainder coming from business rates which were set by the government, and from charges on some services. The major part came in government grant.

The declining importance of the yield from local taxes produced another headache for councils which also confused the public and the media. The 'gearing effect' was the name given to this problem by those officials and councillors who fully understood it. With effective control over only the small proportion of their income which the council tax brought in, any attempt to raise total income meant a disproportionately large increase in the council tax. In the mid-1990s this produced the apparent paradox of local taxes rising rapidly at the same time as services were being cut!

There was little that councils could do about this. The Scottish Office controlled most of council income. Through its 'capping' powers it also effectively controlled the level of council spending and the level at which the council tax was set. Accounting and financial management requirements for particular services gave the Scottish Office very detailed controls and left councils with little real financial discretion. It was particularly frustrating for local authorities that so called 'capital expenditure' – needed to build new schools, leisure facilities, roads, and new houses – was very tightly controlled by the Scottish Office. Councils applied for consent to borrow money to finance these projects and very often were turned down by the Scottish Office. The local government view was that there was always far too little capital spending permitted. The very limited amount that was allowed made it very difficult for local councillors to decide on priorities and provided a regular point of disagreement between districts and regions.

The Introduction of Spending Curbs

A number of significant changes affected local government throughout the 1980s and 1990s. These changes included legislative measures designed to control local authority spending and the introduction of market principles into local government. In the early 1980s the Conservative government introduced a series of measures designed to curb council spending. This meant the tacit abandoning of the principles underpinning the Wheatley reforms. Those reforms had been based on the assumptions that the role and power of local government would continue to grow in a prosperous environment sustained by full employment.

The Conservative government wished to reduce public spending in order to control inflation. The spending of local authorities was a key factor in this equation. In Scotland, local authority spending accounted for about half of the Scottish Office total. The government also believed that local authorities could be made more efficient by exposing them to competition, and by encouraging them to adopt the management methods of the private sector.

In 1981, the ADC and 58 other Scottish local authorities produced budgets which were in excess of Scottish Office guidelines. In June 1981, ADC met to consider a Scottish Office request that expenditure plans be revised in order to reduce the budget. The request was given short shrift! The Scottish Office was advised that the council did not consider its planned expenditure to be at all excessive in relation to the community's needs, and this was the mood of most Scottish councils.

Support was given to an anti-government demonstration and march in Edinburgh. Further action followed as the government repeatedly attempted to control public sector spending. Legislative changes to grant systems, rate-capping powers and capital controls were piecemeal. The government eventually secured very tight controls but at the cost of undermining local autonomy and local accountability.

Councillors and Officials

The relationship between elected councillors and the body of employed council officials was vital to the effective working of local government in all its aspects. However it was a very complex and constantly changing partnership.

Prior to Wheatley, councillors were insufficiently involved in running councils but paradoxically sometimes too closely involved in particular decisions such as housing allocations or planning matters. The key officials, usually the Treasurer and the Clerk, often ran the council. From the point of view of local democracy this clearly left a lot to be desired! The 1975 reform aimed to give elected councillors more control, in partnership with senior officials.

Wheatley recognised two broad roles for councillors: to represent their constituents and to ensure effective service delivery for which they had responsibility in law. Paradoxically the reform immediately made more difficult the basic representational role of councillors by reducing their number and increasing their workload. Quite unlike other elected politicians such as MPs, local councillors were necessarily involved in management. Generally they were involved in making senior staff appointments. Councillors' roles were complex and did not always easily co-exist.

The representational role required councillors to represent local issues and concerns to the council, and at times to represent council policies to the local community. Most councillors valued this part of their role most highly, and it was probably the challenge of being effective at representing the community that brought most councillors into local politics in the first place.

Councillors also had a range of other responsibilities to do with running the council and its services: to set a budget which could not be overspent; to set the level of local taxation; to secure the cost-effective delivery of good quality local services; and sometimes they had to be diplomats and ambassadors. They also needed to oversee and participate in decision-making processes based primarily on service committees and decide on policy and make strategic management decisions. These council-focused roles were very demanding and became even more so during the 1980s and 1990s.

The key policy and managerial decisions were usually taken or ratified in council committees or in the full council. A small group of officials served the council's committees making sure that they were properly supported and that their decisions were recorded. The efforts of this group often went unnoticed but they were vital to the democratic process. Aberdeen District Council was Labour-controlled for nearly all of the 1975–1996 period. As in most councils with a political administration, many of the key decisions were actually taken in the majority party group before being put to committee or to the council.

The complexity of the elected councillor's role was generally not recognised. Arguably it was harder to be an effective local councillor than it was to be a good back bench MP. One indicator of how difficult the role of councillor was is the amount of time which was devoted to it. On average in the 1980s councillors put about 74 hours each month into council work. Of course, in the Wheatley system there was very little reward for this effort as the allowances available to councillors were very low. Research carried out in Wales and Scotland in the mid-1990s suggested that councillors were devoting over 100 hours per month on average to their duties. This demonstrated their high level of commitment, something for which they often were not given due credit by the public and by the media. It also demonstrated that there was an enormous barrier in the way of attracting more citizens to seek election as councillors.

In political councils, councillors emerged from the structures and activities of political parties. Having been selected by their party they then had to win a seat in a process of democratic election. By the mid-1990s councillors in Scotland had higher levels of educational achievement than the general population. However they had no specific training in 'how to be a good councillor'. There was no period of pre-entry training in the nature of local government or in how to run councils. Once elected Councillors could from time to time attend conferences and seminars, but they did not have access to the range and variety of training courses available to officials. And yet, in order to make good decisions, they had to be up to date on a wide range of economic, political and policy issues.

By contrast, council officials were appointed employees, generally on permanent contracts and with career structures. Senior council officials were generally well-paid and sometimes were amongst the best paid people in the public sector. The Wheatley reform made local government much more professional, and established better career paths for officials. Increasingly, officials were employed for their professional or technical qualifications and experience and, for the most part, were appointed for their expertise in the key service areas or because they were trained administrators. The reforms of the 1980s and 1990s promoted better management and led to the appearance of distinct managerial posts and careers within local government. Increasing professionalism and the managerial reforms combined to place more emphasis on improving training to keep officials up to date with new developments and to spread knowledge about best practice.

Generally officials were organised in departments, each of which was charged with delivering a particular set of services to the public, or with providing a particular kind of administrative support within the council. Officials reported to their senior managers and to the department's director. In turn the directors would report to their particular council committee. The Wheatley reform tried to bring the departments and directors together by strengthening the role of the council's Chief Executive as head of the paid employees, and as the head of the council's management team.

The Wheatley Commission wanted to modernise and improve local democracy in Scotland. Amongst other things, this meant clarifying councillors' and officials' roles and encouraging new forms of partnership between them.

However, this was not as simple as it appeared, and though much progress was made, councillor–officer relationships remained an area of occasional difficulty in many councils.

The general role of officials was to implement effectively the policies of the council. However, as the Wheatley Commission recognised, there was very rarely a clear divide between making and implementing policy. Officials advised councillors on policy, whilst at the same time councillors sometimes had to be concerned about details of implementation. The problem, as Wheatley recognised, lay in getting the right balance. In general, implementation and the day to day work of delivering the services was the business of officials. Councillors' main responsibilities lay in setting strategy, deciding on policies and monitoring progress with the support of their officials. The partnership between the two groups needed to recognise this division of labour, but it also had to be sensitive to the fact that, in between, there would often be grey areas. The professional training available to officials did not always serve them well in developing an understanding of the political side of council work, or the democratic agenda bequeathed by Wheatley.

Councils employed a very wide range of staff. At senior levels there were highly paid managers and senior professionals who were needed for their high level of professional experience and expertise, and because local government had become a multi-million pound business which needed good management. At the other end of the scale they employed a lot of low-skilled and low-paid manual workers in occupations such as office cleaning and ground maintenance. Many councils in Scotland, including ADC, wanted to improve the lot of their low paid staff, but this was made very difficult if not impossible by the CCT reforms of the 1980s.

The total number of people employed in the ADC varied as statutory responsibilities changed and as reforms required new ways of working. Unfortunately the data did not support detailed comparisons because of changes in collection methods. In 1981 the answer to a question posed by Councillor Stevenson revealed that the 'permanent' employees of the council, including part-timers, numbered 2,365 in October 1975 and 2,385 in April 1981. Figures collected on a different basis for reporting to COSLA showed 2,564 full-time and 599 part-time employees in June 1995. In 1991/92, about 20% of ADC's £120m revenue expenditure went on staff costs.

In different Scottish councils, and at different times, the character of this key partnership varied. In some councils, officials seemed very much to have the lead role. In others the elected councillors were very much in command. The ADC took some pride in being one where the reins were firmly held by the elected politicians.

Increasingly from the late 1980s councils tried new approaches to strengthening officer–councillor partnership. Information and research services were made available to members. In Aberdeen a Corporate Support Unit was set up in 1991. Policy seminars were organised to help bring councillors up to date with new developments. The planning department was particularly active in supporting councillors in this way. Where new policies or new thinking were required joint working groups comprising officials and councillors would explore the options available.

Leadership in Local Government

Regional and district authorities were complex organisations within which some power was centralised but more was dispersed to key committees. Often the real decision-makers were in the majority party group. The key and often creative aspects of implementation fell to officials. In this complex set-up the roles played by individuals were often critical.

Leadership was exercised at a variety of levels. The local councillor would often take the lead on matters relevant to his or her ward. Committee conveners and departmental directors played a key role for their particular service. Generally the best-run services were those with a good partnership between convener and director. However, such partnerships also tended to produce a 'departmentalist' approach which was not good for the council as a whole, or for local democracy. At the level of individual projects less senior officials played key roles, and increasingly this was done through complex partnerships with other agencies.

In the council as a whole, three positions were of particular importance. The most visible of these was the. Lord Provost. As the ceremonial head and lead ambassador for the council, the lord provost came in for a lot of media exposure. The position though was not merely ceremonial and some lord provosts were very much involved in leading decision-making and reform processes. The role played could be fashioned by the individual concerned and depended on a variety of factors including individual personality and standing in the majority group. In the 1975–96 period Councillors Lennox, Fraser, Collie, Rae, Robertson and Wyness all served as Aberdeen's 'first citizen'.

Each of Aberdeen's lord provosts handled their leadership responsibilities in different ways. The varying issues to which they had to respond and their personalities and viewpoints ensured this. There were occasions when lord provosts seemed to take a different view from or even to disagree with the majority group. These occasions tended to be a source of difficulty and anxiety for senior politicians and officials. However, they may have also have added some colour to the business of local government and helped to bring it more to the attention of citizens.

The 'leader' of the council was the leader of the majority party and holder of the strategically important office of Policy Committee convener. This less visible role was generally the most important in terms of giving leadership to the council's decision-making and policy-formulation. Seven councillors played this role between 1975 and 1996: Councillors Fraser, Sewel, Robertson, Thomson,

Wyness, Paine and Farquhar. All were Labour apart from Councillor Thomson who was leader in 1987–88 during the brief Liberal Democrat–Conservative coalition. Councillor Fraser had the distinction of being leader twice, as the first leader of the new District Council in 1975 and later in the 1980s. Councillor Farquhar was the only woman to play this role right up until the reform of local government in 1996.

The chief executive was head of the officials and the third member of this triumvirate. The ability to form good working relationships with the senior elected politicians was one of the hallmarks of an effective chief executive. However, this was made very complex by the requirement that a chief executive be politically neutral and serve the whole council. In the Wheatley system most councils called their head of paid service 'Chief Executive', a term which was much better known in the private sector prior to 1975. Scotland's cities supported the intention to improve management lying behind this nominal change, but stuck with their traditional designation of 'Town Clerk'. In Aberdeen the position was successively known as 'Town Clerk', 'Town Clerk and Chief Executive' and 'Chief Executive', the changes bearing witness to the growing recognition on the part of councillors of the importance of good management and leadership.

In the 1975–96 period, six officials served in this role: Fergus Watt, John Wilson, Jamus Smith, Donald MacDonald, Anne Mearns and Alan Towns. Donald MacDonald left under a cloud in 1994 confessing to being negligent in claiming spurious professional qualifications. The ADC was not geared up to deal with scandal of this nature and scale and initially a hostile press made hay while they could. This unfortunate episode apart, Aberdeen District Council's town clerks and chief executives were reckoned as good and effective public servants who served the city well.

Management Structures

Decision-making in local government was traditionally organised through a series of committees. The 1973 Act required councils to set up some particular committees, for example education and social work committees in the regional councils. Otherwise, councils had a wide discretion in their committee structure. Prior to reorganisation in 1975, the committee and departmental structure of most local authorities grew like topsy as council functions changed. This tended to result in a large number of committees each dealing with their own particular areas of service. Inevitably this led to a degree of fragmentation of service delivery, as each department looked after its own discrete area of responsibility and to some 'turf wars' where an issue affected more than one department, as real-life issues often did. Co-operation between departments was often weak.

At the same time as the reorganisation of local government was being considered, a management guide was prepared by a working party made of senior local government officials and the Scottish Office. The Paterson Report advocated a 'corporate approach' based on departments co-operating closely in service delivery with a strengthened central core around the position of the Chief Executive. The report made a number of recommendations for the structure and organisation of the new councils and their committees. Behind the recommendations was the idea that there were three main resources available to local authorities: finance, property and manpower.

It was recommended that the full council should be at the head of the structure, with a policy and resources committee reporting to it on broad matters of policy. A separate committee was recommended for each of the three main resource areas. Service committees were to deal with the actual provision of services and report either direct to the council or through the Policy and Resources Committee. The report also recommended the establishment of the post of Chief Executive who in turn would head up a management team consisting of some or all of the heads of both central and service departments. The Paterson Report was the first serious attempt to introduce new ideas of corporate management into local government.

In August 1974 the Shadow Council of the City of Aberdeen met to consider the recommendations of the Paterson Report, together with a further report on organisation and management structures prepared by its own consultative committee. The Shadow Council decided to establish a committee and departmental structure which included policy, manpower and finance committees together with service committees for the art galleries and museums, environmental health and cleansing, housing, industrial development, leisure and recreation, libraries, planning and building control and works. This structure remained substantially unaltered until the 1980s when a number of changes occurred. In 1984, ADC decided to establish a women's committee following Stirling's lead.

By the late 1980s, the council's committee and departmental structure had been in place for over a decade, but had remained largely unaltered. In 1987 a new coalition between the Liberal Democrats and the Conservatives took over power at the Town House. One of their first priorities was to review the internal management of the council. Consultants were commissioned to prepare a report on the cost of the council's central services. Councillors had noted that efficiency gains were made in some of the service areas prepared for CCT and wanted to explore these issues in the central areas of the council.

The consultants' first report was produced in 1988. It did not present a favourable picture of the council's internal management and organisation. As with many reports by external consultants criticisms went both ways. Many councillors and officials expressed considerable reservations about the findings of the review and felt that the review process lacked rigour.

The district council elections in May 1988 returned the Labour party to power. The new administration accepted that the main findings of the initial report indicated a need for further investigation. The consultants' remit was ·

extended to include a thorough review of the council's internal management arrangements and committee structures.

A series of substantial reports emerged in 1988. The most dramatic recommendation to emerge was to reduce council departments from fourteen to seven. This caused considerable unease amongst the council's staff as job security and employment conditions appeared to be under threat. The council resolved early in 1989 that a new internal management structure be created comprising nine departments. Councillor Wyness was Leader at this time and he was closely involved in this effort to restructure and modernise the ADC.

The art galleries and museums and libraries departments were merged with the larger Leisure and Recreation Department into a new 'Arts and Recreation' Department. At the same time, the City Architects Department, which at that time was mainly involved in the repair and maintenance of the Council's housing stock, became part of the Housing Department. The separate departments of Environmental Health and Cleansing were brought together in a new Environmental Development Department. A new Economic Development Department was also created. Responsibility for personnel, information technology and policy and performance review came under the remit of the Town Clerk's Department. Subsequently, a new department, Aberdeen Leisure, was added. This was the contracting department responsible for catering and sport and recreation. The remainder of the former Direct Services Organisation (DSO) became the Contract Services Organisation (CSO).

The following year, the council decided to bring back the consultants in order to review progress and assess whether the aims of the review had been met. The 1992 Local Government Act promised the extension of CCT to a range of activities including legal, personnel, information technology and financial services. The reorganisation of local government in 1996 had the result of postponing the extension of CCT to these services until 1997. Nevertheless, the CCT legislation put considerable pressure on local authorities to adopt more business-like ways of organising and delivering services.

Aberdeen District Council, like most in Scotland, proved that it could win contracts in competition with private contractors. It won all the contracts let in the lifetime of the district council. This had interesting consequences for staff morale. At first the announcement of plans for CCT and some of the early preparations seemed to demoralise staff. The message which the government seemed to be sending out was that councils were inefficient compared with the private sector. Once ADC began to win contracts there was some evidence of a reverse effect. Having won their contract in competition staff felt that they had been unduly criticised and that they could compete on costs with private firms.

The successive annual spending curbs announced by the Scottish Office meant that local authorities were becoming increasingly aware of the need to provide value for money and thoroughly review their use of available resources. The consultants' final report went before the council's Panel for Management

Restructuring in January 1991, together with the observations of the trade unions and the council's own heads of department. This and separate internal reviews cast doubt on whether or not projected savings had been realised. There was an apparent rise in staffing costs but it was not clear whether this was a consequence of the consultants' recommendations, the steps taken to comply with the CCT legislation, or some other factors altogether. Steps taken in 1991 and 1992 reduced staffing levels by 94 posts and produced savings which helped the council to reduce its part of the community charge by 24%. Councillor Wyness spoke proudly of the city's 'outstanding budget'.

The seemingly endless round of management and staffing reviews left many staff feeling insecure and vulnerable to change. Inevitably morale suffered in some departments. Throughout the 1988 to 1992 period the council attempted to keep staff fully informed on the progress of the review; and it pointed to its success in largely avoiding compulsory redundancies when losing posts and in complying with the CCT requirements.

Compulsory Competition

The introduction of CCT for certain local services in the 1980s was one of the most significant changes which affected local government. The Local Government Planning and Land Act of 1980 became operational in Scotland in 1982. Local authorities were required to establish Direct Labour Organisations (DLOs) for construction work and road maintenance. The DLOs were placed on a trading basis and opened up to possible competition from the private sector. The aim was to make DLOs more efficient and cost effective by getting them to emulate private sector management methods.

The attempt to introduce market disciplines into local authorities through the introduction of competitive tendering had two main purposes. Firstly, it aimed to improve efficiency by promoting competition and so requiring councils to look very closely at their costs. In particular councils had to look very closely at their labour costs because the services picked out for CCT were labour intensive. Secondly, it intended to change the nature of top management by embedding a commercial ethos inside local authorities. After the enforced sale of council houses CCT was the most significant aspect of the privatisation programme which Scottish councils experienced.

Virtually all construction and maintenance works carried out by local authorities were affected, including construction and maintenance of highways, general water and sewerage works, construction of new buildings and maintenance works. As far as the ADC was concerned, this entailed a radical restructuring of the Department of Building and Works which carried out building and maintenance works. Before the reform this work consisted mainly of repairs to and maintenance of the housing stock and to other properties owned by the ADC. The council employed a large number of skilled tradesmen to carry out these works, and operated from premises in Jasmine Terrace.

After a brief run-in period in which only 40% of all eligible building and maintenance works were subject to competition, all contracts had to be competed for. The former Building and Works Department became a 'contractor' and had to function as a trading organisation, quite distinct and separate from the rest of the ADC. It had to achieve a rate of return similar to company profits in the private sector. In the event of failure the Scottish Office could step in.

This required radical changes to the council's way of doing things. If the council decided to modernise part of its housing stock it could no longer simply tell its own employees to carry out the work. Instead, the council was required to invite tenders from both their own DLO and also from private building firms. The majority of the staff of the former Building and Works Department were transferred to the new DLO in order to undertake the work should the contract be won. The remainder became a client team working for the council itself. Theirs was the complex responsibility to specify the work to be done, invite tenders and monitor the contracts as they were carried out.

The extension of CCT in 1988 led to the setting up of two further contracting organisations, the Direct Services Organisation (DSO) and Aberdeen Leisure. The focus remained on those council services which were carried out mainly by manual workers. If councils wished to continue in these areas of work, they could only lawfully do so if they won the contract through a process of competition in which the private sector could participate. This time the services included a range of cleaning and catering works, grounds maintenance and maintenance of vehicles. The legislation was phased in over a period of four years. In Aberdeen City the change affected services provided in the main by the Leisure and Recreation Department. The Scottish Secretary was given some powers to extend CCT to new service areas, and the management of leisure facilities was brought into the new system.

The 1992 Act extended the CCT regime to a range of white collar and professional areas of work. The personnel, legal, information technology and finance departments were amongst those brought into the CCT net. The decision to reform local government structures led the government to delay the planned introduction of these changes.

By the mid-1990s there was a growing feeling in Scotland that while compulsory competition may have brought some benefits, nevertheless it was a very heavy-handed approach. It was widely accepted that building DLOs had been made more efficient. Economies had clearly been achieved in cleaning and in ground maintenance, but the situation was much less clear in other CCT services. It became clear that simply complying with the legislation entailed substantial bureaucratic costs which were not usually considered in the comparisons which claimed to show 'efficiency gains'!

CCT was criticised for focusing on costs rather than on the more important concept of quality. Rather than encouraging councillors and officials to seek the best approach to improving quality for their local area, CCT imposed the same regime on every council. Ironically one of the key managerial reforms of the 1980s was criticised for stifling local management initiative.

At the decision-making level, a curious situation arose. The ADC's elected representatives were responsible for instructing the works to be carried out and for awarding the contracts. However, some councillors also sat on the newly-created Contracting Board which was charged with overseeing the operation of the DLO which was competing for those contracts. This role was similar in some respects to that of sitting on a Board of directors of a company. This role was quite distinct and separate from the traditional roles of elected members of the council. In some respects the separation of the client from the contractor tended to divide the elected members.

Though it wasn't noticed much at the time, CCT tended to undermine the corporate objectives of the Wheatley/Paterson changes. Corporate working required open co-operation between departments and a long-term view focused on community needs. By contrast complying with CCT meant focusing on commercial strategies to win contracts, and not undertaking any activities unless they were fully specified in the contract.

The supporters of compulsory competition argued that it helped councillors by forcing them to focus on strategy and on monitoring performance. The critics, who were in the majority in Scotland, argued that it tended further to marginalise elected councillors. They also argued that the costs of change were carried by the manual employees in these service areas. It was their pay and conditions which were often squeezed to win contracts. This rankled in councils which took pride in being good employers. Once again central reforms seemed to be removing local discretion.

The Citizen's Charter

The 1992 Act brought the Citizen's Charter to local authorities. The aim was to introduce a market type of accountability in which citizens would be encouraged to see themselves as individual consumers rather than as people in communities. Local authorities and other public bodies were required to publish 'charters' setting out the standards of service which they planned to achieve. Then once a year they had to publish information on how they were doing compared with the charter standards. The whole process was overseen by the independent Accounts Commission which consulted widely with councils before deciding on the appropriate indicators against which 'performance data' had to be published. Once all the data were available the commission then published 'league tables' showing the 'good', the 'bad' and the 'plain average' of Scotland's councils.

Initially the charter was underpinned by seven principles, but for reasons not explained at the time, equality of opportunity was quietly dropped to leave the following six:

Standards – setting, monitoring and publication of explicit standards for the services that individual users can reasonably expect. Publication of actual performance against these standards.

Information and openness – full, accurate information readily available in plain language about how public services are run, what they cost, how well they perform and who is in charge.

Choice and consultation – the public sector should provide choice wherever practicable. There should be regular and systematic consultation with those who use services. Users' views about services, and their priorities for improving them, to be taken into account in final decisions on standards.

Courtesy and helpfulness – courteous and helpful service from public servants who will normally wear name badges. Services available equally to all who are entitled to them and run to suit their convenience.

Putting things right – if things go wrong, an apology, a full explanation and a swift and effective remedy. Well publicised and easy to use complaints procedures with independent review wherever possible.

Value for Money – efficient and economical delivery of public services within the resources the nation can afford. Independent validation of performance against standards.

The supporters of the charter approach argued that it clearly was having an effect as councils were improving and that this was demonstrated in the published information. The critics argued that the indicators tended to be aspects which were easily measured rather than true yardsticks of quality, and that the costs of collecting and publishing the data outweighed any benefits. They also argued that management reforms had to be locally developed rather than centrally imposed if they were to work.

The Central Services

The council's finance department was the one of four services known as 'central support' services. The others were personnel, legal services and information technology. The ADC was a large and complex bureaucratic machine and it needed these supports to work effectively. In 1991/92, it spent about £5m on these services.

The complexity of its finances required in-house specialists for budgeting and financial control, for advising the large service departments, and for discussions with the Scottish Office. As a large employer and a labour-intensive organisation, the ADC needed personnel specialists to handle recruitment, promotions, retirements, resignations, the payroll, staff training and a host of other issues which were important to staff. The council's authority derived from a complex set of statutes. Specialist lawyers were needed to interpret these and to advise officials and councillors on a host of issues including planning cases, property acquisitions and developments, the use of discretionary powers, and the sale of council houses and other properties.

These three central services evolved in local authorities in the post-1945 period. Their managerial requirements in the 1970s were set out in the Paterson Report. In contrast, the fourth of the support services – information technology – was not considered by Paterson or Wheatley. It was simply too new for its implications to be properly understood.

When they began their work in 1975 the new councils found themselves on the edge of a technological revolution which would gather pace for the rest of the century. Information technology revolutionised office work, transformed the keeping of records and documents, made completely new forms of communication routine, and opened up a wide range of opportunities in service design, delivery and use. Hundreds of staff had to be trained in the new skills required, and then re-trained every time the technology moved on apace; and personal computers and portable 'lap-tops' were made available to councillors.

Two major issues arose for the central services in the 1980s and 1990s. Because they supported all service departments but weren't responsible for any particular external services to the public, their costs were not as closely watched as other parts of local government. The pressure to control these central costs emerged as a by-product of the introduction of compulsory competitive tendering (CCT), particularly after 1988. The result was that, if local authorities wished to carry out certain works by direct labour, they had to win the contract in open competition. In 1992 the government announced its intention to impose CCT directly on the support services. This initiated a process of reorganising those services to face anticipated market competition in 1997.

Precisely because they were central, at times they came to 'control' as much as to 'support'. Officials running the council's key services increasingly complained that financial, personnel and administrative procedures had been designed to suit the specialists rather than to help the council as a whole. In the 1990s the key to this problem seemed to lie in decentralising aspects of the support services to the service departments which used them. This was perhaps clearest in regional councils where some managerial autonomy was devolved to school heads, and financial control was devolved down to middle managers of social work to support 'Care in the Community'. Ironically as steps were taken to decentralise support services to make them more 'user friendly', it seemed that complying with the government's CCT requirements might require the support services to be re-centralised!

Property

The ADC owned a substantial amount of property. The work of selling, buying, modernising and refurbishing went on behind the scenes; this was vital to all of the service departments and to the service users because good quality buildings were part and parcel of good quality services.

The ADC's architects designed new buildings and major refurbishments and generally managed the building work. Their designs had to balance concerns for effectiveness with the need for conservation in the older properties. They also had to have a very broad sense of appreciation of the environmental impact, not just visually but also in areas like energy use. The Property Department generally looked after the whole building stock and, together with the council's lawyers, handled purchases and sales.

The improvements to properties were often to the highest standards. Both James Dun's House and the Tolbooth Museum won awards, as did the sheltered housing development at Taransay Court. In all, ADC architects received thirty-one awards and commendations.

Trade Unions

Most ADC staff belonged to a trade union. Reforms in employment law in the 1980s clarified the rights of individuals to choose whether or not to join a union, whilst European directives provided some new types of employment protection. The 'Transfer of Undertakings Protection of Employment' directive seemed to strengthen employee rights in situations of reorganisation or where contracts were won by the private sector under CCT. Labour councils generally wanted their staff to be in trade unions and provided some facilities for the unions' full-time and lay officers. Across the political spectrum in local government it was recognised that the existence of unions which could speak for most of the staff made the essential tasks of negotiations and some tasks of management much easier.

The councils as employers negotiated with the unions at national level, and salary levels and the main terms and conditions were set nationally. The ADC implemented the national agreements. Many important but smaller issues were locally determined. Consultative procedures allowed the unions to have a say and to exert some influence, particularly over employment issues but also on some broader matters of policy.

Until the late 1980s the government took national pay agreements into account in the funding of local authorities. However, in the 1990s it ceased to fund pay awards, arguing that councils would need to fund any increases themselves through 'efficiency gains'. Both councils and the trade unions resented this move, arguing that the funding of local government was being cut in an underhand way.

Local authorities had a surprising number and range of trade unions. A number of these unions also had members outside local government. The unions went through their own changes of name and amalgamations, generally driven by the need to cut costs as their membership fell in the 1980s. In 1996, in the new City Council, UNISON was the largest union with most of the white collar staff and manual workers. The Educational Institute of Scotland was the largest of the teaching unions, covering school teachers and community education. Skilled building workers tended to be in the Union of Construction and Allied Technical Trades whilst other manual workers were in the Transport and General Workers Union and the General, Municipal and Boilermakers Union. The Fire Brigades Union organised the fire-fighters.

The End of the Wheatley System

After the 1992 election, the Conservative government set about reorganising local government in Scotland. The Scottish Office consultations showed how far the accepted role for the public sector had shifted since 1975:

> Government policies are now designed
> – to increase the choices open to the consumer of local government services;
> – to give the consumer a greater role in determining how those services should be delivered;
> – to encourage local authorities to consider alternative methods of service delivery; and
> – to work in partnerships with the public and private sectors as well as with individuals.

The concepts of value for money, strong financial management and public accountability were to be applied in new ways to local government. Local government was no longer to be viewed as a local monopoly provider of services. Rather it was to be encouraged to see itself as a vehicle for 'enabling' those services to be provided. This might involve more provision by the private sector or by voluntary agencies, and less of a direct role for the council and its employees. Clearly the key values and hopes of the Wheatley Commission had finally been abandoned. Legislation which was implemented in 1996 brought in government's idea of thirty-two all-purpose councils. Once again local government reform reduced the numbers of elected institutions and politicians. In Aberdeen the wheel seemed to have turned full circle as unitary local government was restored to the city.

4: Aberdeen's Economy

The Wheatley Report provided the framework for Scottish local government for two and a half decades, but one thing it said little about was the role of local councils in economic policy. It confined its remarks to industrial promotion in which it thought both regions and districts could play a role. No statutory power to engage in economic development was provided to the new councils in 1975. Nevertheless pressures arising from local needs meant that most local authorities developed such an economic development role during the 1980s. In most cases the main concerns of local councils were to tackle unemployment and poverty, and to help develop new firms and industries which would create local jobs. Generally councils in Scotland developed a good record of working in partnership with the private sector and with government agencies.

Local economies are generally complex systems and Aberdeen's was no exception. Often they involve a wide range of types of industry. In Aberdeen, the range has extended from fishing to advanced electronic engineering for the oil industry. In the case of cities there is usually a complex relationship between the economy of the city and that of its surrounding area. This point was very much in the minds of the proponents of regional government in the late 1960s and early 1970s and was a recurring theme in the Wheatley Commission's review. It was argued that cities and their surrounding areas should be considered together for economic development purposes. Oil came to provide a clear example of this interdependence, with most of the jobs located in the City of Aberdeen, but very many of the employees living elsewhere in the region.

Active economic policy was prominent in Labour Party thinking. The Labour government set up the Scottish Development Agency in 1975. In the same year, the new Aberdeen District Council adopted a comprehensive economic development policy. Councillor Fraser was leader of the council and had a close interest in economic development. The policy was concerned to assist traditional industries as well as the rapidly growing oil sector, in order to help create a 'diversified economic base'. Priority was given to providing land and sites for industrial development.

In order to sustain local economies, the provision of good local services was extremely important. The economy depended on the provision of good quality infrastructure such as roads, water, sewerage, power and housing. Most of the local infrastructure services were local authority responsibilities in the 1975–95 period, though of the services mentioned only housing was a district council responsibility. Modern industry also relied on the availability of the right types of labour and here local authority education services were extremely important. Throughout the period schools were a regional council responsibility as were further education colleges until 1992.

Local authorities were in themselves very important to the economy. They were amongst the largest employers and the most important buyers of goods and services in their areas. In the late 1960s and early 1970s this economic role was not considered terribly important. The Wheatley Commission scarcely referred to it. Sometimes local councils themselves were not aware of their own importance, although it could be argued that 1988 legislation largely discouraged them from taking an overview of their economic role in any case. In the late 1980s and early 1990s, the government tended to downplay the role which local authorities could play in their local economies.

Whatever happened in the economy, the local authority role was very important. If industry was expanding and jobs were being created councils had to do their best to facilitate those trends while protecting the environment and ensuring some balance to the process. The decisions of ADC's industrial development, planning and property committees directly affected the local economy. Where industries contracted and jobs were lost – as was the case in many parts of Britain in the 1980s and early 1990s – it was to the local council that communities turned for support and practical help. In many communities local authorities became closely involved in both processes, supporting and encouraging economic development on the one hand, and assisting disadvantaged and poorer communities on the other. In the early 1980s the ADC began to develop initiatives aimed at helping Aberdeen's unemployed.

In Aberdeen, on most of the criteria which are important to the community, the economy performed very well compared to other parts of Britain over the period. While other councils had to respond to large scale job losses in the steel industry, in motor manufacturing, in engineering, in shipbuilding, or in coal mining, Aberdeen's main challenge was the relatively very pleasant one of growth brought about by North Sea oil. Over the 1970–1995 period the Aberdeen economy changed markedly from a declining one based on agriculture, fishing and traditional manufacturing, to one in which the key firms were hi-tech international leaders and the main industry was of international importance.

Aberdeen's 'Black Gold'

In the mid-1960s Aberdeen was displaying all the problems of a depressed economy. The traditional industries in the city such as fish processing, textiles, shipbuilding and paper making were in gradual long-term decline. Increased mechanisation further reduced the demand for labour. Unemployment was increasing and people were leaving the city in search of better job prospects. The rest of the north east showed a similar pattern. In recognition of the economic situation, the region, in common with almost the whole of Scotland, received Development Area status in 1964. This allowed local firms and industries to receive limited government assistance.

In 1966, the Scottish Office commissioned Professor Maxwell Gaskin of Aberdeen University to conduct a study into the development potential of the north east: the report was published in 1969. It was possibly the most advanced regional economic study of its day. It predicted that there would at best be only limited scope for economic growth in the region and that this would be primarily in the service sector. Ironically, 1969 also saw the first big oil strike in the North Sea – Amoco's Montrose Field.

By the mid-1960s, oil and gas exploration in the central and northern North Sea was already underway and the industry was looking to the city as a possible base for its activities. Discussions between oil companies – who were anxious to secure important facilities – and the Aberdeen Harbour Board began in September 1964, and in 1965 Hall Russell of Aberdeen built the first UK oil rig supply vessel. The first big oil discovery in 1969 was closely followed by the huge BP Forties Field in 1970 and the news that other explorers had struck black gold.

By the early 1970s the 'gold rush' was well and truly underway though the long term implications of oil were not widely appreciated until 1973/74. Central government set up fiscal and licensing arrangements to help make the North Sea economically attractive to the major companies in the industry. The government wanted quick exploitation of oil to end Britain's dependence on producers in the Middle East and to help the balance of payments. The need for quick exploitation meant that the multinational oil companies had to play the leading role as they had the available expertise. Central government largely confined itself to a watching brief setting up and chairing a standing conference on North Sea oil.

The city corporation and the county of Aberdeen were also quick to see the possible benefits if the industry located in Aberdeen. However, it was by no means certain that the industry would choose the city as its base. Other settlements on the east coast were considered: Dundee, Montrose or Peterhead could have provided the industry with harbour space and industrial land. Dundee had a strong higher education sector, but Aberdeen had some advantages over the others. Perhaps the most significant of these was the existence of an airport which had the potential to be developed to accommodate the needs of the industry.

The role of the local authorities was also of vital importance in convincing the industry that Aberdeen should be the heart of the administrative and service support for oil production. The local authorities' main concerns were to ensure that land and sites were made available, to provide the necessary infrastructure, to try to balance conflicting pressures for development, and to minimise any adverse effects on the environment. The corporation had limited land available within its boundaries and the brunt of the land requirements fell on the County Council which purchased sites at Dyce in 1968 and Bridge of Don in 1969 for industrial purposes. The corporation purchased land at Altens on the south side of the city from the county of Kincardine in 1970 for use as an industrial estate. This land was incorporated within the city boundaries in 1970 and became a key resource for ADC's economic strategy.

Preparing for Oil

The Gaskin Report helped to shape the local government response to the early years of the oil boom. The report recommended the co-ordination of economic development and industrial promotion on a regional basis. It led directly to the establishment of three agencies: the North east of Scotland Joint Planning Advisory Committee (NESJPAC), the North East of Scotland Development Agency (NESDA) and the North East of Scotland Tourism Association (NESTA). The ADC role initially developed within this framework. After regionalisation in 1975, the council continued to collaborate effectively on many aspects of economic development but also developed an independent role.

NESJPAC offered advice to the local authorities on the likely impact of oil and co-ordinated their planning efforts. It helped to prepare structure plans and local plans as introduced by the Town and Country Planning (Scotland) Act 1969. NESJPAC quickly recognised that it would have to pay immediate attention to the rapidly changing scale of oil activity. By the early 1970s the oil industry was making heavy and largely unforeseen demands for harbour facilities, industrial sites, office space, infrastructure, hotels, housing and labour. The scale of expected future development was so great and so imminent that an overall regional strategy and structure plan was urgently required.

In the early 1970s land use planning in Aberdeen was based on a development plan which had been produced in 1953 and updated in 1963. By the late 1960s the Development Plan was being amended at a rate of four times per year. The planning framework was proving to be quite unsatisfactory and the local authorities found themselves in a difficult dilemma. It was unlikely that even the basis of a structure plan could be produced much before mid-1974. In the meantime, the oil industry was actively looking for an administrative and support base for its offshore operations and the local authorities were anxious to ensure that Aberdeen and the surrounding area would be chosen.

NESJPAC developed a number of 'holding strategies'. These alerted local authorities to the sheer scale of what was happening and offered advice and guidance. These holding strategies were really an attempt to influence development in order to prevent excessive demands being placed on the resources of the local authorities in acquiring land and providing essential infrastructure, and to help avoid the construction industry becoming over-stretched. NESJPAC had only an advisory role. It spelt out these strategies clearly, but it did not specify how they could be achieved. Some of the potential impact was lost.

The local authorities were in a position to influence the pace and location of development in the exercise of their planning function. They adopted a 'dispersal' strategy in an attempt to spread the pressure of development around the north east. However the local authorities did not feel able to use discriminatory planning policies in order to achieve this aim. As a result, the vast majority of oil related businesses chose to locate in or around the city close to the administrative centre and within easy reach of the harbour and airport.

Planning applications began to flood in for new industrial and commercial premises and for housing and offices. The corporation had to balance its roles in facilitating development whilst still retaining a measure of control over it. It also lacked an adequate planning framework in which to achieve this. The corporation granted developers planning permission subject to a number of conditions. These were designed to inhibit 'speculative' developments and to protect the environment of the city. However, no one wanted to do anything that was likely to 'frighten' the industry away.

NESDA was a pioneering partnership agency. It was set up in 1969, and through it local authorities and the private sector worked together. It was widely regarded as a model. For some time the SDA left its development work in the north east to NESDA. In June 1973, NESDA took part in a business mission, which the Press and Journal organised, to the Houston Oil Show in Texas. This paved the way for later participation by the local authorities, and for the annual promotion of Aberdeen in Texas by the ADC.

The north east had a strong tradition of voluntary public–private partnership, even by Scottish standards. NESDA's role was to co-ordinate economic and industrial development in the north east. It promoted the region and tried to attract business to the north east. It operated through district offices but did not have one of these for the city area. This made ADC's own role even more important. The council worked in partnership with NESDA but also developed its own role.

In 1975, NESDA became the economic development arm of the new GRC. From this point on, ADC felt the principle of successful partnership had been undermined, the GRC having assumed the driving seat. The fact that the regional council was Conservative and the district council was Labour did not help matters. ADC continued to collaborate with NESDA whenever possible. On a number of occasions it called for NESDA to be re-established on the 1969 principle of voluntary and equal co-operation. In 1990 the regional council established an Economic Development and Planning Department into which NESDA was finally merged.

Aberdeen's economic development needs were different from the wider region in some respects and similar in others. With so much oil-related development taking place, there seemed little need separately to promote Aberdeen for economic expansion. Promotion of the city was often carried out by NESDA in conjunction with the Harbour Board and airport management. However, ADC vigorously promoted Aberdeen whenever opportunities arose.

Aberdeen District Council took its promotional efforts south to a high profile industrial development event in London in 1979. In 1980 the council supported an unsuccessful GRC bid to have the Scottish Exhibition Centre located at Bridge of Don. An agreement with Aberdeen Football Club helped ADC promote Aberdeen at the club's away games in Europe. This agreement was used when Alex Ferguson's young, all-conquering team won the 1983 Cup Winner's Cup in Gothenburg and the so-called 'Super Cup' in Hamburg.

The council also pursued promotion by bringing people to the city. The first annual Aberdeen oil exhibition took place in 1975, under canvas. The successful annual event moved to the Exhibition and Conference Centre after it opened in 1985. The ADC also promoted Aberdeen at two other major annual oil events in Houston and Stavanger.

The council worked with the GRC to promote Aberdeen's case to be a pilot 'Freeport' in a new central government initiative. Councillors and officials thought that the bid was strong. In February 1984 the council told the government of its 'deep disappointment' at not being chosen.

In 1994, ADC and Stavanger launched a new initiative to develop trade opportunities. The World Energy City Partnership involved six cities by 1996. An unsuccessful bid was made by the council and Grampian Enterprise to host the UK/Ireland Corporate Games in 1995. The strength of this bid led to Aberdeen being named host to the Games for the following year.

The ADC saw the provision of land and sites for industry as one of its key economic roles. Its consistent policy was to provide the maximum land for industry which was permitted by the planning framework. A large number of sites were provided at East and West Tullos, Altens, Mastrick and Northfield. The council also developed its own advance factory units in Cotton Street to help new businesses get on their feet.

In 1979, the government began a review of regional policy as part of a general effort to reduce state involvement in the economy. The eligibility status of an area for regional funds was largely determined by its unemployment rate. In Aberdeen and the north east, unemployment was relatively low and it quickly became clear that the whole area's regional status – and with it a range of government grants – was at risk. The ADC and GRC lobbied unsuccessfully against this change, and had the support of local private sector leaders in the Chamber of Commerce. Councillors Bonney, Kelman and Sewel represented the district council in a north east delegation which went to London to press home the case to Industry Department and Scottish Office ministers. The ADC argued that the whole concept of regional policy should be re-worked to give assistance to particular industries rather than whole areas. This view did not fit in with the sharply free market orientation of central government. In 1982 the whole north east was removed from regional policy assistance.

In 1981, ADC set up the Aberdeen Industries and Development Authority, affectionately known as 'AIDA'. This became the centrepiece in the council's economic role during the 1980s and it helped to provide a vehicle for policy after the regionalisation of NESDA. AIDA was intended to be a very broad forum but was weakened at the outset when both the GRC and the SDA turned down invitations to sit on the new body.

AIDA commissioned academic research into the decline of the city's industrial base, caught as it was between enormous development pressures and competition for resources on the one hand, and a very high cost environment on the other. The studies showed a more rapid decline than in most of Britain, with a 21% drop in manufacturing jobs between 1977 and 1981 and the expectation that the downward trend would continue. The studies helped to inform the campaign over regional policy and formed the basis for the strategy document adopted by AIDA in 1984.

The loss of regional assistance meant that the local councils had to take the lead in providing help to industry. NESDA developed a loans scheme for the north east which was regarded as 'best practice' by councils throughout Scotland. The ADC used s.83 of the 1973 Act to provide loans to firms in Aberdeen. Specialist NESDA staff helped ADC staff to assess the applicants.

In 1983, ADC opened the first of three enterprise centres. The network formed by the Aberdeen, Riverside and Granitehill centres worked to help small companies in a variety of ways, in particular by providing short-term accommodation which they could afford. This allowed companies to test the Aberdeen market without first having to take on very expensive premises. In 1994/95, fourteen companies with 185 employees used the centres. In 1984, following approaches by the Chamber of Commerce and the Aberdeen branch of the National Westminster Bank, ADC gave its support to Aberdeen Enterprise Trust. The AET went on to provide advice and support to new and small firms. In 1993, ADC helped to fund a new Grampian Business Information Centre in Albyn Place. This was a partnership project which involved the AET, the GRC, the Chamber of Commerce and Grampian Enterprise.

From Boom to Bust ... and Back Again?

The North Sea environment presented a lot of problems to the oil companies with the technology available in the late 1960s. Production lagged some way behind the initial discoveries. The first oil was brought ashore from Hamilton Brothers' Argyll Field and then from the BP Forties Field in 1975. Brent oil came on stream a year later with Ninian following in 1978. The oil was piped or taken ashore at three major locations: Cruden Bay to the north of Aberdeen, Sullom Voe on Shetland and Flotta on Orkney. Total started the first major gas production in 1977, piping the gas to St Fergus near Peterhead.

Exploration continued throughout the early years of production. The pace of exploration was driven by a range of factors including the oil price and profit forecasts, the increasing technological ability to tackle more difficult environments, and government energy policy. The development area was extended north of Shetland, but Aberdeen was already established as the key centre for supporting the oil and gas industries.

By 1992, 54 oilfields were in production and 15 were in advanced stages of development. Four small ones had ceased operating. The GRC forecast that a further 90 fields would be developed in the coming two decades, though these would tend to be smaller.

The first two decades were not without problems. While the popular press sometimes portrayed Aberdeen as a sort of north-eastern 'Klondyke' where everyone was getting richer, this caricature was far from the truth. Those closely involved knew that any industry of this importance brought with it a degree of vulnerability. In the case of oil the key issue was the price per barrel, quoted in US dollars. In 1986, what the experts feared happened: the dollar price fell sharply sending shock waves throughout the Aberdeen economy.

In 1981, the price peaked at $40 per barrel. In 1985, it fluctuated between $28 and $30. The following year the price fell as low as $8.40. Late 1987 saw the price back above $16, well above the key level at the time for most North Sea producers. In the intervening months jobs were lost; at the worst point recorded redundancies were running at 1,000 per month. House prices fell and the retail and leisure industries were badly hit. Planning applications to ADC fell away sharply, undermining the fee income of the Planning Department.

The national media swooped on Aberdeen, anxious to find out about the city that had apparently gone from boom to bust overnight. The six o'clock news reported that the oil boom was over and that Aberdonians were going back to fishing and farming! The economic future of the area looked to be in the lap of the gods. Cars were seen around the city displaying stickers which read 'Please God give us another chance and we promise not to throw it away again'. A new type of promotional challenge emerged for the local authorities – to restore confidence in the local economy for residents and for potential inward investors alike.

In the event, divine intervention was not required and oil prices gradually recovered, almost regaining their all time high of $40 a barrel for a short period following the outbreak of war in the Middle East in 1989. Nevertheless, confidence had been dented. 1986 marked the end of the major expansionary phase for Aberdeen's oil economy.

The response of the industry was to closely re-examine its costs. The ensuing programme of cost reductions meant that pre-1986 employment levels would never return. After the profound psychological shock of 1986 there was more willingness to discuss 'life after oil', and to face the fact that one day the valuable resource would eventually run out. Prior to the price slump of 1986 these had seemed to be issues which could be put off for a long time.

After the price crash the local authority role broadened. Concern was again expressed over the difficulties which economic growth caused outside the oil industry. The local authorities campaigned unsuccessfully to have Assisted Area status restored. They tried unsuccessfully to involve the oil companies in the campaign, but the companies took the view that this was a matter to be resolved between local and central government – the councils began to look more to Europe and their international links, and they encouraged longer term strategies for all the local industries, building on AIDA's studies. This involved re-emphasising the importance of traditional industries such as fishing, farming, food processing, manufacturing, textiles, papermaking, forestry and tourism. If the future of oil was one of 'downsizing', then other sectors would have to create wealth and jobs. Export opportunities would need to be found for oil-related 'know how'. There was a new recognition of the city's rich resources in education, research and development. With this came the recognition that more could be achieved if the public and private sectors worked together.

In 1986 the Scottish Development Agency launched the 'Aberdeen Beyond 2000' project to look at the long term economic future of Aberdeen. The project was primarily a forum of business leaders on which the local authorities were represented. The GRC launched its own 'Grampian Initiative' to examine the longer term issues for the wider regional economy. Both projects stressed the importance of strong public–private partnerships, the need to develop new overseas markets, the importance of higher education, and the need to support growing industries such as tourism.

Aberdeen District Council supported the wider initiatives and launched its own 'Look Local First' campaign in an attempt to encourage support for local businesses. Promotional materials were distributed encouraging residents and businesses to buy local produce whenever possible. Campaign pens had to be quietly withdrawn when they were spotted to be 'Made in Italy'!

The late 1980s and early '90s saw the opening of new advanced technology facilities such as a science and research park, an offshore technology centre, and an international drilling centre. These were partnership initiatives involving the SDA, local authorities and the private sector in the best traditions of the north east.

The events of 1986 also made local authorities look again at the ways in which their economic development and promotional functions were carried out. In 1992, ADC set up a full Economic Development Department for the first time. This replaced the former industrial development section and built on the work of the council's economic development team, a small group of Chief Officers brought together in 1984 to co-ordinate the council's activities. In 1993, ADC's central management strongly recommended a more corporate approach examining the economic impact of all council activities. Even the council's farms were put under the microscope – the 1993 review showed that ADC had 'secure long term investments' in some 2,370 acres. It recommended that these be made as cost effective as possible, and that their contribution to the economy be assessed.

In 1988, the GRC opted for a high-profile and wide-ranging strategy. 'Together to the Future' stressed the need for new partnerships to be forged between the public and private sectors. It also stressed the need for co-ordination of the region's various economic development and strategic planning functions. In

1990 a new Economic Development and Planning Department was established, bringing together the existing Physical Planning Department, NESDA, the Grampian Initiative and elements of the Education Department's vocational training role.

A key element in the economic development strategies of both councils after 1986 was the realisation that the area as a whole had to be more outward looking and that new markets had to be found for local businesses. They began to look towards Europe and further afield in order to secure the long term economic prosperity of both Aberdeen and Grampian region. The ADC looked more closely at the economic potential of its twinning links in other countries.

The Rapid Growth of the Oil Sector

The local authorities had to respond to intense development pressures and in some way every local authority role and service was involved from education to housing, from planning to the fire brigade, from the police force to the roads department. The local authorities had to tread a difficult tightrope, trying to support and facilitate development while minimising adverse impact on the environment and the community.

The withdrawal of government help for industry meant that the public sector effort was primarily that of the local authorities. Local authority estimates suggested that between 1975 and the early 1990s council expenditure on oil-related developments was well over £100m per year throughout the Grampian region. The great majority of this was expenditure by the GRC which estimated that in some years 12% of its budget was directly oil-related. The ADC did what it could with the smaller resources available to it. Councillors and officials took the lead in meeting the senior managers of the oil companies, introducing them to the city, to local government and to the workings of the council. This helped to secure company sponsorship of council projects in later years.

Government departments like energy, trade and industry and the Scottish Office played a role in helping to establish the new industry. The Scottish Development Agency also played a part, particularly through its Aberdeen-based oil and gas division. In 1991, the SDA was replaced by Scottish Enterprise. Its local arm, Grampian Enterprise Limited, covered the city area and most of the north east of Scotland. The local authorities were quick to develop partnerships with GEL. The city's higher education institutions became involved. In July 1980, HRH The Prince of Wales opened the offshore survival centre, an initiative taken by the Robert Gordon Institute of Technology, which was to become a world leader. The RGIT worked closely with NESDA analysing the training needs of local industries. Aberdeen University established an offshore medical support centre, which also became an internationally recognised centre of expertise.

As the industry developed, the importance of training was increasingly recognised. The Cullen Enquiry which followed the Piper Alpha disaster of 1988 highlighted the importance of training and safety as never before. Generally in the 1980s it was government policy to leave training decisions for employers to take in the light of market forces. However a statutory training body was set up for the offshore petroleum industry. It was based in Montrose and developed training expertise in relation to dealing with a wide range of situations from oil spillages to major platform incidents. After a few years the training body was taken over by its industry and its statutory basis was removed. The Offshore Petroleum Industry Training Organisation also became internationally renowned. Trainees from as far away as Australia regularly attended its courses in Montrose.

Oil Capital of Europe

The status of 'oil capital' was built on particular industry roles which the local authorities helped to shape. The heavy engineering and fabrication work associated with the initial development of the industry in a new production location was carried out in other parts of Scotland, for example Methil in Fife and Ardersier near Inverness. Some of the later development-type work was carried out from foreign yards. In some cases North Sea contracts were carried out as far away as Korea! There was simply no particular need for this part of the industry to be locally-based. Intense international competition gave rise to employment problems for those fabrication yards which were based in Scotland.

Aberdeen's roles were focused on the key activities which supported production – administration, servicing, supply operations and communications – and were best located close to the production activities. These activities were more stable in that large numbers of manual workers did not tend to be dependent on one contract for their employment. They supported a broader range of enterprises and occupations. They also provided a better opportunity for locally-based firms and those which had chosen to base themselves in the north east to grow and become international forces. The expansion and diversification of the Wood Group is an example. Initially the expansion of local firms was perhaps easiest in areas such as engineering where relevant skills and management expertise already existed. By the 1980s there was also a large and growing service sector within which a number of locally-based firms operated.

The city's status as Europe's oil capital was assured when the large oil companies, the so-called 'majors', established offices in Aberdeen. Most did so during the 1980s: Shell, Chevron, Total and Amerada Hess went to Altens, BP set up at Dyce, Conoco and Marathon went to Rubislaw, and Elf to Bridge of Don. These companies were all international in nature. While they all established a highly significant presence in Aberdeen this did not include their most senior levels of management. The ADC campaigned for key government functions and oil-related civil service jobs to be moved from London to Aberdeen. Some success was achieved, and over fifty Civil Service jobs in the Department of Trade and Industry moved north in 1993.

The growth in oil employment up to the mid-1980s brought people from all over the UK. Some came from outwith the UK in search of new opportunities. The staff of the oil majors came from a variety of countries. Employment change brought new communities, new perspectives and new cultures to Aberdeen. The role of oil capital also made the city look outwards in new ways. Stavanger, Houston and south east Asia became partners in a world-wide industry rather than merely exotic and faraway places.

The Impact of Oil

North Sea oil affected almost every part of Aberdeen's economy and society. Prior to the mid-1970s the population had been in decline. The impact of oil was roughly to stabilise the city's population which stood at nearly 213,000 in 1971 and just over 211,000 in 1991. The largest population gains arising from oil were in the commuter settlements close to the city: Ellon, Inverurie, Westhill, Banchory, Portlethen and Stonehaven. While Aberdeen's population remained at roughly the same level, the nature of that population changed dramatically with consequences for council services. In the 1971–91 period, the city's employment level rose by 58%, from 94,700 to 159,500. In 1976, 15% of city jobs were oil-related. This proportion rose to 31% by 1991, the comparable figure for the whole of Grampian region being closer to 20%.

The attractiveness of Aberdeen and the surrounding area to people seeking work – in the late 1970s between 5,000 and 6,000 people were entering the area each year – meant the arrival of families with school age children, heightening the demand for school places. Most of the area's new housing was built on the outskirts of the city, or in existing towns within commuting distance of Aberdeen, and new schools had to be provided in these areas. This placed considerable financial burdens on the GRC as education authority. However, many of the area's incomers were foreign nationals working in the oil industry, and American, French and Dutch schools were established in the city.

The well-paid nature of many of the jobs increased car ownership with consequent pressures on the roads, the bridges over the Don and Dee, and the environment. High income levels also increased the demand for shopping and leisure facilities. The ADC had to respond to a wide range of new pressures.

Many of the new jobs in oil and oil-related work were well-paid. Between 1976 and 1993, male earnings in Grampian were consistently above the British average; the same was not true of female earnings, however. Throughout the period they were below the British average, and by 1993 had fallen to 90% of the British level.

The growth in employment possibly had its most visible impact in the housing market. Between 1975 and 1991, some 15,000 new houses were built in Aberdeen, with many more built elsewhere in Grampian. Most of the new housing was built on the edges of the city at Bridge of Don/Danestone, Dyce, Lower Deeside, Cove Bay and Kingswells. House prices were high for most of the period, reflecting the high level of demand. In the late 1970s and early '80s, house prices in the Aberdeen area were rising at the rate of 18% a year. Indeed, throughout most of the twenty year period Aberdeen prices were above the British average, and the second highest in the UK after London and the south east of England. The exceptions were the late 1980s when the fall in the oil price in 1986 and consequent job losses led to a slump in the housing market.

The relative prosperity which came with the oil industry increased the demand for retail activities. Between the mid-1970s and the early 1990s some 100,000 square metres of retail floor space were opened. The Trinity, St Nicholas and Bon Accord shopping centres were opened in Aberdeen. The ADC had planned ahead by acquiring some of the land and property on which the St Nicholas and Bon Accord centres would be developed. The remainder of the land and property came into the council's ownership as part of the development agreement negotiated between the council and the two developers. As ground landlord and as planning authority, the council was closely involved in the detail of these developments.

When new patterns of shopping and leisure activity seemed to be posing a threat to Union Street and the city centre, ADC joined with Grampian Regional Council, Grampian Enterprise and Scottish Homes in a new City Centre Partnership which was formed in March 1991. The aim of the project was to promote and revitalise the heart of the city. By the mid-1990s, the city centre had undergone significant improvement, and Union Street was reckoned to be one of the most profitable retail pitches in Britain. Some 1300 new homes were created and the resident population of the central area was on the increase.

The growing economy needed more space for offices and for industry. Between 1972 and 1991, over 430,000 square metres of major new office development took place, Shell's 34,500 square metre complex being the largest of these. The new high prestige offices of the oil companies constituted one of the most striking physical impacts of oil on Aberdeen. Large new industrial areas were developed at Altens, Bridge of Don and Dyce.

Aberdeen Airport

The airport was perhaps Aberdeen's trump card when it came to winning the key role in servicing oil. Largely as a result of oil the airport grew rapidly. In the early 1970s, Aberdeen had a relatively small regional airport handling around 120,000 passengers per annum. In 1975, the airport was taken over by the British Airports Authority and, in recognition of the role that the airport could play in support of the oil industry, a major expansion programme costing £10 million began. A new passenger terminal building was opened in 1977. In 1993 over 2,000,000 passengers travelled on routes to and from Aberdeen. A high proportion of these were helicopter passengers, indicating the importance to the airport of the movement of oil workers. By the mid-1980s, the combined passenger movements of the airport's three helicopter carriers – Bristow, Bond and British International Helicopters – had made Aberdeen the busiest civil heliport in the world.

The massive growth in the airport brought many benefits to Aberdeen and to the north east. For a city such as Aberdeen which is some distance from the main centres of population and their markets, the ability easily to access the rest of the UK and the world is of vital importance. There was a significant increase in the number of scheduled services to airports in the UK and Europe, with many destinations being made available in response to the needs of the business community. The ADC generally supported the applications which operators made to the Civil Aviation Authority to fly new routes from Aberdeen – around 80% of the airport's passenger activity was business travel. By the 1990s, passengers could fly to all major UK airports and a range of European destinations. The increased wealth and prosperity of the area led to the introduction of an increasing range of holiday charter flights from Aberdeen.

Nevertheless, the presence of a busy airport on the city's doorstep created its own dilemma. Since the early 1970s the local authorities were concerned to ensure that the disturbance caused to people living in the vicinity of the airport was kept to a minimum. This involved BAA carrying out a detailed study of noise levels in the vicinity and making sound insulation grants available to residents within the 'noise footprint' of the airport. In 1973, the County Council took the decision to attach conditions to the grant of planning permission to BAA for the construction of the new terminal building. The condition was that no flights would be allowed to take off or land at the airport between 2150 hours and 0630 hours, except in the case of an emergency. The ADC assumed planning responsibility for the area surrounding the airport in 1975 and kept these limits in place. A public enquiry took place in 1976, and the council's stance was endorsed by the Scottish Office. Over the years, a number of applications were made by the airport authority in an attempt to gain a greater degree of flexibility in this, primarily in order to allow delayed flights to take off and land outwith the airport's normal operational hours. Despite some lobbying by business interests and airport management, the restrictions remained in force in 1996.

With so many passengers passing through the terminal building each year, safety and security became increasingly important. The airport acquired its own full time police presence in 1975, and a dedicated and highly skilled fire and rescue service the following year.

Aberdeen Harbour

The development of the port was also vital to the oil industry and to Aberdeen's position in it. The port grew rapidly from handling 2,000,000 tonnes of shipments in 1979 to twice that level in 1991. It became one of the largest ports in Scotland and one of the most modern in Europe. Much of the growth came from the oil industry. However the port provided facilities and services for all the

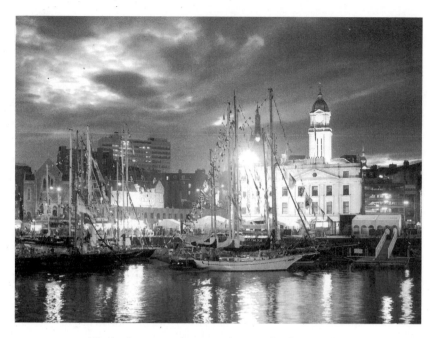

The harbour provides a grand setting for the Tall Ships

region's industries. It changed markedly in character from a traditional port dominated by the fishing industry to one of the most modern in Europe, home to the high technology vessels servicing the oil industry.

In 1994 it became the first Scottish port to be approved by HM Customs and Excise for the export of meat; it also had a purpose-built terminal for forest products and a dedicated grain export terminal. A wide range of products pass through the port, including that other 'liquid gold', whisky.

The port provided the main 'gateway' for the island communities in Orkney and Shetland. General cargo vessels travelled regularly to Norway, Sweden, Denmark, the Faroes, Finland, Belgium and Holland. The port was also important to travel and to tourism. In the late 1960s and 1970s, major quay reconstruction took place. The Harbour Board financed the work by borrowing from the Government and latterly from the European Regional Development Fund. The ADC was represented on the Harbour Board and generally supported its work.

The oil companies needed round-the-clock operations. Some wanted their own quays, some were content to share facilities and others preferred to leave offshore supply to specialist firms. The Harbour Board tried to ensure that they were all accommodated. In May 1984 the Secretary of State for Scotland opened the port's ninth oil base.

The port took on a new appearance and role. In the late 1960s, visitors would have observed a large but traditional harbour dominated by a fleet of mostly small fishing boats. Trends in the fishing industry reduced the number of boats with larger vessels becoming common. By the late 1970s Aberdeen was in the process of transition to a very modern port built largely on meeting the needs of the oil industry. By the mid-1980s oil supply provided about half of the Harbour Board's revenues. At the same time other industries had to be catered for; general cargo accounted for about 50% of total shipping movement in the port.

The port's tradition of ship repair and its dry dock facilities were needed by the oil and oil supply industries. The Harbour Board turned the former shipyard into the Telford Dock in 1994, named after the great engineer who designed the modern harbour. The £12m cost was the largest single investment in the port this century. The dock provided a multi-berth ship repair facility capable of handling the largest oil support vessels as well as large cargo ships.

Aberdeen became a popular port-of-call for cruise ships during the 1980s. The Harbour Board actively promoted the port in this way, joining the Cruise Europe organisation for that purpose. In 1991 there was a highly successful visit of the Cutty Sark Tall Ships Race. The 70 ships are estimated to have attracted 600,000 spectators, and the very high public interest in the event led the Council to bid successfully to host the 1997 race in partnership with its twin city of Stavanger.

Traditional Industries

The growth of oil to some extent both concealed and hastened the decline of employment in the older local industries of traditional engineering, shipbuilding and ship repair, paper making, textiles and fishing. Traditional manufacturing was in decline throughout Britain due to recession and international competition for most of the 1980s. There is no reason to think that Aberdeen could have 'bucked the trend'. However, the decline of local industries concerned the ADC, and studies of the problem were commissioned in the early 1980s. A number of initiatives were taken to help the industries and to offset their decline.

Fishing was in decline as effort and pressure on stocks both increased. 1970 saw the handling in Aberdeen harbour of the largest tonnage of fish in the post-war period, but after that landings declined and, in 1979, ADC began a series of discussions with the industry. The decline was put down to a range of factors including the problems caused to some fishing boats by rising fuel prices, restrictions imposed by other countries, and the diversion of the inshore fleet away from Aberdeen. The main beneficiary of this move was Peterhead where fish landing charges were lower, primarily because its harbour did not come under the Dock Labour Scheme. The abolition of this scheme, in 1989, helped to lower Aberdeen's costs and restore some of its competitiveness.

The availability of grant aid from Europe helped to convince the Harbour Board to reconstruct Commercial Quay West and the adjacent fish market.

Queen Elizabeth and Princess Anne opened the new market in August 1982. However the decline of the industry continued. Employment fell as fewer, larger and more mechanised boats went to sea, trends which were to be seen throughout Britain's North Sea fishing communities. As the decline threatened jobs and people's livelihoods so the regulatory framework – in particular quotas imposed by the European Union to protect fish stocks – became a matter of controversy. By the mid-1980s fishing contributed only about ten per cent of Aberdeen Harbour Board revenues from ships and goods.

Fish processing was an important sector. The mostly small companies in it were dispersed over a large area and were often in inappropriate properties. The ADC and GRC met with the industry. In the mid-1980s a strategy emerged in the form of the Aberdeen Sea Food Project. This brought significant improvements, particularly to the industry's premises. The project was regarded by the local authorities as one of the most successful partnerships in economic development. The local authorities, the industry, the Harbour Board, the SDA and British Rail all contributed.

The meat industry and meat processing were also important to Aberdeen. The removal of the livestock market from Kittybrewster to Thainstone made sense – a modern city could not easily stop to let cattle pass through. However the change

'Something fishy?' – the Fish Market at work

72

also lost the colour brought to Aberdeen by the regular visits of farmers and merchants. When pig slaughtering ceased at Lawsons of Dyce in 1979, one result was six redundancies amongst ADC's meat inspectors. A few years later, when all the activities of the plant were moved to England, ADC protested at the futility of a system of regional incentives which simply lured jobs around the country rather then stimulating new enterprise.

Shipbuilding remained significant in Aberdeen until well into the 1980s. Some thirty-nine ships, mostly small in terms of tonnage, were built between 1975 and 1985. The industry was nationalised by the Labour government in 1977. At this time, the well-known Hall Russell company was Aberdeen's main presence in the industry. Policy was reversed and the industry was returned to the market by the Conservative government in the 1980s, during a period of international recession. The manner of deregulation raised a clear threat to the future of shipbuilding in the north east, and the council campaigned to keep the industry in Aberdeen. A long tradition of shipbuilding effectively ended with the demise of Aberdeen Shipbuilders Ltd in 1991.

These processes of decline in the traditional sectors may have been hastened by oil. The traditional industries, facing increased competitive challenges, found that oil pressures were pushing up costs in the local labour and property markets. Highly skilled workers could often find better-paid opportunities in the oil sector. At the same time the new industries provided more attractive opportunities for investment and employment.

Unemployment and Deprivation

The scourge of unemployment returned to Britain in the mid-1970s. Unemployment was a problem internationally throughout the following twenty year period. Contrary to the expectations of the political leaders of the 1970s, the problem did not quickly disappear with the next economic boom. Unemployment proved to be a very difficult problem to which no country found a convincing answer. The prosperity brought by oil insulated Aberdeen to some extent from the national and international problem. Between 1975 and 1995, the unemployment rate in the city was consistently lower than elsewhere in the country. In 1976, the total number of people out of work in the whole of the north east was only 5,300 or 3.3%. In the summer of 1991, when 9.2% of Scots were unemployed, the proportion in Grampian was 3.8%. However for the relatively small numbers without work the high living costs of the north east made for a very difficult time.

Unemployment and consequent poverty existed in parts of the north east and in parts of the city. In 1993, when male unemployment in Aberdeen averaged 7.5%, the proportion out of work exceeded 12% in the wards of Balnagask, Tilllydrone and Grandholm. The government's expectation that a healthy free market would see a 'trickle down' of benefits to everyone didn't seem to offer much to the most deprived areas. Youth unemployment was a particular problem in the city areas of Northfield, Brimmond, Ferryhill, St Machar and Woodside, whilst long term unemployment was a problem in Northfield and Seaton.

The level of poverty in the city was often overlooked or even denied because of the prosperous image of the oil capital. When government figures became available, the scale of the problem which existed in parts of the city surprised many. The 1991 census showed that in Fersands, 62% of children were in households with no economically active adult; and the figure was also high in Middlefield, Printfield and Alexander/Hayton.

The Government provided large-scale employment and training programmes for young and adult unemployed people. These were financed by the Manpower Services Commission, and then by GEL after 1991. Local authorities in Scotland were vital to the effectiveness of these programmes, providing over 70% of Community Programme places, and number of ADC departments provided valuable opportunities to unemployed people through these programmes.

The ADC worked both to help the unemployed and to try to provide new jobs. In 1984 the council set up a steering committee on unemployment. It entered into talks with the Unemployment Centre Steering Committee which led to a centre for the unemployed, with education and training facilities, being set up. The council began to investigate using European Community funds to tackle unemployment, but was hampered by its own lack of development status within the UK. It supported the Aberdeen Employment Restart Centre which opened in Frederick Street in 1993 and provided valuable retraining to unemployed people.

In addition to providing loans to companies, it worked with the Scottish Co-operative Development Committee (SCDC) to promote workers' co-operatives as a new and alternative form of employment. A temporary development post attracted supporting funding from Europe's Social Fund. In 1994, there were ten co-operative enterprises supported in some way by ADC's efforts.

The local authorities sought to tackle the problems of urban deprivation, and formed a Joint Steering Committee on Urban Renewal in 1983. The councils played an important role in targeting resources towards areas with particular needs, but the residents in those areas also wanted to help themselves. Area forums of local residents were set up in Ferrier, Sandilands, Printfield and Northfield. Interesting initiatives followed, such as the establishment of the north of Scotland's first credit union in the St Machar area of the city. This provided savings and low-cost loans facilities for communities which had difficulty accessing commercial financial services.

The oil industry undoubtedly brought great benefits to the city in terms of employment, prosperity and enhanced opportunity. However, behind this outward show of prosperity lay many of the same problems encountered elsewhere in the country. The challenge to local authorities in the 1970s, '80s and '90s was to tackle these problems and to do so against a background of public expenditure cuts. In Aberdeen this was made more complex by the pressures of oil. By any reckoning, that was a formidable challenge indeed.

5: Planning the City

Good planning was essential to Aberdeen, particularly given the intense pressures created by the oil industry. The planning function also provided the most pervasively influential role of local government. The main purpose of planning – focusing on the use of land and buildings – was to strike a balance between the need for change and development on the one hand and the interests of the community on the other. The availability of land was more or less fixed and, as the one piece of land could often serve different purposes, there were often competing proposals on how best to use it. The local authority role in mediating between competing demands and protecting the community interest was both central and vital.

The planning function had to be exercised in the light of forecasts on how the demand for land and its use seemed likely to change. Economic forecasts were particularly important, involving judgement and estimates as well as science. There was room for disagreement, and on a number of occasions the ADC and GRC differed on the forecasts for the future of the oil industry and the development pressures which would follow. The local authority role had to be exercised within the framework of planning law.

Local government set the planning framework in partnership: with the Scottish Office, who provided national guidance; the GRC provided a strategic perspective; and the ADC drew up local plans. Private developers worked with local authorities to ensure that their proposals were appropriate. The services of the local authorities themselves – for example, the siting of schools, sheltered housing and community facilities – had to be consistent with the overall planning framework. In all of this a balance between development and conservation had to be struck and maintained.

Planning affected almost every aspect of the city: the location of new buildings, the conservation of old ones, the siting of infrastructure, the development of the port and the airport, the provision of new houses, the regulation of hot food take-aways, the location of industry and offices, the modernisation of the fish market, the management of land on the edge of the city and around it, the provision of land for burial grounds, the development of community and leisure facilities, and the development of transport were all matters which required planning. Many less visible aspects of city life were also shaped or influenced by local authority planners – changes of use for buildings, the protection of land corridors for the oil and gas pipelines, and the use of the wayleaves for cabling are examples. Local authority planning designated land for housing, offices, industry, schools and leisure facilities. It shaped the environments in which people lived, studied, worked and played.

Every city has unique aspects which planning must take into account. Much of old Aberdeen was built from granite, but local sources became exhausted as the development pressures associated with oil grew in the 1970s. In an attempt to retain this aspect of its identity, the ADC stockpiled granite once commercial quarrying ceased. The city had a wide range of buildings and areas which were of historical importance and developments affecting them often caught the public's imagination and sometimes proved controversial. Maintaining a vibrant city centre required the sensitive handling of developments along the city's granite mile of Union Street, whilst the redevelopment of historic Castlegate and Green areas proved controversial. Public feeling often ran high when developments were proposed in environmentally sensitive areas of the city.

The Old Aberdeen Conservation Area provided a good example of this, where proposed developments – such as new student accommodation – were closely scrutinised by the council and also by local residents. Protecting the Green Belt around the city remained a priority, but the intensive pressure to identify land suitable for development within the city's confined boundaries sometimes led to a conflict between the two. Planning proposals affecting any of the city's fine buildings were closely scrutinised, not only by the council, but also by conservation bodies such as Historic Scotland and the local civic society, and by the citizens of Aberdeen as well. The Town House, Aberdeen Central Library, His Majesty's Theatre and the Music Hall were all extensively refurbished during the 1980s and '90s, and the planning process had to ensure that the works were carried out in a way that would enhance the buildings. Where buildings changed use, the concern was to ensure that the proposed use was in keeping both with the building itself and also with the area in which it was situated. Of particular concern was the conversion of buildings in the city centre into licensed premises. A major concern was to maintain the fine balance between the city centre as a housing district, commercial and retail centre and area for entertainment and leisure.

The Evolution of Town Planning

The formal planning role of local government began early in the twentieth century. An Aberdeen and District Joint Town Planning Scheme was drawn up in 1933. Post-war planning was shaped by key legislation of 1947, and by subsequent Acts of the late 1960s and early 1970s. The local authority's direct role was strongest during these decades. In the late 1940s the legacy of war-time destruction and the need to clear city slum housing both required a strong local government role. At this time the prevailing ideology in central government favoured strong, central and rational approaches to planning. At local level, councils were expected to take a broad approach to the planning of their areas.

By the 1980s, the government's view had altered to favour the private sector. Local government's planning role was changed to prioritise the enabling of private sector developments and the supporting of public–private partnerships for development. The language of planning evolved with 'management' displacing 'planning' to some extent. Most people in local government – councillors and officials – were not in favour of this trend and saw it as a weakening of the local government role. Whether, as a result of the change, the overall planning system was made better or worse for a particular area was a matter of opinion, and opinion was divided.

The Development of the Framework

In the post-1947 period, Scotland evolved a complex and distinctive approach to planning. This involved partnerships between the Scottish Office and local authorities and between the public and private sectors. As is often the case in matters to do with local government, legislation aimed to generalise what the best councils were already doing. The radical 1947 Act required councils to produce comprehensive statutory development plans. This process which was already underway in Aberdeen. 'Granite City', a very comprehensive development plan for its day, was published in 1952. In the same year the area south of Skene Street became the first part of the city to be designated for comprehensive development.

The 1947 system quickly came under criticism as inadequate. It did not provide an adequate framework for linking land use and economic planning. Land use issues were given priority over social and economic issues. The development plan approach did not seem comprehensive enough, and this made it difficult to manage the development of public services or to encourage private initiative in a co-ordinated way. Critics argued that some of its provisions simply discouraged the private sector. The system for planning did not allow sufficient public involvement and its critics felt that within it decisions of key local importance were being concealed or fudged. Planning was felt to lack the flexibility required in a period of rapid change.

The inadequacies of the system were much discussed in the late 1960s and early 1970s, at the same time as the Wheatley Commission was pondering the future of local government as a whole. In 1972 a Parliamentary Select Committee advocated a national planning framework for Scotland as a whole. This suggestion was never pursued but in response to it the distinctive position of the Scottish Office was developed.

The planning system which evolved in the early 1970s had three main layers: the guidance and advice issued by the Scottish Office mainly in relation to issues of national importance, strategic structure plans and detailed local plans. Scottish Office guidance is often thought to have been most valuable in rural areas, but much of it was highly relevant to Aberdeen and the other cities. The 1978 guidelines for large scale shopping developments were an example. The guidelines and advice of the Scottish Office represented a major effort to offer strategic direction to planning in Scotland, and to overcome the deficiencies of the earlier system. Yet the new approach was far from comprehensive. It did not include urban regeneration or economic planning, both of which proceeded separately under the direction of different government departments.

The local dimension of planning had three elements. The first was regional strategy. The NESJPAC was set up in 1970 to foster co-operation and co-ordination on strategic planning issues between Aberdeen and the other councils of the north east. This voluntary form of regional co-operation brought together the Corporation, the counties of Aberdeen, Kincardine, and Banff, and the joint County Council of Moray and Nairn.

NESJPAC was active in preparing both for the impact of oil and for the needs of the emerging Wheatley local government system. In 1972 NESJPAC appointed a regional planning adviser whose first task was to report on housing in Aberdeen. The report pointed to large and imminent development pressures, requiring perhaps 16,500 new houses over five years, and called for a full structure plan to be prepared. In 1973, concerns were repeated to the British Airports Authority over the delays in providing new terminal buildings and runway extensions.

The Scottish Office and NESJPAC agreed what the key elements of the strategy for the north east should be in 1972. NESJPAC's early work was the first to alert the local authorities to the sheer scale of development pressures which oil was likely to bring. Taking this forward became the responsibility of the adviser and his small Regional Planning Unit. Much was expected of regional reports, but in practice this layer of the system was rather quickly dropped.

The remaining elements were structure plans and local plans. These were intended to be managed together by individual local authorities at regional and district levels. Part of NESJPAC's role was to co-ordinate the structure plans of neighbouring authorities prior to the 1975 local government reorganisation.

The local planning system was not intended for two different tiers of local government, and yet this was what the Wheatley reforms gave Scotland in 1975. Once the different functions were allocated to different councils the system became more difficult to operate, slower to work, and more costly than its designers had expected. The Wheatley system advocated planning for the city in the context of the larger region within which it was located. There was little disagreement with this principle.

In the late 1960s, Aberdeen recognised that the supply of housing had to be tackled on a 'city region' basis. A joint Town Planning Committee, comprising the city and Aberdeen and Kincardine counties, tried to co-ordinate planning issues in and around the city. The North East of Scotland Development Agency (NESDA) was set up in 1969 as a voluntary partnership initiative with a pioneering role in economic development. NESDA was instrumental along with the Scottish Industrial Estates Corporation in developing industrial sites at East and West Tullos.

The 1975 local government reforms removed Nairn to the new regional council for the Highland area. The voluntary approach of NESJPAC was replaced in the Wheatley system and NESJPAC itself was wound up. In its place the very unequal regions and districts were harnessed together to move the planning system forward. The districts ceased to be structure planning authorities.

The cities, having opposed two-tier local government, particularly resented the two-tier planning system. Within this system the regions took on the strategic task of structure planning. Not surprisingly they tended to regard this role as the more important, after all the local plan had to conform to the region's strategy. This rankled in the cities. With some justification they felt that their concerns were every bit as 'strategic' as those of the Regional Councils, and that the local plans were closer to communities and their needs. In any case planning was as much art as science. There were legitimate differences of view between professionals and between politicians. Key concepts, even 'strategy' itself, could be understood in different ways, and it was impossible for any structure plan to be completely unambiguous. Attempts to avoid ambiguity tended to sacrifice the very flexibility which good plans needed.

The different layers of the planning system were intended to be complementary, and to provide 'checks and balances', with the system as a whole providing the framework for development. The clearer the system the better for all parties. Individual developers could appeal if their planning proposals were rejected, and between 1984 and 1991 some 280 appeals were pursued against planning decisions taken by the city. More than 80 of these went to public enquiries overseen by Reporters appointed by the Scottish Office. In 1980, the council submitted objections, on safety grounds, to the proposed liquid gas pipeline from St Fergus to Mossmorran in Fife. The Energy Secretary overruled these objections and the development went ahead.

In cases where it was proposed in some way to alter a building which was 'listed' because of its historical or architectural importance, the approval of the Scottish Office was required. In December 1984, Planning Convener Councillor Bonney moved that the committee seek the Secretary of State's approval to erect a banner on the Arts Centre in King Street showing the unemployment figures for the city. Once the banner was up, Aberdeen Unemployed Centre wrote in complaining that the figures were the official 'registered unemployed' which it believed understated the real extent of the unemployment problem.

ADC decisions could be 'called in' by the GRC if it considered them to be inconsistent with the Structure Plan. In 1994, GRC called in decisions to site new houses at Glashieburn and Middleton Park. In both cases the Scottish Secretary considered that it was really a matter for ADC and the plans went ahead, but such decisions did not always go the city's way. At times the checks and balances became means for pursuing disagreements between the different institutions involved in the planning system.

At times neighbouring district councils disagreed over issues of common concern just as Aberdeen Corporation had at times differed with its neighbours. In 1975, the ADC inherited different approaches to Green Belt management which had been developed by the counties of Aberdeen and Kincardine. At the beginning of the 1980s the city had disagreements with neighbouring Gordon and Kincardine and Deeside districts over land allocations for housing developments.

Planning probably provided more cases of friction and disagreement between regions and districts than all the other local government services put together. This was a Scotland-wide problem, within which the ADC and GRC had their share of disagreements. The press and media were often quick to seize on these highly visible and easy targets. At times the difficulties of the system were greatly overstated, whilst disagreements between local government tiers were unfortunate and generally led to expensive delays and some public rancour. In the worst cases one council would seek to blame the other for all the problems. However, for every case of friction or conflict there were scores of examples of good, timely planning decisions which were based upon and required co-operation. There were also many cases of good partnership working between the ADC and GRC.

The evolution of the planning system presented further, unique difficulties for Aberdeen. By the early 1970s much of Scotland was beginning to feel the painful decline of traditional industries and the loss of jobs. The main pressure was to encourage a planning stance to facilitate almost any development for the jobs it might bring. By contrast Aberdeen's economy was rapidly expanding. By 1973/74 the oil majors had arrived and the consequent development pressures were imposing great strains on an inadequate planning system. Aberdeen's particular situation required a robust and clear planning system which simply was not available. The inadequate system grafted on to the Wheatley local government reform did not begin to produce sophisticated plans until the end of the 1970s, a decade too late. It could be argued that the ADC and GRC made an inadequate system of planning work reasonably well, and that they did so despite the most intense planning pressures.

These pressures were uniquely intense amongst Scottish local authorities. Between 1984 and 1991 the Planning Department responded on average to more than 2,300 planning applications and over 2,900 applications for building warrants each year. In the early 1990s responding to applications took up nearly half of the department's time.

Critics of ADC's planning efforts sometimes argued that Stavanger or Shetland got more benefits for the community from oil than did Aberdeen. This perhaps was the case, but the critics overlooked the inadequacy for the purpose of the planning framework available to the corporation in the key years of the late 1960s and early 1970s. They ignored the weaknesses and the problems caused by the slow development of the two-tier planning system. They failed to point out that Shetland may have benefited from having a single, all-purpose council and unique locational advantages to bolster it in discussions with the oil majors. And they simply failed to recognise the sheer scale of the development pressures to which the Council's planners had to react or that these pressures tended to dominate the meetings of the Committee.

The critics also tended to forget the real doubts about the future of North Sea oil which existed until the 1973 war in the Middle East. Until then many in Aberdeen felt that oil would be a 'here today, gone tomorrow' affair, with any benefits going to the American companies and not the local area. There were doubts about how large the oil reserves were, and about whether the technological problems in extracting the oil could be solved. The oil companies themselves at this point had only a token presence with small offices and very few staff. After the 1973 war, the oil majors became more positive towards the North Sea, in part because of the political stability of Scotland and Norway. The sharp international oil price rise of 1974 changed the economics of the industry, and the North Sea became potentially much more profitable. Also, the UK government became more enthusiastic, anticipating tax revenues from the industry and a big contribution to the trade balance.

Planning and the City of Aberdeen District Council

Despite the local government upheaval of 1975 and the changes in the planning framework which saw the new GRC become the structure planning authority, there was a remarkable continuity in the underlying approach to planning in the city. Between 1947 and 1995 the city had just four Directors of Planning. The earlier ones helped to produce 'Granite City' and all four were heavily influenced by it.

The approach which evolved in the city was one of modernising and updating the early report and making it more flexible and responsive, in particular to the needs of the oil sector. From 1975 this was expressed through the two-tier planning system, namely local plans and ADC's responses to GRC structure planning. Both levels agreed that Aberdeen was the heart of the north east, and its centre for work, shopping, leisure and communications.

Within the new planning system the GRC initially produced two Structure Plans, one focused on oil and the Aberdeen area, and the other on the rural hinterland. The plans were major projects in their own right and their completion was a considerable achievement. The first plans were not fully approved by the Scottish Secretary until May 1981.

Land for Housing

This approach included instructions to the GRC to look again at housing provision and to accommodate a major increase in Aberdeen city. In the late 1970s, the council's Planning Committee believed that suitable land for housing was running out. There were only two sites left and these could probably only provide about 500 new homes. Attention switched to Dyce, to land at North Denmore which had previously been thought unsuitable, and to finding smaller sites. The heavy demand for new housing taken with the shortage of land and escalating house prices created a situation which the council was keen to avoid.

Pressures from the building industry and the government's policy of deregulation led to proposals to relax some building standards. Action by ADC allowed the public to glimpse the likely consequences. The building control section borrowed a 'show house' from Edinburgh District Council and erected it beside St Nicholas House. The so-called show house had been built to the minimum permissible standards. It was eventually donated to a charity which used it as a children's play house! Proposals to amend building regulations to allow the construction of very small houses did not find favour with the council who refused a considerable number of applications preferring instead to maintain good housing standards. As households changed and the numbers of elderly people grew, demand for smaller houses increased, but maintaining housing standards remained a council priority.

The 1986 Structure Plan for the Aberdeen area included new housing forecasts. The ADC disagreed with these, considering the GRC forecasts to be overestimates, and produced its own alternative strategy based on its own housing projections and on local plans. In particular the committee considered the projected demand for housing to be too high in part because it was based on the boom years of 1984/85 and not the somewhat harsher climate of 1986, and it objected to the proposed distribution throughout the city. The Planning Committee also thought that the GRC was underestimating future growth in the population of elderly people, and their housing needs. This would make it more difficult for the council to meet Scottish Office guidelines on the provision of sheltered housing.

There were particular objections to GRC proposals for Kingswells, East Brimmond and Cove. The council favoured housing development on its land at Cairnie. However, this didn't fit in with the Structure Plan, and there were objections from Gordon District Council, in whose area the land lay. The ADC argued its preference for a 'new settlement' to be created, in effect a new town to take some of the housing pressures off Aberdeen. In 1991 the GRC produced one plan for the whole region, and from 1992 it sought developer interest in a new settlement to be built in the north east.

Public opposition led to this policy being set aside. New housing continued to be dispersed to the city and the surrounding towns. Planning and market mechanisms ensured that in broad terms housing needs were met. The price was high though and the area had some of the highest cost housing in the UK. This created problems for those entering the housing market and those on low incomes. In 1975, the committee noted that 535 families were living in caravans: in 1994, there remained 410 residential caravan places, though many of them were unused.

The growth in population not only created demand for new houses in which to live, it also required more land for disposing of the dead. The 1952 development plan thought that the city's population would not grow beyond 200,000 and burial grounds were made available at that level. The Kaimhill crematorium met demand for the whole north of Scotland from Kincardine to the islands. A new crematorium was opened at Jessiefield in 1976. In 1978, the committee thought that 92 acres of burial ground would be needed compared with the 66.5 acres which were available.

Local Plans

Local plans were developed by ADC, initially for inner areas of the city. Consultations over the local plan for Cove took place in 1977, followed by plans for Lower Deeside and the north of the city. The focus then moved to considering Aberdeen as a whole. A single local plan for the city was formally adopted in 1992, which was the first of its type in any of the main Scottish cities.

The planning process was guided by the production of a series of policy statements and development briefs illustrating the council's position with regard to future developments. The council formally adopted a Green Belt Policy Statement in 1982 which clearly stated that there would be a presumption against new building within the city's Green Belt except in specified circumstances. Similarly, the council formulated a number of other policies dealing with a range of specific issues such as the development of office premises in the west end and a guide to the use of dormer windows in the city.

Through the publication of a number of development briefs, the council was able to influence and guide development in certain areas of the city. One of the earliest of these outlined proposals for the development of the Science and Research Park at Bridge of Don. This was followed, during the 1980s, by a series of briefs for the redevelopment of some parts of the central area such as the Castlegate, The Green, and the St Nicholas 'triangle'. Plans to redevelop the sea beach area were contained in a comprehensive guide entitled 'Links to the Future'.

Whilst the concept of development briefs was a new one, some of the ideas on which they were based were not. Proposals to redevelop certain areas of the city had been outlined in 'Granite City' and some even predated that. By the mid-1990s some of these proposals had come to fruition whilst others were only beginning to take shape.

Public Participation in Planning

Planning allowed, and to some extent required, the participation of the public at certain points in the process, and steps were taken to review and improve the mechanisms for encouraging such participation. While these remained far from perfect, planning was generally ahead of other council functions in seeking to involve and consult the public. There were statutory consultations. People could examine the detail of draft plans and of individual planning applications. They could and frequently did object. Often a specific issue seemed to dominate the public's reaction to planning proposals. In 1988 the Planning Committee noted that there had been a healthy 500 responses to consultations on the draft local plan. However about two thirds of these were about housing proposals in Cove. The committee also noted that only four council departments and three councillors had responded. In 1990 a Planning Handbook was published to help raise public awareness of planning processes and issues. In 1994 proposals to develop land within sight of Lover's Walk at Peterculter brought a storm of protest. The Planning Department received 470 objections and a 1,700-signature petition. Public pressure resulted in a compromise being reached when the ADC attempted to secure access agreements along the north bank of the Dee from the city to Peterculter.

The Planning Committee was particularly concerned to liaise with organisations which could advise on the needs of disabled people in relation, for example, to ease of access to buildings for those with mobility problems. Policy was adopted in October 1975 and was reviewed annually, an important management device for checking on progress. Liaison took place with the Disabled Persons' Panel on Planning and Building Control Matters and the committee adopted design guidance notes to advise developers about the key issues and help them to respond. In 1991 the panel became the Disability Advisory Group, in a change which the Planning Committee supported, believing that it would further improve services to disabled people. In June 1993 the Planning Department responded to a request from the Women's and Equal Opportunities Committee by publishing detailed guidance notes and illustrations as policy and so further raising the profile of these important issues. A Disabled Access Officer was appointed in 1991.

Following proposals from the City Planning Officer, the council set out on a new approach to involving people in the 'Planning for Real' initiative in 1995. This focused on the Bridge of Don area where local people wanted more community facilities as well as a halt called on new house building. Twelve hundred people attended the first public meeting and in-depth seminars involving councillors, officials and residents took place. Discussions were helped by the provision of three-dimensional models which gave participants a clear image of the proposals. Planning convener Councillor Maureen Irons described the new approach as 'a listening exercise' and stressed the importance of a partnership approach. Housing convener Councillor Ramsay Milne agreed and looked forward to the full involvement of the community: local people made over 3,000 suggestions for the area. Invitations went out to community organisations, the GRC, the health board, Scottish Homes, Grampian Enterprise and others in an effort to build a multi-agency partnership which listened to and involved the local people. This led to a Community Plan and a formal partnership agreement.

The Herald and Post welcomed the 'historic agreement'. 'Planning for Real' was one of the largest and most thorough projects of its kind to take place anywhere in Scotland.

The City Centre

The development of the city centre was a long-standing concern of the Council. The centre's potential as well as development problems, including congestion and car parking, were identified in 'Granite City'. This was the first thorough study of the issues in any Scottish burgh. In 1953 the corporation recognised that car parking was a growing problem, and the economic growth which came with oil meant that car use and ownership grew rapidly from the late 1960s.

In 1975, the first car parking standards were adopted by the Committee. Car parking was one of the policy areas where the two-tier local government system caused confusion. The GRC provided car parks, and both tiers adopted their own parking standards. The ADC developed and updated standards for off-street parking, and increased the available car-parking space by requiring provision in office and other developments. It became common in Aberdeen for areas which had previously been rear gardens to become car parking space as the buildings were turned into offices. It wasn't until 1984 that the GRC and ADC began to liaise closely to ensure that they adopted common standards for car parking in the city centre. These were incorporated in the GRC transport policies and plans for 1986–91.

The committee supported a series of recommendations by the City Planning Officer on the future of the city centre in August 1985. The council subsequently brought in consultants to look at the future of the centre and Union Street in particular. They identified a strong demand for housing in and around Union Street. In 1978, the Planning Committee expressed its desire to safeguard a 'living city centre'. In many cities in Britain and North America development patterns seemed to be encouraging people to move out of the central area, and Aberdeen wanted to avoid this. The report noted that the centre's population was markedly older than the city as a whole and that this would have implications for the provision of public services, particularly housing.

Three new shopping centres – Trinity, St Nicholas and Bon Accord – provided Aberdeen with a standard of shopping above that of most British cities – but there was a price to pay. The new shopping centres hastened the decline of small and specialist retailers. In the city centre and especially Union Street 'To Let' and 'For Sale' signs proliferated. In 1991, there were some 50 vacant shops in Union Street alone, although this was an expected part of the adjustment process for the area following major development.

A working party was set up to examine how to tackle the problem: in 1991, the City Centre Project was launched. It involved ADC, GRC, Scottish Homes and Grampian Enterprise. Its remit was to revitalise the commercial area and to ensure the balanced development of the central area. Its early success led to the formation of the City Centre Partnership. It was a catalyst in turning round Union Street's fortunes, not only by helping to get shops re-opened but also by finding ways to use the accommodation above shops which often lay empty. By 1995, there were less than a dozen vacant retail properties out of nearly 200 in Union Street.

The Partnership was behind some 140 projects which took place between 1991 and 1996. Floodlighting helped to enhance historic buildings such as Marischal College to make them more attractive for residents and visitors. The Partnership helped to provide 1,400 houses, and 3,000 residents were brought into the city centre's population. Private sector money was raised to pay for much of the cost of a 53-camera closed circuit television scheme to deter crime and to make the centre a safer place. The Denburn Pocket Park project – which won an Aberdeen Civic Society award in 1996 – transformed a piece of urban wasteland into an attractive landscape.

The City Centre Partnership also provided the catalyst for the implementation of a number of measures designed to tackle problems of traffic congestion in the city centre. Separate bus lanes appeared in Union Street and King Street and a number of other traffic calming and management schemes were implemented. Other experiments were attempted with differing degrees of success, such as the pre-Christmas pedestrianisation of Union Street and the 'Park and Ride' scheme. By the 1990s the council had developed a very clear policy designed to encourage housing in the city centre. The policy was contained in the Aberdeen City District Wide Local Plan adopted in 1992 and the Housing Plan 1991–96. The use of 'brownfield' sites (vacant sites within the built up area) was encouraged as was the re-use of existing buildings. Existing housing was improved through the Housing Action Area Programme and the use of improvement grants. The policy proved to be a success with housing developments taking place throughout the central area of the city including the Castlegate, The Green, Middle School and George Street. Many of these developments were the result of successful partnerships between the council, Scottish Homes and the other public and private sector housing providers in the city.

The council's policies for the city centre sought to encourage housing and other forms of development in order to create an attractive and vibrant environment. They also recognised the importance of the city centre for recreational purposes. Between 1986 and 1993 the number of licensed premises in the centre almost doubled. This proved to be a source of controversy. City centre residents complained about street disturbances in the early hours of the morning as licensed premises closed. This presented a problem for the police who were responsible for maintaining law and order. At times the blame was placed at the door of the council's Licensing Board for granting too many licenses or extensions beyond the statutory 11pm closing time. Yet when these were not granted the board stood accused of being a 'kill joy.'

The problem was considered by the board, the council's Licensing Committee and the police. Councillors even went on night patrol with the Police to see the problem at first hand! In 1993, the council revised their guidelines for the control of residential use and licensed premises in the city centre. An earlier experiment to provide late night buses to take people away from the city centre was withdrawn when it proved to be uneconomic. However, the council in conjunction with the City Centre Partnership continued to look at the need for late night transport.

Shopping

Rapid changes in retailing and shopping arose from increased car ownership and use, and changes in technology and business organisation. In some areas of retailing larger units were needed to make efficient use of new methods and to provide the necessary car parking. By 1981 over 52% of Aberdeen households had one or more cars, a little above the average figure for Scotland. In the wider GRC area the figure was over 61%; and the car was used for more and more journeys, whether these were for leisure, shopping or to get to work.

In 1977 consultants were brought in to report on the new trends. Their report stressed the importance of limiting large scale retail developments on the outskirts of the city in order to preserve Union Street and the surrounding area as the retailing heart of Aberdeen. However, the council also recognised the need to develop the area in order to provide modern, high quality shopping facilities to match the city's prosperous economic image. Three major shopping malls were planned for the centre of the city. The first of these was situated on the site of the historic eighteenth-century Trinity Hall on Union Street, and opened its doors for business in 1982.

The council was anxious to ensure that redevelopment of the site did not result in the loss of the listed building and so an agreement was reached with the developers that the hall would be retained and incorporated into the development. The council also wished to ensure that the facade of the new mall did not detract in any way from the remainder of Union Street and therefore insisted on the use of granite.

During the 1970s and early 1980s compulsory purchase orders were used by the ADC to buy up large sites in the areas of St Nicholas Street and George Street. In 1979, a two-stage plan for the comprehensive development of the central area was approved. The CCDA was expected to take four and a half years to complete but took considerably longer. In October 1983, Lord Provost Collie laid the foundation stone for the St Nicholas Centre, and, in 1985, Lord Provost Rae opened the centre with its twenty shops, 96,000 square feet of retail space, and 14,000 square feet of offices.

The Bon Accord Centre was the heart of the second stage of the CCDA, and did not receive full planning permission until November 1984. The original outline proposals of the developers were modified substantially by the Scottish Office as a result of planning enquiries. The old buildings around Schoolhill were retained and extensive use of granite and other traditional materials was made. The development was a priority for the ADC. Councillor John Sewel, the leader of the council, was closely involved in driving the plans on to fruition. However the development, like the St Nicholas Centre before it, was also controversial in that it altered the historic street layout by building over part of George Street. The Bon Accord Centre was officially opened by the Queen in August 1990: it had 54 shops on two floors and was linked to the adjacent John Lewis store. The whole shopping complex employed well over 1,000 people.

The Bon Accord Centre aimed to provide the most modern shopping facilities and to link them with work, leisure pursuits and ease of access through parking provision: it provided a 500-seat food court, playcare facilities for children, and 1,200 car parking spaces and, in 1990, it was voted the Best Kept Shopping Centre in Scotland. The centre also incorporated an ADC leisure facility with an international standard bowls hall. More than 55,000 people entered the Bon Accord Centre each day in the 1990s. However, while many people welcomed the retail and recreational opportunities offered by the St Nicholas and Bon Accord Centres, others regretted the demise of St Nicholas Street and George Street which had been major shopping areas for decades. There were also some regrets that the streetscape of the city had been permanently altered.

In 1988, consultants carried out a major survey of shopping in Aberdeen for ADC and GRC. It noted a growth of 75,000 square metres of shopping floorspace since 1975. There were 'superstores' in operation at Dyce, Middleton Park, Berryden, Garthdee and Portlethen, and three more were being developed. A number of 'retail warehouses' had also opened. The survey clearly showed that the trend for 'out of town' shopping was as popular in Aberdeen as elsewhere in the country. Whilst the ADC welcomed new shopping facilities, they were also very much aware of the need to preserve both the traditional retail heart of the city and the smaller shopping facilities serving local needs.

The ADC was approached by several disabled citizens who had heard about an innovative access scheme in Wales and who wanted this to be replicated in Aberdeen. 'Shopmobility' was the result. Lord Provost Robertson opened the project in Flourmill Lane in 1992. The scheme allowed people with permanent or temporary mobility problems to have the use of powered or manual wheelchairs and scooters so that they could shop or use town centre facilities. Volunteers were available to help. On average 60–80 people used the scheme each day, though demand was far higher than this at Christmas. The ADC and the GRC provided about 75% of the costs with the rest being met through fundraising.

The Needs of Industry

The rapidly growing economy needed more land for its industries. Expanding and relocating companies boosted the demand for office space, as did the 1975 local government reform. Throughout the 1970s industrial land was taken up at the rate of 50 acres per year, and by the end of the decade 600 acres remained available: at Dyce, Bridge of Don and Altens.

The GRC, ADC and SDA were all involved in the provision of sites for industry. The council felt that it would be more sensible if it had the sole responsibility within the city, and it made this recommendation to the Stodart Committee of Enquiry. In 1995, less than a year before local government reorganisation, the GRC sold off industrial estates at Bridge of Don and Altens. It faced a budget crisis and argued that the sale was needed to balance the books. The ADC was furious at this and thought that the proceeds of the sale would benefit other parts of the region more than the city. City councillors condemned the sale as an 'asset strip', which would deprive Aberdeen of important resources for economic development.

The idea for developing an Aberdeen Science Park to promote new hi-tech industries was first put forward in 1980. The council supported the concept of the park from the outset but the initial planning application submitted by the SDA and GRC was refused primarily on the ground that the proposed site was situated within the Green Belt. However, following considerable discussion with the SDA and the preparation of a development brief by the Planning Department, the sensitive development of the site at Balgownie was approved.

The demand for office space put particular pressures on the West End and on this aspect of the GRC Structure Plan. After a number of call-ins by the GRC, a compromise office policy was worked out in 1981. This allowed development in one part of the West End while seeking to discourage it in the other part. This policy was reviewed and updated in 1993.

Transport

The importance of oil to the nation undoubtedly accelerated the modernisation of roads to Aberdeen, particularly from the South. Some developments attracted higher than normal rates of Scottish Office grant such as the dualling of the main route north to Aberdeen from Perth. Many improvements to the trunk road network came about as a result of successful campaigning by the public and private sectors. However, even co-ordinated campaigning sometimes failed to achieve a quick result. The campaign for the electrification of the rail link from Aberdeen to Edinburgh (CREATE), which ADC supported, was still active in 1996. The campaign failed to win the backing of the Government which was more intent on privatisation of the railways at this time.

At local government level transport was viewed as a strategic service and was the responsibility of the GRC. Transport plans were drawn up for the whole region. Subsidy was offered by the region to 'social' routes without which rural communities could have become more isolated, and to some commuter routes to try to encourage the use of public transport.

The ADC was critical of GRC transport plans, feeling that at times there was under-investment in roads and that the city's needs were neglected within the broader exercise of regional planning. By 1981 the use of public transport was in sharp decline, accounting for only 35% of journeys to work. The ADC made particular criticisms of the bus services which the GRC provided until deregulation in 1986. In September 1981 the Planning Committee approved Councillor Clyne's motion to call on the GRC to transfer responsibility for city bus services to the ADC.

Perhaps the single most important failure of the two-tier system was the inability of the city and the GRC to agree on an additional road bridge over the Dee. The ADC favoured a new bridge at Hilldowntree, some 600 metres upstream from the existing Bridge of Dee. The GRC disagreed and in 1989 applied for planning permission to build a new crossing just 22 metres from the existing bridge. In 1996 the much needed third bridge seemed as far away as ever. Much debate took place on the case for a third road bridge over the River Don. This was strongly opposed by communities such as Tillydrone, while road users' organisations and Gordon District Council campaigned for the development.

The airport at Dyce expanded rapidly. The main terminal was opened in 1977 and further expanded in the 1980s. In 1979, planning permission was sought for a heliport in anticipation of the huge increase in helicopter traffic of the 1980s. In order to deal with the planning issues an Aberdeen Airport Consultative Committee was set up. Relations between ADC as local planning authority and the airport's management were good throughout the period.

The main issue of disagreement related to airport use. The original planning permission for the airport's modern development was approved by the Scottish Office in the 1970s. It included a restriction which meant that flights could not land or take off after 10.30pm, except in cases of emergency, to minimise disturbance for the nearby residents. This restriction was increasingly criticised by the business community which wanted more flexibility. The ADC recognised the problem and, in 1992, senior officials in the Planning Department were instructed to enter into talks with airport management.

In 1993 the 10.30pm rule was relaxed, for a football game! The international match between Scotland and Switzerland was scheduled for 8 September. The airport management knew that after the game it would be impossible to get all of the expected Swiss supporters onto their planes and in the air before 10.30pm. While the Swiss supporters had a good reputation, the Chief Constable thought that there could be problems if they had to stay over until the next day. In July, the Planning Committee agreed to lift the airport restriction on this occasion.

The issue of granting flexibility to the airport so as to accept delayed

scheduled flights was hotly debated during 1994. The ADC refused planning permission preferring that the airport's permitted operating hours remained the same.

The rapid growth of residential areas on the outskirts of the city placed considerable strains on the existing road network into the city centre. Proposals for two new crossings of the River Don to the north of the city and the River Dee to the south emerged. A lack of resources as well as fundamental differences of view between the ADC and GRC held up progress. In 1996, after considering fourteen options, the GRC Structure Plan proposed a western peripheral bypass to ease pressure on Anderson Drive.

As Aberdeen's economy grew so too did the transportation by lorry of all kinds of industrial and consumer goods. Lorry parking emerged as a problem. In 1973, the police estimated that there were 1500 cases of indiscriminate lorry parking each week. The provision of a lorry park at Altens on the outskirts of the city, and the introduction of lorry routes bypassing the central area, helped to ease this problem.

Green Belt

The ADC tried to protect the Green Belt around Aberdeen against the development pressures of the oil industry and the housing market. The Green Belt was needed to protect the edge of the city and the surrounding countryside, to prevent the city expanding and encroaching on neighbouring towns, and to provide amenity and recreational facilities. By the late 1970s, the pressure to develop sites on the periphery of the city was intense. This was particularly so in Lower Deeside. The council inherited a Safeguarded Area Policy from Aberdeen County in 1975 which was extended to the area of West Culter/Anguston and thereafter adopted an interim development policy for Lower Deeside. This defined urban groups split up by 'green wedges' where development was not generally permitted.

By the early 1980s, it was recognised that there was a need for a comprehensive policy to protect the green fringes around the city. The Planning Department consulted widely on the most appropriate policy. It received a large number of replies from individuals, companies, government departments, the Rowett Research Institute, the GRC and neighbouring district councils. In 1982, a widely supported policy update emerged and this was incorporated in local plans. The adoption of the policy generally strengthened ADC's case for resisting development in the Green Belt around Aberdeen but nevertheless, the pressure to develop new areas, primarily for housing, remained substantial. In 1984, the council expressed its total opposition to a proposed housing development within the Green Belt at Kingswells. The whole community was opposed to the development, but following a successful appeal to the Secretary of State, it went ahead.

The district wide local plan promoted the concept of countryside around towns. The countryside areas were in the original Green Belt and would be considered for development if and when appropriate proposals emerged. This approach was intended to help control development and to safeguard other parts of the Green Belt in the longer term.

An Aberdeen Urban Wildlife Project emerged in 1990. Some 170 sites of interest were identified and catalogued. Three priority areas – Donmouth, Den of Maidencraig and Scotstown Moor – were developed as local nature reserves in partnership with Scottish National Heritage. Texaco provided private sector sponsorship initially at Donmouth. A wide range of local organisations became involved in the planting of trees and shrubs and the general tidying up of the areas. In 1993, ADC became involved in an innovative partnership along with Forest Enterprise, the Scottish Agricultural College and Aberdeen Enterprise Trust which sought to improve public access to and enjoyment of the countryside around the city. The Four Hills Project focused attention on the countryside areas of Brimmond, Elrick, Kirkhill and Craibstone and its aim was to provide easy access to them from the built up areas of the city.

Conservation

Most of the city's efforts at conservation focused on the built environment. The concern to protect individual buildings was an old one, as it had been a priority concern of local authorities from the late nineteenth century. In 1974, an archaeologist and an assistant were appointed, the costs being met by the Society of Antiquaries, with the council providing office space. In 1979, the Art Galleries and Museums Department took on these two specialist employees.

In 1991 – in line with the new management thinking in the council – the City Planning Officer and the City Arts Officer reported together on the need for a nature conservation strategy to be developed for Aberdeen. This was published in 1993 along with a Community Woodland Plan.

Legislation was put in place between 1953 and 1979 to protect ancient monuments and buildings. The council surveyed Aberdeen's stock of historic buildings and found there were 1647 'listed' buildings of which 53 were 'Category A' and deemed to be of national importance. Ownership of the 53 'A' listed buildings was divided. The city had nineteen including the Art Gallery, the War Memorial and the Cowdray Hall. The others were owned by the GRC, the Kirk, and the University of Aberdeen. Planning proposals involving any of the city's listed buildings were closely scrutinised. For example, the nineteenth-century Marischal College, once perhaps unkindly described as a 'maister monsterpiece', was in fact the world's second largest granite building after Madrid's Escorial. In 1995, proposals to convert part of the building into a luxury hotel proved controversial. Following much debate over the details of the redevelopment, the proposal was approved.

In late 1986, the Planning Committee discussed the state of the city's historic buildings. The University of Aberdeen was actively involved in conserving its buildings and worked in close partnership with the Council. However, some city buildings gave grounds for concern, particularly some of the older church buildings (churches had been exempted from listed building controls). These concerns were not new. In 1981, a baluster fell on the pavement from Greyfriars Church, though fortunately no one was injured. This led to the church carrying out a structural examination, and to the University of Aberdeen doing the same for Marischal College. In 1986, several pieces of Langstane Church fell to the ground. One of these was estimated to be 30-40lbs in weight. Again, fortunately, no one was hurt. The council had a statutory responsibility to ensure that the buildings were made safe but it was also keen to ensure that the spires of Aberdeen remained a strong landmark on the city's skyline. The most significant restoration project was the dismantling and total rebuilding of the sandstone steeple of the Gilcomston South Church on Union Street. The ADC helped to meet the costs in order to retain an important city centre landmark, whilst Historic Scotland made a substantial contribution to the project.

The city's broader conservation policy developed under legislation of 1967 and 1974. These Acts focused attention on conserving whole areas. The policy aimed to ensure a high quality of design and building, improved landscaping and environmental management, the 'disciplining' of motor vehicles and the creation of pedestrian areas. The council designated Conservation Areas within which development was tightly controlled. These were Old Aberdeen – in which the University of Aberdeen played a prominent role – Union Street, Bon Accord Crescent/Crown Street, Albyn Place/Rubislaw, Great Western Road, Cove Bay, Ferryhill, Lower Deeside (Pitfodels and Footdee). Special measures were taken to ensure tree preservation: by the mid-1990s the Planning Department had over sixty Tree Preservation Orders in place.

Recreation/Community Facilities

The two-tier local government system led to both councils providing community facilities. Co-ordination was weak until the early 1990s, when ADC and the GRC got together to try and look systematically at the issue. Their joint study showed poor provision in a number of parts of the city: Stoneywood, Danestone, Denmore/Dubford, Hazlehead/West End, Ferryhill, Cults (east), Milltimber and Culter. The council prioritised the provision of new facilities at Airyhall and Constitution Street to add to its stock of eighteen community centres. This was later supplemented by new provision at Ferryhill and Peterculter.

One of the major planning proposals which emerged in the 1990s concerned the redevelopment of the beach area. The proposal aimed to supplement the existing facilities at the Beach Leisure centre and Linx Ice Arena to make Aberdeen beach one of the major tourist attractions in Scotland. In 1995 proposals were approved for the construction of a nine-screen cinema complex, restaurants, a night club and other entertainment facilities. Planning permission was granted for a new hotel with conference and leisure facilities at Links Road to the north of the Beach Boulevard.

The years between 1975 and 1996 saw some remarkable changes take place in Aberdeen. The most visible of these occurred in the physical layout of the city and the uses made of its land and buildings. The planning process played a key role in helping to shape these changes. The arrival of the oil industry in the early 1970s brought intense pressure to develop the city in ways which the authors of 'Granite City' could never have imagined just two decades earlier. At the same time, the reorganisation of local government split the planning function between the regional and district councils. These two factors combined in Aberdeen to make the task of planning the city very complex and onerous indeed.

The ADC worked with a wide range of public and private sector bodies in order to create the Aberdeen of the 1990s. Between 1975 and 1995 the built up area of the city expanded by 16%. Whether particular developments have enhanced or detracted from the overall character of the city is of course a matter of opinion. Nevertheless, the council consistently worked to shape the city in a way that would provide the quality of environment which Aberdonians and visitors alike would enjoy, and assist the development of the local economy.

6: Good Housing for the Citizens

Introduction

If the weight of councillors' mail-bags provided the main clue to the relative importance of different services, then housing would undoubtedly top the list. Even in the regional councils, which had no role in providing council houses, councillors often found that they got more enquiries from constituents about housing than any other issue! The importance of the issue to the public lay in the size of the council's role – as owner of one third of the city's homes in 1995 and with some 32,000 tenants – and in continuing levels of housing need. In the district arena, housing was of more concern to the public than anything else. Given that shelter and housing were among the most basic human needs, this was not really surprising.

The public sector was the major provider of housing in Scotland in the decades after the Second World War, far more so than in England and Wales. Their role developed throughout this century and peaked in 1981 when it was estimated that around 55% of all houses in Scotland were publicly owned. In Aberdeen in 1981, almost 53% of all households lived in council-owned accommodation. By the 1990s, the dominance of public sector housing had begun to wane, although local authorities remained a major provider of Scotland's housing. The growth of public sector housing came about as a direct result of legislation.

In the 1980s and 1990s new legislation changed the role of local authorities in housing. In addition to encouraging the spread of home ownership, the housing reforms of the 1980s and '90s focused on the revitalisation of the private rented sector; more effective use of public finance; and on changing the role of local authorities by placing less emphasis on the direct provision of council housing, and more on developing a new role 'enabling' the provision of housing by other bodies.

The district councils' housing role was perhaps more affected by the government's reforms than any other local authority service. And with each change in the law affecting local authority housing, the role of the council changed. Many of these changes were strongly opposed by the ADC, as they were in most of Scotland. The changes were seen as an erosion of the traditional council role in the provision of affordable housing for a large proportion of the population.

The Growth of Public Sector Housing

Local authorities have had an interest in housing since the nineteenth century, but it was not until the end of the First World War that they began building houses in significant numbers. During the second half of the nineteenth century, a local council's interest in housing was largely focused on the eradication of unsanitary conditions and on the problems of overcrowding. The 1848 Public Health Act did not extend to Scotland. This left the responsibility of doing something about the health of the nation in the hands of local government. The adoption of police Acts led to a measure of improvement, including the demolition of some insanitary buildings and the laying out of streets etc., but the provision of housing rested very much in private hands. A number of Acts relating to housing were passed in the late nineteenth and early twentieth centuries. These were of limited impact as local authorities did not have the resources to implement any major building programmes.

In Aberdeen, the corporation proceeded – under the Housing of the Working Classes Act 1890 – to clear out slum houses between Exchequer Row and Chapel Lane, which were described as 'receptacles of filth' providing 'facilities for the commission of crime, and the escape of criminals'. In 1897 the corporation took the decision to construct artisans' dwellings in the city's Urquhart Road, Roslin Street and Park Road area, so beginning their involvement in the direct provision of housing. The 1890 Act provided the legal powers. The sixteen tenements were to be 'plain but substantially built'. By providing facilities which are taken for granted now but were rare then – such as sinks and water in the kitchens and WCs – the council sent out a clear signal about the housing standards which Aberdonians should have. However, the bulk of the population in Aberdeen and elsewhere in Scotland continued to be housed in private rented accommodation, much of which was overcrowded and lacking in the most basic amenities.

The state of Scotland's housing was the subject of a Royal Commission which reported to Parliament in 1916. The report was a damning indictment of the failure of the private sector to meet housing needs, particularly in Scotland. The commission's view was that 'no satisfactory programme of housing can be carried out unless a definite obligation is placed on some person or Authority to see that a sufficient number of suitable houses is systematically provided'. Lloyd George's coalition government promised the men who fought in the First World War 'homes fit for heroes' on their return. In 1919, the obligation to provide those homes fell on the shoulders of local authorities. The significance of the Housing (Scotland) Act 1919, known as the Addison Act, was twofold: firstly, it made council building obligatory, and secondly, it provided state subsidies to local authority housing where none had existed before.

Following the First World War, attention was given to the clearance of slums and the demolition of insanitary dwelling. Almost 3,000 slum houses were dealt with in Aberdeen. The population displaced by slum clearance or demolition were mainly re-housed in the new housing estates within the city.

In 1920 the corporation began its first post-war housing scheme, comprising 156 dwellings at Torry. The larger housing estates were started after 1924. The Housing (Scotland) Act 1924, known as the 'Wheatley Act' was the main success of the first Labour government. It increased the subsidy available from the government for the construction of houses. The Scottish Office ensured that this subsidy continued even when it was threatened or reduced south of the border.

Between 1924 and 1936 the corporation was responsible for the construction of some 6,434 houses in the city. The largest scheme was to the south of Woodside in the Hilton, Middlefield and Cattofield areas where the houses were predominantly flatted. Corporation schemes also sprang up at Powis and to the north of School Road comprising mainly three and four storey tenement flats. Flats were constructed at Ruthrieston and a mixture of house types was constructed at Torry. The majority of granite or brick houses constructed by the corporation during the inter-war years stood the test of time remarkably well.

The Housing (Scotland) Act 1935 directed local authorities to carry out surveys of housing conditions within their areas. The results, published in 1939 showed that, despite the considerable progress that had been made throughout the 1920s and '30s, around one third of all houses in the city remained overcrowded, unfit for human habitation, or both.

This unsatisfactory state of affairs was made worse by the Second World War. In Aberdeen, as in most other cities, the building of new houses was virtually brought to a standstill, although the corporation did manage to complete 852 houses between 1940 and 1945. Some 200 houses were destroyed or had to be demolished as a direct result of war damage. Many more were damaged. This left the city with an acute housing problem and an estimated requirement of some 15,000 new houses.

After the Second World War, local authorities and central government worked together to repair the damage caused by air-raids, and to clear slum housing. With a post-war shortage of building materials and skilled labour, the housing problem could not easily be addressed. Nevertheless, by 1950, around 4,000 new houses were built, including some 1,500 temporary homes. During the 1950s, the construction of a number of permanent housing estates was commenced, the largest being at Cumming's Park, Northfield, Kaimhill, Garthdee, Kincorth and Torry.

The corporation, like other housing authorities, began to experiment with the use of non-traditional building materials. Quality remained extremely important and the corporation's policy was to ensure that a least 50% of all new post-war housing was constructed of granite or suitably faced brickwork.

Initially the main approach, throughout Britain, was to demolish the old and replace with new housing. There was a general belief that renovations would end up as a subsidy to the inefficient private sector. Some of the new developments were built to radical designs with new materials and building processes. Aberdeen avoided the excesses of the 'high rise' approach which predominated in a number of Britain's larger cities. There were 57 multi-storey blocks in the city built from 1960 onwards, providing a total of 4,447 homes.

The new houses provided better living conditions than the ones they replaced. Many of the new buildings won awards. However the sense of community which existed, even in some slum housing, could not easily be replaced. In some cases the new houses gave rise to problems – dampness, and poor insulation for example – which only became obvious years later when the local authorities lacked the resources to put the problems right. In addition, the construction of houses outwith the central area of the city was often not matched by the provision of adequate community facilities and this was a problem which ADC had to tackle in later years.

By the 1960s the local authority sector was the largest in the housing 'market', and it was common for the local authority to be the main landlord in its area. Throughout the 1960s and most of the 1970s local authorities continued to build houses for rent. However, despite the fact that 41,000 public and private sector houses had been built in Aberdeen since the end of the Second World War, more housing was required. The corporation had virtually exhausted all of the land which had been zoned for housing purposes in the development plan, and a review of the housing situation in the Aberdeen area was urgently required. At the same time, the Wheatley Commission was considering the future shape of local government in Scotland.

The Housing Legacy

The Wheatley Commission thought that many of the local authorities of the 1960s were too small to deliver an effective housing service. It argued that housing required a certain scale to be efficient. In addition councils had to be able to co-ordinate their housing, social work and education policies. The Commission rejected the idea that Scotland should have a single, centralised approach to housing. Instead it saw the new, stronger local authorities playing the key role.

Housing became the main responsibility of the 53 districts in 1975. The housing committee was the most prestigious service committee and councillors were keen to serve on it. Providing good quality housing for the citizens of Aberdeen was seen as one of the council's most important functions.

The ADC's housing role included house building, letting of houses, rent collection, estate management, repair and maintenance of council stock, the provision of accommodation for homeless people and the administration and payment of improvement grants in the private housing sector. The council had responsibility for the licensing of the city's nine sites for mobile homes and, from 1989, for the travellers' site at Clinterty.

In order to discharge this wide range of functions, ADC established three committees: Housing (Building and General Purposes), Housing (Improvement

Grants) and Housing (Management). These committees reflected the council's priorities at the time. In addition to the day to day management of the existing stock, the council pursued an extensive programme of building new houses and improving the standard of its older stock, as well as administering the payment of a large volume of improvement and repairs grants to the private sector. This committee structure was altered over the years to take account of the changing priorities of the council.

By 1995 the council's role had become considerably more complex than it was in 1975 and its decision-making process reflected this. There was one housing committee with overall strategic control. The committee operated with a considerable degree of power delegated to it by the full council, subject to matters of policy or resources being approved by the Policy Committee. There were five standing sub-committees, liaison groups and working parties which in turn fed into the Housing Committee. These were the Housing Cases sub-committee, Housing Plan Working Party, Housing Initiative Areas sub-committee, a Joint Co-ordinating Committee on Housing and Social Work, and a Forum of Housing Activity sub-committee. In addition there were a number of specific groups such as a working group with tenants' representatives, a review of the Scheme of Allocations Working Party, and a Domestic Violence working party.

Planning the Service

In 1975, one of the new council's first priorities was to establish an up-to-date assessment of housing need in the city. The corporation had produced a report on housing in 1959 to cover the period from 1960 to 1976, and a second report in 1965 which extended the period up till 1984. The situation had been reassessed in 1971 to take account of the city's boundary extensions which had added areas to the north – west of the city at Whitemyres and Greenfern and to the south at Altens. NESJPAC and GRC's regional report had examined housing, and the council took these reports into account. The ADC's report was produced in 1977 and showed that, as at March 1977, there were 78,884 houses in the city of which 36,057 were council-owned. 7,653 houses were below the tolerable standard, lacking in basic amenities: the vast majority of these were in the private sector.

The ADC inherited a situation that was unique to Aberdeen. By the early 1970s, North Sea oil was beginning to have an impact on the housing market. The most obvious effect was in the private sector where rents and house prices rose rapidly – by the end of the decade, the level of house prices in the city had risen to such an extent that they were second only to London and south east England. One of the effects of the escalation in private sector prices was to make it considerably more difficult for first time buyers to enter the 'bottom rung' of the housing ladder. Prices in the private rented sector rose rapidly. During the 1970s, changes in the law also had the result of diminishing the size of private rented sector. These factors increased the already high demand for public sector housing.

'1,000 Houses a Year'

The completion of 1,000 local authority houses per year became a target for the ADC in the 1970s. It had inherited a situation where council house completions were at an unsatisfactory level largely because of shortages of skilled building workers. The arrival of the oil industry created an unprecedented demand for office and industrial buildings, and for both public and private sector housing, whilst building contractors in the city were mainly engaged in non-housing work. In an endeavour to accelerate house completions, the council considered the possibility of establishing 'work camps' around the city to accommodate incoming building workers. By mid-1975, the recession in the building industry nationwide created new interest in local authority contracts from both local and national builders. In the two decades from 1975 the council built more than 6,600 homes in the city.

However, although the housing stock available to the local population was greatly improved, the high level of local authority completions did not provide a major source of accommodation for incomers to the city. Until 1981, in line with legislation and local authority practice, the council's allocations procedure gave clear priority to applicants who had been resident in the area for at least six months. The high number of completions may also have inadvertently created an expectation that the level of investment in housing would continue. In later years, as public expenditure cuts began to take hold, this was an expectation which the council was unable to live up to.

Improving the Housing Stock

The ADC's housing programme placed considerable emphasis on the rehabilitation and modernisation of the existing stock. Housing improvement became an even higher priority in the 1980s and '90s as the council's house building programme began to be curtailed by new legislation. Much of the stock was in need of substantial refurbishment. Many of the council's older properties lacked facilities such as modern kitchens, bathrooms and central heating, while some properties lacked effective insulation or had problems of dampness or condensation.

Substantial investment was needed in order to improve the overall condition of the stock. The council embarked on an ambitious programme of improving houses according to their need and age. Many of the improvement schemes had a dramatic impact on the overall quality and appearance of the houses involved – the addition of pitched roofs along with general improvements to the fascia of 1930s housing at Pittodrie Street and Linksfield Road greatly improved their appearance.

In February 1982, the council set up a pilot scheme in the city which was intended to supplement the ongoing house improvement programme. The

Tenant's Grants Scheme was available to tenants who wished to upgrade their homes in addition to or in advance of the council's own improvement programme. Tenants were able to obtain a grant from the council for a specified range of improvements such as kitchen or bathroom renewal, window replacement, and more recently the installation of central heating systems. The pilot scheme was extended in 1983 and, in the following years, a number of alterations were made to the scheme in order better to target resources. By the 1990s around £2m a year was spent in this way.

In 1989/90, and then in 1994, the council assessed the condition of all housing in the city. The 1994 survey confirmed that significant improvements had been made in the overall condition of Aberdeen's housing since the 1970s. In particular, a large proportion of below tolerable standard (BTS) housing in both the public and private sectors had been brought up to standard. The 1994 survey showed that the number of BTS houses had been reduced to 2461, 85% of which were in the private sector.

The council embarked on an extensive programme of improvement including window replacement and measures designed to improve energy efficiency such as insulation and replacement of heating systems. Safety was improved by installing smoke alarms in all council properties. Despite the high levels of investment some council estates in the city had particular problems such as a high number of 'difficult to let' properties, a poor environment, vandalism and general signs of degeneration.

In 1993 a Housing Initiative Areas sub-committee was established to monitor trends across the city and to identify areas where particular initiatives were required to tackle housing and environmental issues. Many of these problems were tackled through the council's 'Selective Urban Regeneration Exercise' which sought to improve the quality of life in areas such as Balnagask, Printfield and Seaton. Ground floor verandahs were enclosed to improve security

Improving the environment throughout the city was an important element in the council's housing programme. Landscaping and fencing brought environmental improvements. Car parking and traffic management initiatives were carried out in some housing schemes in association with GRC's Roads Department. In 1994, the council sought to make the environmental improvements programme more responsive to area needs by establishing separate area environmental improvements budgets. This allowed Housing Officers to instruct minor improvements in their areas.

The installation of controlled entry systems in the city's multi-storey blocks greatly improved security. However, in some multi-storey properties, vandalism remained a persistent problem. The introduction of a concierge system at Tillydrone in 1994 improved security and reduced vandalism. In turn this greatly improved the appearance of the flats.

The council was also conscious of the social problems often associated with high rise living. The provision of community rooms or community facilities in the council's sheltered and special purpose multi-storey blocks gave tenants more opportunity to meet for social and recreational purposes.

Improving the Private Sector

The council's responsibilities extended across the whole housing market. It had responsibility for securing improvements to houses in the private sector. Surveys carried out in the 1970s revealed that a large proportion of the city homes which lacked basic amenities were in the private sector. Housing Action Areas (HAAs) were set up to tackle the problem. Householders in those areas gained access to grants for the repair and improvement of their homes. Between 1974 and 1995, the council declared 65 HAAs covering a total of 2,990 dwellings. The 1994 House Condition Survey confirmed that significant progress had been made in improving the overall quality of private sector housing with the majority of BTS houses brought up to standard. During the 1990s, financial constraints meant that it became increasingly more difficult for the council to fund improvements in the private sector. As a result, no new HAAs were declared after 1991 and Repairs Notices were only used in the most serious cases.

Other Providers

The other providers of public rented housing in Scotland during the 1970s and 1980s were the Scottish Special Housing Association (SSHA) – which had been set up as a government agency in 1937 – the New Town Development Corporations, and housing associations. The private sector provided housing, generally for purchase rather than for rent. The SSHA was a non-profit making agency set up to supplement local authority housing provision, particularly in areas of rapid economic expansion, and played an important role in meeting oil-related housing needs in Aberdeen. Between 1971 and 1981 it provided 1,750 new houses in the city. There was no residency requirement for allocation of an SSHA house and incoming workers were helped to find accommodation. By the early 1980s the SSHA's house building programme had tailed off in Aberdeen mainly because of the shortage of suitable sites.

Shifting the Balance

By 1980, local authorities were the main providers of housing in Scotland. The existing legislation gave them considerable discretion in formulating their individual housing strategies. The extent of the local authority house building programme in Aberdeen during the 1970s was a good example of this, but perhaps the very strength of public sector housing in Scotland was the main reason for later retrenchment.

During the 1980s and '90s, Conservative governments legislated to exercise a far greater degree of control over the local authority housing role. The result was less and less autonomy for local government. Housing policies in Scotland increasingly followed those south of the border. The 'right to buy' legislation and the relentless pressure on local authorities to raise rents applied equally throughout Britain. Responsibility for local authority housing rested with the Scottish Office Development Department (SDD) rather than with the Department of the Environment in London, but this seemed to make little difference to the main policies.

The Effect of Spending Curbs

In 1978, for the first time in more than 50 years, local authorities did not provide a majority of the new houses completed. However the major change came in the 1980s. Government policy favoured home ownership and greater variety in housing tenure. These policy changes required some reduction in the local authority's direct role as housing provider and landlord.

Local authorities generally subsidised council house rents by using some of their rate income. At the end of the 1970s the rates subsidy to housing expenditure was typically about 14% in Scotland. This was made more difficult during the 1980s, and councils were forced to raise rents to generate the income needed to pay for repairs and maintenance. By the end of the decade the subsidy had all but ceased and council housing was effectively self-financing. Many regarded this as unfair since home owners could still receive financial support through mortgage tax relief.

Between 1979/80 and 1987/88 average council rents in Scotland rose by more than 60% in real terms. In 1980, the average weekly rent for a council house in Aberdeen was a little under £7 and the income from rents accounted for 41% of the housing budget. Government grants accounted for 47% of the annual budget. By 1994/95 the average weekly rental had risen to £24.38, and the income from rents accounted for 93% of the housing budget. Despite the virtual ending of subsidies and the rise in rents, ADC took pride in keeping rents lower than other cities in Scotland.

The 'Right to Buy'

In 1980 the Government gave council tenants the right to buy their homes. The sale of council houses to tenants was not new but was much more common in parts of England than in Scotland. Aberdeen County Council sold houses to sitting tenants at market value between 1971 and 1975. Some 59 of these were in the city district area.

The Conservative government's policy had distinctive features. In particular the extension of new rights to all tenants effectively made the policy compulsory as far as councils were concerned. Sales were to be heavily discounted below real market values and it was clear that councils would not be free to use the income from sales to finance the new building which they would like. Most councils including Aberdeen opposed this new policy. In 1980, members of the Policy and Housing (Management) Committees met to consider the terms of the Tenants Rights etc. (Scotland) Bill. Policy Convener Councillor Sewel moved 'that the Bill, in so far as it relates to the sale of council houses represents an unwarranted intrusion by central government into the affairs of local government'.

The reform allowed tenants to buy after three years, and this was later reduced to two. Large discounts were offered so that tenants were able to buy their homes at much less than the market value. Discounts of up to 60% on the market value of the property were available. In 1987, the discount was raised to 70% – large discounts and rising rents provided tenants with strong incentives to buy their homes. Not surprisingly the policy rapidly became very popular with tenants, particularly those in the better properties; supporters of the policy saw it as one of the most successful and popular strands of the privatisation programme. After 1982 more than 11,000 council houses were sold annually in Scotland. In 1994 the average purchase price for a council house in Aberdeen was £16,412.

The council, like many others in Scotland, was criticised for the slow processing of 'right to buy' requests. Between 1980 and mid-1994 nearly 15,000 Aberdonians made enquiries about buying their house and about 9,000 went on to purchase. By the late 1980s, the backlog in processing purchase applications had become critical as councils faced the risk of financial penalties if applications were not processed on time. At one point in the late 1980s, tenants could wait up to one year to receive the title deeds to their home, and the council took the unprecedented step of contracting a proportion of the work involved to private legal firms in the city in an effort to reduce the backlog. In 1981/82, 147 properties were sold; in 1993/94 more than 1,100 were sold, and the council expected this rate to continue throughout the 1990s. The ADC's aim was to make applicants an offer of sale within two months.

The 'right to buy' policy created difficulties within councils as the council stock and landlord role decreased with every sale. The best types of property were the most popular and the policy simply removed most of these from the council to the private sector. In some of the better council estates in the city, as many as 40% of houses had been purchased by 1995. Overall, nearly 70% of Aberdeen council houses had been purchased by their tenants by the early 1990s. Flats were much less popular: only 100 multi-storey flats had been sold by the early 1990s. In 1994, figures showed that 21.1% of ADC's total stock of all types of property had been sold to tenants. Councils felt that the quality of their stock was diminished, and they were not allowed to use the income from sales to replace the houses purchased, even though the income was a lot less than the market value of the assets which were sold: and of course a reduced stock also meant less rental income.

By the 1990s, the council's role in building new houses was largely restricted to providing sheltered housing for elderly and vulnerable people, and to working in partnership with other agencies. 1993 was the last year in which the council was able to build new general purpose housing – only 82 council houses were completed, though this was actually the highest level since 1986.

The government policy of privatising council housing was predicted to run out of steam when the pool of tenants who wanted to buy and who could afford it was exhausted. New initiatives were introduced to encourage public sector tenants to buy. In April 1991 the 'Rent to Mortgage' scheme was extended to cover local authority tenants, who were able to transfer their tenancies from the local authority and then convert their rent to a mortgage through a scheme administered by Scottish Homes. As councils predicted, this initiative was largely unsuccessful: by 1994, only 66 tenants had taken this route into home ownership in Aberdeen.

In 1987, the government introduced a White Paper establishing a new direction for local authority housing. The Housing Act 1988 and the Local Government and Housing Act 1989 introduced a number of policies to expand choice and to promote an 'enabling' role for councils. In 1989, a new agency – Scottish Homes (SH) – brought together the SSHA and the Housing Corporation in Scotland. It also became a major landlord in its own right by inheriting the housing stock of the SSHA. The establishment of SH was not wholly welcomed by Scottish local authorities – most saw it as a further threat to the local authority housing role. It was also seen as a non-elected body, lacking the legitimacy and accountability of the ballot box.

Tenant Choice

Scottish Homes was set up to provide low cost properties for rent and for first time buyers, and to help in the housing aspects of urban renewal. By 1990 the SH stock in Aberdeen had grown to more than 1700, but from then on the agency reduced its landlord role. Tenants were given some choice over which landlord they wanted to transfer to. Local authority control was not an option. This policy of 'empowering' tenants gave rise to housing co-operatives emerging as community-based landlords. By 1994, there were four of these co-operatives in Aberdeen – St Machar, Sheddocksley, Deeside and Mastrick – owning more than 590 properties.

The setting up of Scottish Homes was also an attempt to promote more diversity in the housing market. The agency took on responsibility for supervising and financing housing associations. In Aberdeen there were seven housing associations which all kept waiting lists. Attempts were made to co-ordinate the waiting lists of the council and the housings associations in order to provide a more co-ordinated approach to housing allocation across the city, but this proved difficult. Castlehill was set up by the very active and entrepreneurial Voluntary Services Aberdeen in 1970. Castlehill had 564 properties in 1994. Grampian and

Langstane were locally-based as were two smaller associations – Aberdeen Soroptomists and Aberdeen YWCA. In addition to these, two national associations, Hanover and Margaret Blackwood, operated in Aberdeen. In total the associations provided just over 1800 homes in 1994, and had over 9,000 applicants on their waiting lists.

By 1994, the council's direct role as landlord was considerably reduced as a result of government policies of the 1980s and early 1990s. However it retained over 32,000 properties, about one third of the total stock in Aberdeen. The council remained a major landlord, and probably had a more complex role in relation to the overall housing market than in 1975.

The Tenant's Charter

In December 1991, the government launched its Tenant's Charter for Scotland. The charter, affecting all public sector tenants including tenants of the local authority, outlined government proposals for improving public sector housing. In many respects, it was a reflection of some of the good practices and initiatives already pursued by many local authorities, including the ADC. The charter restated the existing rights of tenants but it also introduced a number of significant changes. It promoted home ownership and introduced a new 'right to repair' provision. It also proposed that local authorities adopt new measures to improve their standards and performance. Many of the proposals were made law in 1993.

The 'right to repair' provision attracted considerable publicity when it was launched. By law, local authorities were already duty bound to maintain their housing stock in a wind and watertight condition and to carry out certain repairs. Many local authorities had a good record of planned maintenance of their stock, although their repair and maintenance programmes had been affected by increasingly stringent controls on local government spending. Typically, councils would prioritise repairs: a burst pipe might be fixed within a day, while a few weeks might be taken to repair a window sill – Aberdeen distinguished 'emergency', 'urgent' and 'routine' repairs. In 1993/94, 95% of 'emergency' repairs were completed within the target time of four hours and 81% of 'urgent' repairs within the ten-day target. In total, in 1994/95, over 128,000 repairs of all kinds were carried out in response to notification by tenants.

The 'right to repair' addressed the issue of the quality and speed of council house repairs. It was aimed at encouraging local authorities to have a good repairs service and to set timetables for the carrying out of repairs. It also gave tenants the right to instruct private contractors to carry out urgent repairs up to the value of £250 if the council did not carry out the repair within a specified period of time.

The Tenant's Charter proposed that local authorities set standards for the provision of housing services. Tenants were to be informed of these standards which were to be monitored and the results published. This meant that ADC had to publish information on a wide range of things such as the time taken to carry out repairs, to answer letters, to sell houses under the right to buy legislation, and so on. The introduction of housing management plans, performance indicators and proposals for CCT were all part of the government's drive to raise standards, increase accountability, provide value for money and alter the nature of accountability.

Towards a Housing Strategy

One of the underlying themes of the government's housing policy in the 1980s and '90s was to encourage local authorities to develop a more strategic role in the provision of housing. The introduction of legislative and financial controls made this change both necessary and inevitable. The government issued a White Paper on the future direction of local authority housing in 1987. It set out the government's position quite clearly by stating that 'local authorities should increasingly see themselves as enablers who ensure that everyone in their area is adequately housed but not necessarily by them'.

The Council modified its housing strategy as its role changed. An important step towards the development of a comprehensive housing strategy was made in 1993 with the adoption of a Housing Objectives Statement, which was revised in June 1994 to take account of feedback received from public consultations. Five core objectives were identified as being central to the strategy, and these formed the basis for the strategic development of the council's housing role.

Partnerships

The changes in the local authority role meant that councils had to consider new ways of providing an effective housing service. This resulted in an ever increasing number of agreements and 'partnerships' being forged between councils and other bodies with a role in housing.

Partnership working in one form or another was not a new idea as far as ADC was concerned. A tripartite forum – of ADC, the Scottish Office and the SSHA – met regularly throughout the 1970s and '80s in order to discuss housing issues. After Scottish Homes came into being in 1989, it was recognised that the partnership needed to be redrawn in order to reflect the changing roles of the 'partners'. In February 1991, the council and Scottish Homes signed a Strategic Agreement in which they agreed 'to work together to identify and tackle housing needs in the city'. The partnership between the two gradually evolved over the course of the next few years, as it was increasingly recognised that more could be achieved by harnessing the resources of Scottish Homes to the strategic vision of ADC. One of the most significant results of the partnership was the provision of new homes as part of the regeneration of the central area of the city. The council and Scottish Homes reached an agreement to establish a combined waiting list covering all the public and voluntary sector housing providers, and to improve information through an 'option shop'.

In its strategic role, ADC had to ensure that best use was made of all available housing stock. In 1988, the Forum for Housing Association Activity was established. This brought together ADC, Scottish Homes, and the Housing Associations active in Aberdeen. The four housing co-operatives joined the forum when they were established. The aim was to co-ordinate the work of all housing providers in the city in an effort to make best use of all their resources.

The council worked closely with organisations representing tenants and residents. Involving tenants in the housing service was a priority of both central government and the ADC. In 1993, the Tenant Information Service was given the task of working with tenants to develop and support their participation. Over the course of the following year tenant representatives and councillors met to discuss various housing management issues. By 1994, thirty-one tenants' associations had been established in the city. In 1994, a Participation Development Group was established by tenant representatives to look at housing issues on a city-wide basis and to consider the future direction of tenant participation. The following year the Council established a Tenant Support Unit in order to promote participation. The Fersands Housing Development Project was established in 1992 with help from the Urban Aid Programme. This helped the community to examine future housing management issues and tenure change, including the setting up of a housing co-operative.

In 1995, the council adopted a policy against racial harassment. This made racial harassment a ground for eviction from a council tenancy. The policy was the result of a successful partnership between the council, Grampian Police and the Racial Equality Council. It resulted in the ADC winning a local authority Race Award.

Community Care

From 1 April 1993, the council, together with GRC, Grampian Health Board and the voluntary sector, became involved in the implementation of the government's policies for care in the community. The provision of sufficient and suitable housing was an extremely important aspect of the community care policy. The council entered into annual Housing Planning Agreements with the Social Work Department of the GRC and the Health Board in order to identify the future housing needs of community care client groups – by liaising with the other housing providers in the city, the council acted as an 'accommodation broker' in order to secure an adequate provision of housing.

The implementation of the legislation placed additional demands on the ADC as housing authority. The Joint Community Care Plan for 1994–97 set out the intention of the GRC and Grampian Health Board to reduce the provision of beds in the city's hospitals and residential homes for the elderly despite predictions that the elderly population would rise during that period. During the 1990s, ADC's housing programme placed emphasis on the provision of sheltered and supported housing. This was achieved through a combination of new build properties and the conversion of some of the council's existing stock. By 1994, there were 2,545 sheltered housing units in the city of which 1886 were provided by the council.

The council became involved in the regional council's Community Alarm Scheme, which was a highly successful project operating throughout the region from 1984. It involved connecting elderly households to a central control room which they could contact in an emergency. Aberdeen District Council contributed to the success of the scheme by paying for and installing the necessary equipment in all council homes occupied by an elderly person.

The council had to secure the provision of suitable housing for other community care groups such as those with physical handicaps or learning difficulties. Again, the joint Community Care Plan set targets for a significant reduction in hospital beds and a corresponding increase in the demand for specialist housing. Throughout the 1990s all new housing provided by the council was built to 'barrier free' standards which meant that it was suitable for wheelchair users. The council provided most of the accommodation for people with physical disabilities, with the other main provider being the Margaret Blackwood Housing Association which provided supported accommodation at Raeden Court and Eday Gardens. Housing for people with learning difficulties or mental health problems was provided by ADC and voluntary organisations. The demand for accommodation was considerable and was highlighted in 1993 by the controversial plans to close Kingseat and Woodlands hospitals.

Homelessness

The ADC had a statutory responsibility to assess and meet the housing needs of homeless people. The Housing (Homeless Persons) Act 1977 increased local authority responsibilities for the homeless and transferred responsibility for them from regional social work to district housing departments. The council fulfilled this responsibility by providing a range of temporary and permanent accommodation.

By the 1990s the number of homeless applicants had increased substantially, particularly those assessed as having a priority need – such as those with responsibility for children and those vulnerable because of old age, mental or physical disability. The two main reasons for homelessness were matrimonial disputes and family or friends being no longer willing or able to accommodate the applicant. The increased demand for accommodation placed a considerable strain on the Housing Department as it became more and more difficult to place applicants in permanent accommodation. In 1993/94, the department was assisting over 370 households with temporary accommodation.

The ADC's record in providing permanent housing was consistently above the Scottish average during the early 1990s, but the situation still gave the council cause for concern. It became increasingly difficult to allocate permanent housing to homeless persons who had been temporarily housed in bed and breakfast establishments, and this in turn placed greater demands on the supply of temporary accommodation. The council decided to increase the provision of short stay accommodation at the Accommodation Assessment Unit in Bon Accord Street by a further ten places. The council's Homelessness Strategy was also reviewed. Amongst other things, it sought to ensure adequate provision for women who were made homeless by domestic violence and for young single homeless people.

The ADC established a Domestic Violence Working Party in January 1991 in order better to co-ordinate and improve services. The working party considered a report in 1991 which showed that, during a three month period earlier in that year, 147 women had applied for accommodation in the city's refuges and that only 47% were successful. The council worked with Aberdeen Women's Aid and Grampian Women's Aid in order to provide additional refuge accommodation

Only the best will do – sheltered housing, Janesfield Manor

and bring provision in the city more into line with national guidelines.

The Aberdeen Single Homeless Review Group was set up to help homeless young people aged 16–18. The group included representatives from ADC's Housing Department, the GRC Social Work Department, the voluntary sector, Scottish Homes and housing associations. Further initiatives followed with the setting up of a Young Single Homeless Project in 1992 which offered supported temporary furnished accommodation to young people between the ages of 16 and 18. A Young People Leaving Care Committee was also established to consider the housing needs of young people leaving local authority care and moving into Council accommodation.

Housing Management

Housing management had to change in line with the council's housing responsibilities. In 1981 the Housing Department produced a series of reports entitled 'Towards an Effective Housing Service'. This led to a number of fundamental changes in the approach to municipal housing management. One of the main recommendations of the report was that there should be further decentralisation of the housing management service.

The reports also recommended that elected members should concentrate on developing a clear overall housing strategy for the city and not become involved in the day to day administration of the service. The proposals contained in the series of reports were mostly adopted and laid the basis of housing management within the ADC in the 1980s. They led to the creation of four sections within the Housing Department: administration, finance, allocations and estate management.

Decentralisation of housing management was a key proposal. An area office already existed in the Mastrick area of the city. The creation of an East Team in 1983, based at Tillydrone, and a West Team in 1984, based at the existing Mastrick office, brought the administration and management of the housing service closer to tenants. Offices were also set up in the 'difficult to let' estates. In 1989, a blueprint for the further decentralisation of the housing service was discussed. The proposal was that there should be four principal area offices and a network of satellite offices and rent collection points. This proposal fell foul of cuts in funding and was not implemented.

Despite the lack of resources a number of other changes were made to provide a better service to tenants. By 1995 the East and West teams provided a full range of services, including estate management, and administration of housing benefits and rent arrears whilst, throughout the city, tenants benefited from the council's investment in new computerised systems for paying rent. The new payment points could be used 24 hours a day, 365 days a year. In 1995 the Council brought in a pioneering helpline to deal with disputes between neighbours – tenants were able to get advice outwith normal office hours.

In the same year the council offered preferential insurance rates for home contents which tenants could pay along with their rent. The 'big freeze' over the 1995 Christmas holiday had shown up the problem of council tenants being under-insured or having no insurance. The enquiry by the Scottish Select Committee showed that these problems were greater in Scotland than elsewhere in the UK and suggested that the costs of insurance were probably the main factor. Under the ADC scheme, minimum level insurance was made available to pensioners for 56p per week and to younger tenants for 72p. More than 1,100 applications to join the scheme were received in the first few months.

In the mid-1990s, ADC was preparing for another management shake-up to help it meet the challenge of CCT for housing management. The government had intended to impose this on councils earlier, but the local government restructuring of 1995/96 required a delay. Under CCT, the council would only be able to manage its own stock if it won that right in competition with other bidders. The government's plan was to let 30% of the work in 1998, and the remainder by April 1989. CCT would involve many of the key aspects of management, including the day to day housing management activities of rent collection, property letting, tenancy management, administration of repairs and maintenance and caretaking and cleaning. Local authorities would retain responsibility for ensuring an adequate supply of housing in their area, allocating properties, setting rents and capital programming.

The Future of Local Authority Housing

The housing reforms of the 1980s and '90s dramatically changed the role played by local authorities in the provision of public sector housing. Despite this changing role, ADC remained a major landlord in Aberdeen. But councillors regretted what they saw as an erosion of the council's ability to respond adequately to the demand for public sector housing. Many councillors felt that the introduction of CCT and increased financial stringency would further undermine the council's role. By 1994, the number of applicants on the council's waiting list had risen to over 5,000. Many councillors felt frustrated that the council could not adequately respond to rising housing needs.

At the same time, councillors had the opportunity to look at new and innovative ways of providing a quality housing service to the public. They began to forge new relationships with other housing providers in the city. They worked hard to make the most of the available housing stock. They also increasingly tried to involve tenants in making decisions about their own housing and local communities. The role played by the council in the provision of public sector housing in Aberdeen changed dramatically in the two and a half decades of Aberdeen District Council's existence. But one thing which did not change was its enthusiasm and commitment towards providing the citizens of Aberdeen with one of the highest standards of housing anywhere in the United Kingdom.

7: The Environmental Services for a Clean and Healthy City

Many of ADC's environmental services were essential but largely 'unseen' by the citizens of Aberdeen. Many of the public may have been unaware that it was council workers who collected their household refuse, who kept the city's streets clean and who provided a multitude of other services which either safeguarded health, or contributed to the clean environment in which people lived and worked.

The reality was that the work carried out by the ADC's Environmental Health and Cleansing Departments had a significant effect on everyone in the city. The departments had to collect and dispose of domestic and trade refuse; it had to monitor atmospheric pollution and ensure that the air people breathed was reasonably clean and free from pollution; it carried out routine inspections of the city's water supplies to make sure that they were wholesome; it inspected establishments in which food and beverages were produced, sold and consumed; and it provided a wide range of other services such as the provision of public toilets, the dog warden service, and the management of the city mortuary, crematorium and burial grounds.

Environmental services underwent substantial change between 1975 and 1996. This was due to the combined effect of new legislation and the heightened public profile of environmental issues. The impact of these changes was complex. Local authorities retained considerable discretion for local action and recycling, resulting in 'green' initiatives. The council's regulatory role grew as new legislation was introduced. New national and European standards reduced the amount of local discretion which local authorities had in their regulatory and enforcement roles. In some areas standards were set, and councils simply had to get on and ensure that they were met. After 1988, the extension of CCT altered the council's direct role. In Aberdeen and elsewhere, the emptying of dustbins and the cleaning of streets became more of a business and less a social service.

European legislation probably had a greater impact on the environmental services than on any other local government function. The public became aware of the European influence when it affected their everyday lives. At times this was seen as unwelcome interference by Brussels and at times it appeared ridiculous. The city's Fishmarket was prohibited from using wooden fish boxes, and these had to be replaced with supposedly more hygienic plastic ones. If the unfortunate fish did manage to make it to the local fish and chip shop they could no longer be served in newspaper! The traditional 'dram' had to be measured out in millilitres rather than the well-known quarter or fifth of a gill. And when legislation forced the GRC as water authority to remove the harmless peaty tinge from the city's water supplies, it appeared to some that Europe had simply gone too far! Yet these and other directives were the law and the local councils had no option but to implement them.

The Early Development of the Services

Local government first became involved in environmental health in response to insanitary living conditions. Early initiatives were concerned with providing a clean water supply and a sewerage system. As the population increased, additional measures had to be taken in order to prevent the spread of disease. Insanitary housing was cleared, food and beverages were inspected, domestic and trade refuse was collected and disposed of and local authorities had a legal duty to take whatever steps were necessary to prevent the spread of infectious diseases. In 1964 when Aberdeen was dubbed 'the beleaguered city' due to an outbreak of typhoid, it was the council which traced the source of the infection to a consignment of South American corned beef. As a result the epidemic was swiftly contained. By 1975 a wide range of environmental services were provided by local government. However, they all had common aims – to preserve the environment and to promote public and private health.

The 1975 Reforms

The Wheatley Commission looked at the environmental services as a group, with the exception of water and sewerage services which were seen as a special case. Wheatley's recommendations were accepted and the GRC became responsible for water, sewerage, and consumer protection. The ADC assumed responsibility for the remainder of the environmental services and for refuse collection. Environmental services were among the most important district-level responsibilities – in 1991/92, the net cost of these was £5.5m.

Prior to the 1975 reorganisation, the city's fleet of street sweeping vehicles covered some 286 miles of streets. After reorganisation, they had to sweep an estimated 430 miles. Levels of services had to be standardised across the new city district: and there were more shops, offices, factories and restaurants to inspect. In the first year alone, 467 additional premises were visited under the requirements of the 1963 Offices, Shops and Railway Premises Act, and inspections under the 1961 Factories Act increased by over a hundred – a large abattoir and meat processing factory at Dyce came within the city's new boundary. The corporation's existing staff was supplemented by an additional two veterinary meat inspectors and a further thirteen meat inspectors. Before 1975 local authorities had responsibility for some personal health services including health visiting, home nursing and vaccinations and immunisation. The National Health Service (Scotland) Act 1974 removed these services from local government and integrated them within the restructured NHS.

The new division of responsibilities between the two tiers of local government created some problems in the early days. Staff from ADC's Environmental Health Department were responsible for carrying out routine inspections of catering establishments to ensure that they were clean and safe. But they had no responsibility for food sampling. Staff from the GRC's Consumer Protection Department also had to visit the same premises in order to carry out checks. Although it caused some confusion, the system worked fairly well primarily due to the good working relationships between officers in the GRC and the ADC. This anomaly was rectified in the 1980s and responsibility for food sampling passed to the ADC following the recommendations of the Stodart Committee.

In 1975, the council established two departments to carry out its environmental responsibilities. The Cleansing Department was responsible for street cleansing and refuse collection and disposal; and the Environmental Health Department was responsible for the remaining services. The council's Cleansing and Environmental Health Committee was responsible for overseeing both departments. This structure remained basically unaltered until CCT appeared on the scene in the late 1980s.

The council called in consultants to advise on restructuring in preparation for CCT. In 1990, the Contract Services Organisation (CSO) was formed with responsibility for all services subject to CCT. These included street sweeping, refuse collection, waste disposal and recycling. The staff of the former Cleansing Department who were directly involved in providing services were transferred to the CSO, while the remaining staff became a small client team responsible for drawing up the new contract specifications and overseeing the work as it was carried out.

CCT shifted the managerial emphasis to identifying, reducing and controlling costs and to planning the service as if it was a business. The CSO had to compete in the market for contracts. Investment in new technology and the use of new methods reduced staffing levels. Through natural wastage and early retirement packages, staffing levels were reduced by about a quarter and payroll costs were brought down. The council took some pride in achieving this without any compulsory redundancies.

In the 1990s, the Client Services section monitored the delivery and performance of CCT services. In 1991/92, its net budget was £4.3 million, about £20 per head of population. The services were provided by a Cleansing and Environmental Development section and a Contracting Board. The section managed and maintained the city crematorium and burial grounds: in 1991/92 its net budget was £169,000. The Contracting Board disposed of domestic and commercial wastes and operated the council's vehicle workshops. It managed two treatment plants, three landfill sites and community waste and recycling centres: in 1991/92 it disposed of 90,700 tons of domestic waste. Comparisons between cities suggested that Aberdeen's relatively high disposable incomes made for more wasteful lifestyles. In the same year it had a net expenditure of £1.1m and disposed of 414,600 tons of trade and builders' waste.

The Cleansing and Environmental Services section also ran the services which were not exposed to CCT. These included public health, food hygiene and standards, health and safety at work, atmospheric pollution, noise and meat inspection. This part of the service cost £1.1 million in 1991/92. The Cleansing and Environmental Development Committee was responsible for the oversight of all the environmental services.

Expectations and Standards

Maintaining the level of service which the local community had come to expect remained a key objective. Aberdonians expected their household refuse to be collected twice a week, their waste paper once a week and their garden refuse and larger items to be uplifted on request. There were more than 14,000 special uplifts in 1994/95!

Care was taken to specify the key 'quality standards' in the CCT contracts. The CSO won its contracts on price or quality, but not without the occasional complaint from a private operator claiming that the rules were unfair. The reality was that all the main rules were set out by the Scottish Office in guidelines and other instruments!

The ADC also provided civic amenity sites where unwanted items could be disposed of. In 1993, Aberdeen was voted 'Britain's Cleanest City', proving beyond a shadow of a doubt that high standards were being maintained; and the service was efficient. In 1994/5, the published performance information showed that in Aberdeen the cost of collecting domestic and commercial refuse, and uplifting bulky items was £21.76 per premises. This was almost one third less than in the three other Scottish cities. In the more environmentally aware 1990s, the public seemed to have a better grasp of the council's roles. The council's 1994 survey showed that more than 80% of the public thought that the refuse collection service was good or excellent and this compared with the best placed councils in Britain.

Environmental Health Services

The term 'environmental health' described a diverse range of services although the protection of public health and safety was common to them all. The ADC was responsible for inspecting food hygiene in restaurants and licensed premises, ensuring the safety and proper labelling of food, monitoring noise, atmospheric and chemical pollution, pest control, regulating slaughterhouses and abattoirs, dealing with complaints concerning public health nuisances, operating the city's crematorium and mortuary, providing a dog warden service and the provision of public conveniences.

The environmental health services were not exposed to CCT, but this part of the department still underwent considerable change. There was a dramatic increase in the amount of work that the council was legally required to carry out. This was particularly noticeable in the areas of food hygiene, health and safety and pollution. More and more time was spent enforcing regulations and less was available for the discretionary side of the service. From the 1970s onwards, environmental health officers increasingly specialised in particular aspects of the service. The need for professional training assumed even greater importance. Restructuring in the late 1980s and early '90s resulted in a change in the balance between office-based managerial or supervisory staff, and officers on the street.

Food Hygiene

The department's environmental development section had wide-ranging statutory responsibilities for the regulation of food hygiene standards. It had powers to inspect premises in which food was manufactured, prepared and sold.

The ADC influenced food hygiene standards by advising proprietors of the safest and most hygienic ways in which to manufacture, store, prepare and provide food and beverages. Ultimately they could resort to legal enforcement if standards were not maintained. Chemical and microbiological samples of food were taken for analysis. In 1993, a food hygiene merit award system was introduced providing further incentives for food establishments to maintain high standards. The council's environmental health officers were also responsible for investigating and dealing with complaints from members of the public. The council had to enforce the food control legislation in some 1,600 establishments. In 1991/92, 1,302 visits were made and 222 complaints by individuals about food quality were followed up.

The same section of the department was responsible with enforcing occupational health and safety legislation in some 3,700 business premises. In 1991/92, 1,167 inspections were made; about 150 work place accidents were notified to the department. The publication of Citizen's Charter performance data showed that ADC was successful in fully meeting its own targets in its workplace safety inspection programme.

Pollution Control

Pollution became an increasing problem throughout the 1970s and '80s, but this was part of a nation-wide trend and not peculiar to Aberdeen. Vehicle exhaust fumes, fumes from the city's domestic, commercial and industrial premises and increased noise levels all polluted the environment. The council monitored noise levels in the city and particular attention was paid to the area around the airport at Dyce. As housing was brought back into the city centre, it was increasingly important to monitor noise level from entertainment establishments, particularly late at night. Increased traffic levels caused much of the background noise in the city, particularly near major roads and the absence of a major city bypass did not help the situation. But ADC took whatever measures it could to minimise and alleviate the effects of noise. In 1991/92, 280 complaints of excessive noise were investigated.

Steps were also taken to monitor and minimise unpleasant odours. Catering establishments were required to have effective means of discharging odours, particularly where the premises were near housing. These aspects of the fish processing industry were closely monitored.

In 1979, officers reported on atmospheric pollution in Aberdeen. Lead, sulphur dioxide, hydrocarbons and other pollutants were monitored around the city. The council considered declaring certain areas of Aberdeen 'smoke control areas', but this was not followed up primarily due to lack of resources.

The council had statutory powers to control pollution in general, and they enforced those powers where necessary. But much of their work involved trying to prevent pollution in the first place through education and advice and in reducing it through persuasion and negotiation. Environmental health officers advised the Planning Committee on the environmental effects of new developments. The also advised the Licensing Committee and Board on particular aspects of licence applications.

The Dog Warden Service

The council provided the city's dog warden service, which extended beyond the rounding up of stray dogs. It primarily aimed to encourage responsible dog ownership. The 'nation of dog lovers' often forgot that one person's much-loved pet could be another's nuisance. Fouling was one of the issues about which members of the public complained most.

In 1978 the council began a 'Dog Control' campaign. Leaflets, a code of conduct, and advice were distributed to dog owners, along with the annual dog licence reminders, each year after Christmas in an attempt to encourage new dog owners to look after their pets properly. Owners were encouraged to keep their dogs under control and to clear up after them: special dog waste bins were provided in the city's parks and other public places. As part of a nation-wide initiative to encourage responsible dog ownership, an innovative dog micro-chipping scheme and register was introduced in October 1992. This made the task of tracing and identifying stray dogs that much easier – council tenants wanting to keep a dog had to obtain the Council's permission and register their animal.

Who says it's a dog's life? Alison Adam, dog warden

Public Conveniences

The ADC was responsible for providing and maintaining the city's public conveniences. These ranged from the original Victorian toilets in the city's Union Terrace to 'space age' automated public conveniences! In 1952, the authors of 'Granite City' had complained that the city's conveniences were 'so carefully placed, either for reasons of delicacy or to avoid obstruction, as to be very difficult to find.' The council's research indicated that, in 1994, over 60% of households used these facilities and that over 70% rated then good or excellent. Their availability and image was also important to tourists and visitors.

The council invested in providing new public conveniences and in upgrading old ones; the net expenditure in 1991/92 was nearly £700,000. Improvements included the provision of baby changing facilities and the installation of showers at the beach esplanade. The council's policy of employing attendants in many of the city's toilets, combined with a programme of regular inspections, ensured that high standards were maintained. Often local people were appointed as attendants. The public convenience at Old Aberdeen even doubled as a 'tourist point' when the attendant began providing information about the area to visitors!

In 1995, the media reported that Aberdeen was 'flushed with success' after winning several awards in the Scottish 'Loo of the Year' competition: the council toilet at Beach Central won an award and the facilities at Bridge of Don and Footdee were highly commended. In 1995, the council set up a Public Convenience User Group in an effort to look at how buildings could be further improved. This was thought to be the first of its kind in Scotland.

The Litter Issue

The council tackled other issues which affected the city's environment. In 1976, it launched a campaign to tackle the growing problem of litter. The aim was to make everyone aware that the proper place for litter was in a bin and not on the streets. Some initiatives were specifically targeted at schoolchildren to educate them on the problem and on proper disposal. Competitions were organised on the theme of litter prevention. Schoolchildren and community groups were encouraged to care for their environment and some even played their part in improving the city's environment by organising litter picks.

In 1983, thirty-one unemployed people were involved through the government's community programme in the rehabilitation and maintenance of the city's land reclamation sites. They took part in a number of schemes, including the removal of litter from existing tipping sites, the construction of a new civic amenity site at Ness Tip, and the removal of graffiti from buildings.

The use of plastic refuse sacks contributed to one of the city's most publicised environmental issues – seagulls! The sacks offered no resistance to the beaks of the gulls some of which had adapted well to urban life and could eat almost anything.

Their noisy foraging at first light in mid-summer brought lots of complaints to the council. The problem was at its worst in the city centre where the council continually looked at ways to combat the nuisance. Large numbers of gulls were found to be nesting on buildings around the city centre and controlling them was not a simple task. In 1992, a pilot scheme was introduced to remove nests and eggs from the top of buildings and whilst this had a measure of success, it failed to make a long term impact. The council looked at how other cities had tackled the problem and considered the use of poisons and 'stun guns'; but the main problem was to remove the gulls' food source. Burst refuse sacks were found to contribute significantly to the problem and it was in this area that the council concentrated. The introduction of plastic bins and 'wheelie bins' improved the situation as did an initiative to promote the responsible disposal of refuse and litter. Households and food outlets were encouraged not to put their refuse out the evening before collection.

The ADC was responsible for some aspects of health and safety both in the workplace and in the home. The Home Safety Check scheme was introduced in 1984 and was made available to all householders: council experts checked homes for hazards such as faulty wiring and electrical equipment. As well as carrying out these checks, the council carried out some types of repair for people who were not able to arrange this for themselves.

Recycling

Recycling and re-use became major environmental issues in the 1980s and '90s. In many countries in the EU government subsidies were made available to promote recycling and improve the environment. In Britain the government thought that the issues should be left largely to market forces. Where there was high demand then recycling would be profitable, or at least viable. The government did take some steps to try to stimulate market forces, such as the introduction of a landfill tax in the mid-1990s to encourage councils to look at other methods of disposal. It also set targets, exhorting councils to recycle 25% of household waste by the year 2000.

The ADC considered the introduction of bottle banks as early as 1979, although no action was taken because of the difficult economics of recycling. A year later a scheme was introduced and glass recycling centres began to appear across the city. The scheme was extended to aluminium cans and paper. In the mid-1990s, paper shortages made this type of recycling very attractive. Recycling centres were positioned strategically across the city and smaller mini recycling centres followed. ADC's recycling plan aimed to provide one facility for every 5,000 people. Local businesses and schools were invited to sponsor or provide space for recycling facilities. In recognition of their efforts in recycling, the council received several awards and commendations. By 1994, about 14% of household waste was being recycled, a low figure compared with cities in Holland, but a much better figure than was achieved in Glasgow. In Scotland, only Dundee recycled a higher proportion of household waste.

An Environmental Charter

The ADC was proud of the fact that it had successfully limited the potentially negative environmental effects of the city's growth and the arrival of the oil industry, but it also knew that there was a need to redefine its strategy. The growth in the city's housing stock, new industrial estates, increased levels of pollution and changing lifestyles all had effects on the environment. By the 1990s there was a growing public awareness of the need to have positive strategies for environmental protection and, in 1993, ADC adopted an environmental charter which redefined its priorities. It identified eight main areas for action: energy, recycling, pollution, nature conservation, environmental education, land use, heritage and the built environment.

Aberdeen is famous for its Environmental Charter, and places great importance on educating its citizens from an early age

Clean and Green

In 1994, ADC launched its highly successful 'Clean and Green' campaign. The aim was to involve the whole city in making Aberdeen a cleaner and greener place. One of the first initiatives to be tackled was to clean up a stretch of land along the banks of the River Dee and to carry out environmental improvements such as creating a walkway, providing seats, information boards and planting bulbs. Much of the work was carried out by inmates from the city's Craiginches prison, and by local schoolchildren. The clean-up was a major success for the council. The campaign sought to heighten awareness of environmental issues in the city and to encourage people to do what they could to improve the environment. Schoolchildren undertook such things as litter picks and bulb planting assisted by the 'Clean and Green' team. The campaign's mascot 'Spotless' captured the public's imagination, and helped to spread the message that it was up to people to keep their own city clean.

Water and Sewerage

Water and sewerage were very much 'environmental' services in the broader sense of the word. Local authorities developed their water and sewerage functions in the eighteenth and nineteenth centuries. At the time of the Wheatley enquiry thirteen regional boards made up of local councillors administered the water service. Drainage and flood prevention was the responsibility of the burghs and landowners, whilst river purification was the responsibility of nine river purification boards.

Water and sewerage were defined as strategic services and became the responsibility of the regional councils. The GRC became the water and sewerage authority for Aberdeen in 1975. However, two decades later many people still referred to the GRCs Water and Sewerage Department as the 'Water Board!'

Water and sewerage services were an essential part of the city's infrastructure and vitally important to the environment. Aberdeen's growth in the 1970s and '80s created an unprecedented demand for the services to be extended to new housing estates and new industrial and commercial premises. Some major developments, such as the water treatment works at Mannofield, were brought forward. The substantial costs of providing the additional infrastructure had to be provided by the GRC.

In 1995/96, responsibility for water and sewerage were transferred from local government to three new government appointed bodies. The North of Scotland Water Authority covered Aberdeen. The government argued that local authorities couldn't raise the finance needed to bring water and sewerage up to the new European standards, and it pointed out that it was responding to public opinion by keeping the services in the public sector, unlike England and Wales where they had been privatised. The critics argued that the real financial problem was government's strong control over capital spending and they should let councils borrow if they wished. A referendum conducted by Strathclyde Regional Council provided strong evidence that the public was opposed to the government's plans.

The formation of the government appointed Scottish Environmental Protection Agency (SEPA) continued the trend of weakening the local government environmental role. SEPA took key responsibilities in pollution monitoring and control from ADC and the other districts.

Trading Standards and Consumer Protection

In 1975, the GRC became responsible for trading standards and consumer protection. These services were sometimes confused with ADC's responsibilities for such things as food hygiene and health and safety. The GRC's responsibilities included weights and measures, pricing, consumer credit and consumer safety. In the 1980s and '90s they began to provide debt control and money advice. A relatively small department looked after these services, with a budget of £1.3m in 1994/95

In the rushed 1995/96 reforms the government suggested that the roles of districts and regions was a source of confusion to the public. Actually the regional and district roles were quite different. Local authorities thought that the signs suggested that the government was confused rather than the public. In the various Scottish Office consultative documents there was no recognition of the fact that key aspects of the regional services were actually overseen by the Department of Trade and Industry in London!

8: Arts, Leisure and Recreation

If housing needs were the source of the citizens' greatest concerns, then arts, leisure and recreation were perhaps the best appreciated of ADC services. This was scarcely surprising. People associated these activities with their free time, and with pleasure; many of the facilities and opportunities were high in quality and low in cost to the user. Between 1975 and 1996, the ADC provided a wide range of services including parks and open spaces, allotments, children's play areas, an art gallery, museums, sports facilities and country parks. It was responsible for some of the city's major entertainment venues including His Majesty's Theatre, the Music Hall, Arts Centre and the Beach Ballroom. It organised or provided financial assistance for the diverse range of entertainments and events which took place each year. Yet, until 1983, the council had no clear statutory duty to provide such services, although both the regional and district councils were given powers to provide 'amenity' services. After 1983, the statutory duty to ensure that there was an adequate provision of facilities in their area for recreational, sporting, cultural and social activities was placed squarely upon the shoulders of the district councils. The range and quality of recreational facilities in Aberdeen was a source of pride to the district Council and its predecessors.

The quality of the services provided over the years earned Aberdeen numerous accolades such as 'The Flower of Scotland', 'City of Roses' and 'Scotland's Most Sporting City.' The city's reputation was the direct result of considerable investment by ADC. Between 1990 and 1995, £23m was spent on sporting facilities alone: in a single year (1991/92), the total amount spent on providing leisure and recreational facilities was £20m, approximately £87 per head of population. That investment benefited Aberdonians, people living outside the city and using its facilities, and tourists. His Majesty's Theatre, Aberdeen Arts Centre, the Music Hall and the Lemon Tree regularly drew audiences from all over the north east. Similarly, the city's major sporting facilities such as those provided at the Beach Leisure Centre, Linx Ice Arena and the international standard Chris Anderson Athletics Stadium were used by the region as a whole.

But the role of ADC in backing arts and recreation was not limited to the provision and management of facilities. It supported a range of festivals as well as artistic, cultural, sporting and recreational activities.

During the 1980s and '90s in particular, there was increased recognition of the importance of the amenity services to local communities and the local economy. In the city the provision of good quality facilities had a number of effects. It ensured a high quality of life for Aberdonians and those living around the city. It attracted people into the city and ensured that Aberdeen remained the cultural and recreational heart of the region. Attracting tourists to the area relied on providing an attractive city and good quality recreational services. Similarly, attracting large conferences and cultural and sporting events had a beneficial effect on the city's economy. In the 1990s it was estimated that the Aberdeen Alternative Festival generated around £500,000 annually for the local economy.

The Growth of Recreation and Leisure

Local authority involvement in the provision of recreational facilities was a relatively recent development. In 1878, the council took over responsibility for Victoria Park and Union Terrace Gardens which had previously been looked after by the Police Commissioners. As people began to have more time for leisure pursuits, the range of parks and leisure facilities within the city began to grow. The parks and open spaces and sporting and cultural facilities provided the citizens of Aberdeen with a range of opportunities to fill their leisure time; and the open space and fresh air was important to public health at a time when a large proportion of people lived in overcrowded and unhealthy accommodation. Later, as 'the silver city by the golden sands' became a popular tourist resort, these facilities were also enjoyed by visitors to the city.

Changes in taste and fashion, advances in technology, the growth in ownership of the motor car and increased affluence all influenced how people wanted to spend their leisure time. The ADC responded to those changes to ensure that leisure provision in the city matched those interests.

Before 1975, the corporation took great pride in the quality of its services. However, when the Wheatley Commission came to consider the reorganisation of local government, it found that the position was somewhat different in many parts of Scotland. The research revealed that councils provided parks and open spaces, sports facilities, museums, art galleries, libraries, arts facilities, entertainment venues, community centres, cemeteries, crematoria and a host of other services. These were loosely grouped together and administered by one or more council committee. The level and quality of services varied considerably from council to council as did the names which they gave to their committees.

This did not really surprise the commission as local government's role in the provision of leisure and recreation services had developed in a largely unplanned way; and of course councils were responding to varying local needs. Wheatley decided to look at those services collectively under the title of 'amenity services'. The commission realised that some services were provided for the benefit of the locality only whilst others benefited a wider area or supported tourism and the local economy. It recommended that the regional and district councils be given powers to provide leisure and recreation facilities, with the regional councils having the additional responsibility of ensuring an adequate provision of such facilities within their region.

Wheatley's recommendations were accepted and both regional and district councils were given powers to provide amenity services. The Paterson Committee suggested that both tiers might work together in order to maximise and co-ordinate the services provided. In practice co-ordination between the tiers was often reluctant and sometimes poor. The GRC and ADC generally reached agreement where there was joint use of facilities and consulted on the provision of community facilities, but this level of co-operation took some time to emerge, and not all the issues were satisfactorily resolved.

Before the 1975 re-organisation, the shadow ADC considered the provision of amenity services in the city. It came to the view that the new district council should take responsibility for all amenity services already provided by the corporation and the county of Aberdeen within the new city boundaries. It thought that there should be close liaison between the two tiers over the provision and management of 'joint use' leisure and recreational facilities, such as those attached to the city's schools. Facilities, such as the city's art gallery and museums which benefited the region as a whole, should continue to be provided by ADC with financial contributions from neighbouring district councils.

Rationalisation

In 1981, the Stodart Committee reported on the division of responsibilities between the two tiers of local government. Amongst its recommendations was that responsibility for the provision of leisure and recreation should rest solely with the district councils. The district councils acquired a statutory duty to ensure that there was an adequate provision of facilities in their area for recreational, sporting, cultural and social activities, and they had a considerable degree of discretion over what facilities and services to provide. This responsibility was to extend to the provision of museums, art galleries, theatres, parks and free standing community centres. The regional councils were to retain a residual power to make a financial contribution to the running costs of facilities where the catchment area was wider than the district involved. Responsibility for the provision and maintenance of community centres was to transfer to the district councils except where they were an integral part of regional council educational buildings.

Stodart recommended various ways in which regions and districts should co-operate in managing community facilities. Little progress was made with this particular aspect of the Stodart Committee's recommendations in the city, although the GRC and ADC did co-operate in the joint use of some facilities such as the swimming pool located at Dyce Academy.

The issue gave rise to a bone of contention between the city and the GRC. The ADC wanted control of the Beacon Centre at Bucksburn. It wasn't attached to a school but the GRC resisted any change arguing that the centre was a vital resource for the community education service. The transfer did not take place.

Administering the Service

In order to administer the service, three committees were established. One controlled the city's libraries and a second looked after the Art Gallery and museums. All other amenity services were administered by the new Leisure and Recreation Committee. The Art Gallery, Museum and Libraries Committee involved non-elected members with expertise in the area. Various sub-committees and working groups, such as the Committee of Management of the Cowdray Hall and the MacDonald Art Committee, were responsible for particular aspects of the service. Other working groups were set up as required to look at particular issues, such as Christmas lighting, the bicentenary of Union Street, the erection of a North Sea Memorial and the Beach Leisure Centre. During the late 1980s and early '90s, the council established various trusts to administer particular facilities or events, including the Duthie Park Trust, Aberdeen Recreational Facilities Trust and the Lemon Tree Trust.

This committee structure remained substantially unaltered until the late 1980s, when a new all embracing Arts and Recreation Committee was established, with four sub-committees for arts, art galleries and museums, libraries and sport. Whilst some councillors may have regretted the change, others saw it as a good opportunity better to co-ordinate the provision of services.

The ADC worked alongside a wide range of national and local bodies to provide arts and recreational services. It maintained a close working relationship with the Scottish Arts Council (SAC), the main agency in Scotland for the distribution of grants in support of the arts, but it often felt that the SAC put more of its resources into Glasgow, Edinburgh and Dundee. The general development of sport in Scotland was the remit of the Scottish Sports Council (SSC). SAC and SSC expenditure provided an important source of funding for the arts and sport in Scotland, although investment by many local authorities was greater. In the 1990s, for example, SAC expenditure in Scotland as a whole was typically around £4 per head of population: in 1991/92, the ADC's expenditure on arts and museums alone was £12.79 per head.

Promoting recreation in the countryside around the City was carried out in association with bodies such as the Forestry Commission (later Forest Enterprise), the Countryside Commission for Scotland and, after 1992, Scottish Natural Heritage. At a more local level, there was also close co-operation with the numerous arts and sports clubs and societies which provided facilities and services in the city. Many of these benefited from council grants. In 1979, for example, the council awarded a grant of £2,500 to Culter Football Club towards the provision of new changing facilities, whilst at the same meeting they resolved to award a grant of £142 to the Guizer Theatre Group.

As the financial independence of local government was increasingly constrained maintaining good partnerships assumed even greater importance. Local authorities could no longer fund major new arts and leisure developments solely from their own resources and had to look to their 'partners' to provide the necessary support. In Aberdeen some support also came from the local enterprise company, from industry and commerce, and from the City Centre Partnership.

CCT was extended to certain aspects of the service including grounds maintenance, catering and sports and leisure management in the 1990s. The legislation was phased in over a period of four years. This meant that the council had to invite tenders for certain aspects of its leisure and recreation services including maintenance of the city's parks and open spaces, catering in council-run facilities and the management of sports and other leisure services.

The operational staff within the Leisure and Recreation Department were transferred to Aberdeen Leisure where they had to compete with the private sector to win contracts. One year later, the council reviewed the operation of the new organisation and decided to bring Aberdeen Leisure into a new Contract Services Division although the name 'Aberdeen Leisure' lived on. The council saw some benefits from the new organisational structure. The introduction of competition resulted in a more cost conscious and possibly more efficient service; but some councillors felt that standards in the city's recreational facilities, parks and open spaces fell because of CCT.

A key part of the administration of the service lay in charging policy. This was a difficult area. The conventional wisdom, particularly in Labour councils, was that services should be free, or as cheap as possible, and that where charges were made subsidies should be available for poorer citizens. Generally arts, museums and public parks were run free of charge to visitors while some charges were made for sport and entertainment. Throughout the 1975–96 period, ADC maintained its policy of free entry to the Art Gallery, Tolbooth and other museums.

But this conventional approach was sharply challenged by the government during the 1980s. Some of the right wing 'think tanks' argued that people should be encouraged to pay directly for any services they used. Ideology aside, the growing financial restrictions on councils meant that they had to look closely at every penny which they could reasonably bring in through charges. At the same time, ADC wanted to encourage the maximum use of facilities, involve disadvantaged groups, and provide a wide range of facilities.

The publication of early Citizen's Charter comparative information for sports and leisure in 1994/95 suggested that ADC was successful in balancing these different demands while keeping faith with its principles. Nearly all councils made losses on their facilities. ADC's income for its swimming pools covered just under one third of expenditure, a little below the average of 36%. For its other indoor facilities, ADC covered 41% of expenditure, a little above the Scottish average. The income brought in through charges for outdoor pitches and tracks covered some 86.8% of expenditure and was second in the 'league table' to Edinburgh, which made an operating profit.

Art Gallery and Museums

In 1975, the ADC assumed responsibility for the Art Gallery on Schoolhill. It was already one of the most prestigious galleries in the country and the council set out to enhance further the range of exhibits and services In 1975, the council decided to appoint an Education Officer part of whose remit was to develop the range of events and exhibitions. It was also the council's aim to extend museum provision in the city.

The Art Gallery was already well established as a centre for painting, sculpture, crafts, films, photography and puppetry. It also provided a venue for travelling exhibitions and displays; local and visiting musicians regularly took part in Saturday afternoon recitals in the gallery and the neighbouring Cowdray Hall. Art appreciation was fostered through adult art classes with help from some of the city's art teachers; and the range of exhibits continued to expand as new works of art and interesting artefacts were systematically purchased. By 1983, according to a Scottish Tourist Board survey, the Art Gallery had become the sixth most popular attraction in Scotland. The following year it celebrated its centenary, marked by a series of events and the publication of a guide entitled '100 Paintings' which were drawn from its extensive collection.

The ADC took on responsibility for the city's museums, including Provost Skene's House which was refurbished as a museum of domestic life. The opening of James Dun's House as a children's museum in 1976 was an important addition to the museum provision in the city. The renovation of the seventeenth-century building won the council an architectural award. The museum quickly proved a success with the public attracting over 65,000 visitors in its first four months.

The opening of the Maritime Museum in 1984 was an important contribution by the council towards preserving a vital part of Aberdeen's history. It was appropriate that the museum was housed in the sixteenth-century Provost Ross's House in Shiprow, close to the harbour. It aimed to tell the story of the city's maritime history including the development of the harbour, shipbuilding, fishing and oil. However, lack of space limited what could be achieved. Plans for an extension were already being discussed as the museum was welcoming its first visitors. In 1985, the Council purchased the adjacent Trinity Church with a view to extending the museum but it was not until 1993 that the necessary funding was earmarked and plans were drawn up for the project. The new building was expected to cost in the region of £4m. The plans involved the linking of the two buildings by a futuristic glass-fronted structure and increasing the floorspace five-fold. It was hoped to reopen in time for the return of the Tall Ships Race in 1997. Early in 1996, work began on the extension. The outgoing council placed a time capsule in the foundations containing the plans for the new museum, newspapers, coins and a recipe for the rowie! Lord Provost James Wyness remarked 'future generations of Aberdonians will gain a valuable insight into our maritime history and life in the Granite City in the final years of the twentieth century'.

In 1993, the Council embarked on a project to restore the city's seventeenth-century Tolbooth as a museum of civic history. The Tolbooth Museum on Castle Street opened in 1995 and charted the history of local government in the city. It also illustrated the history of crime and punishment in Aberdeen. Some 36,000 visitors went through its doors in the first six months of operation. The restoration of the building received a special commendation from the Aberdeen Civic Society in 1995.

City in Bloom

The city's enviable reputation in the area of leisure and recreation was largely built on its excellence in the field of horticulture. Aberdeen was fortunate in having a large number of parks and open spaces, including Duthie, Hazlehead, Westburn, Victoria, and Seaton parks, and the Johnstone and Union Terrace gardens.

The city won its first of 'Britain in Bloom' award in 1965 and went on to win it a further nine times over the next three decades. The Scottish title was won a remarkable twenty times! At the height of its success in the 1980s, ADC was invited to exhibit at the Chelsea Flower Show where it won three gold and three silver medals. One of the 'golds' was for the prestigious centre stand. With this record of success, failure in the Britain in Bloom contest in 1993 came as something of a shock!

The local press put it down to the fact that investment in sports centres and ice rinks had prevented spending on the city's appearance – and there may have been something in this. In preparing for the 1996 competition, ADC earmarked additional resources and embarked on a number of projects to improve the overall appearance of the city. It stressed the importance of the contributions made by the city's traders, the Chamber of Commerce and the City Centre Partnership. Councillor George Urquart, the convener of the council's Arts and Recreation Committee stressed the need for a city-wide effort to bring the title back to Aberdeen. He added: 'We all need to work together to improve the city for its citizens, because the local authority can no longer do it on its own.'

Many considered the Duthie Park, with its famous Winter Garden, to be the jewel in the crown amongst the city's parks. The Winter Garden was amongst the top four visitor attractions in the UK after Kew Gardens, the Tower of London and Buckingham Palace. The original Victorian palm house, which was built in 1899, was replaced by the current Winter Garden in 1970. The new facility got off to a flying start by winning a Civic Society Award that year. The Leisure and Recreation Department organised a series of events to celebrate the centenary of the Duthie Park in 1981. The celebrations included a parade of vintage vehicles, open air concerts of popular music from the Victorian period and culminated in a grand fireworks display at the end of the summer. The centenary was also marked by the upgrading of the memorials within the park.

In 1988, the Winter Garden won a British Tourist Authority Award. A number of further improvements were made culminating in the restoration of the Victorian Corridor in 1995. The Winter Garden provided a year-round programme of concerts and other events and were a popular venue for weddings. In 1995, ADC launched its 'Art in the Park' initiative which was aimed at encouraging senior citizens and disabled people to participate in and enjoy painting and drawing. The Winter Garden seemed an ideal venue.

Aberdeen's other parks and gardens also distinguished themselves in a variety of ways. The children's playground in Seaton Park became the first ever winner of the 'Playground of the Year' award in 1976 and the park itself provided the venue for the annual International Football Festival. In 1995 a £240,000 rolling programme to improve children's play areas was announced. The money came from the Aberdeen Recreational Facilities Fund. Committee convener Councillor Urquhart welcomed the opportunity 'to provide better facilities for families and children so they can enjoy the city's wonderful open spaces to the full'.

The largest park – at Hazlehead – was the venue for some of the city's major events such as the Aberdeen Highland Games, the Steam Engine Rally (held

*'One too many?' – Gordon Hay (gardener) and Stewart McBain
count the daffodil bulbs!*

annually since 1982) and the Aberdeen Clydesdale Horse Show. The 1995 Highland Games saw the launch of a new Bon Accord tartan to mark the formation of the new Aberdeen City Council, the Quincentenary of the University of Aberdeen and the 500th Anniversary of the granting of the Torry Charter. The park provided the city with three golf courses and other sporting facilities, and an award-winning maze. It was chosen as the setting for a memorial rose garden – for the victims of the 1988 Piper Alpha disaster – which won an award in 1993. Another rose garden in the park, which was officially opened and named after the Queen Mother, won the Linton Trophy for horticultural excellence.

Aberdeen is famous for its roses. In 1976, the city celebrated the 'Year of the Rose' by organising an extensive rose-planting programme within Aberdeen and sending a gift of roses to its twin city of Regensburg. Important visitors, including the reigning Miss World, were invited to 'plant a rose', and the council agreed to sponsor a Press and Journal competition to choose the city's 'Rose Queen'. But the council did not confine its rose-planting programme to the city's parks. It was estimated that around 2.5 million roses were planted throughout the city and its open spaces. The 67,000 roses in the Nellfield Cemetery won the council a Civic Trust Award in 1982; and if citizens and visitors needed to be reminded that Aberdeen was indeed the 'city of roses', then the annual 'Rose Day', during which roses were handed out on the streets of the city, did just that. That Aberdeen achieved such eminence in horticulture was in no small part due to the expertise, dedication and enthusiasm of its directors of Leisure and Recreation and committee conveners. In 1995, Councillor Collie, affectionately known as 'Mr Parks', had a rose named after him in recognition of his long service as committee convener.

In 1984, the council embarked on a six-year programme during which 11,000,000 daffodils and 6,000,000 crocuses were planted in the city's parks, open spaces and along riverbanks. Once planted, the bulbs went on to multiply three-fold, and provided a huge and welcome explosion of colour in the spring. Other major plantings commemorated important dates, such as the Year of the Child in 1979, and a million bulbs were planted in 1994 to mark the Marie Curie Cancer Appeal.

The council's proposal to redevelop Union Terrace Gardens in the heart of the city proved to be controversial. The plans, first mooted along with proposals to construct the Denburn dual carriageway, involved raising the level of the gardens to provide much needed underground parking space and to create a new civic heart in the city. The plans were supported by a number of organisations in the city and an application was made for Lottery funding. The bid was rejected but some councillors believed that the Victorian sunken gardens were an important feature of the city centre and should remain intact. The gardens in their original state provided a natural amphitheatre in which a number of arts and recreational activities took place.

The City Centre Partnership helped to enhance the central area of the city by creating 'pocket parks' in areas which had formerly lain derelict: Denburn Pocket Park won an Aberdeen Civic Society Award in 1995. It also won an award for the best improvement in 1995 in the 'Beautiful Scotland in Bloom Award' sponsored by the Bank of Scotland.

In October 1995, ADC announced the intention to establish a new community woodland scheme in the city. The project was the joint initiative of ADC and the Forestry Authority. The scheme envisaged the transformation of the city's landfill site at Tullos Hill into a woodland area by re-establishing the remnants of Tullos Wood along the east of the industrial estate. A sheltered footpath from the city's Doonies Farm to the south of Cove was part of the plan.

Culture and Entertainment

In 1975, ADC assumed responsibility for a range of arts and entertainment venues in the city, including the Music Hall, Arts Centre and the Beach Ballroom, all of which they extensively refurbished. In some cases decisions to renovate were taken out of necessity. By the late 1960s, the city's Music Hall – which was one of the major arts and conference venues in Aberdeen – was in need of major restoration. Such was the extent of the work required that the council questioned the viability of such a project. However, in 1972, the corporation put forward their plans and a public enquiry took place. The Secretary of State directed that any upgrading should not significantly alter either the external or internal appearance of the building. It was not until 1984 that the work commenced; two years and £2.5m later the Music Hall reopened in all its former glory, to the sound of the band of the Royal Marines.

The corporation purchased His Majesty's Theatre – which had been in the hands of the Donald family for decades – in 1975. His Majesty's was one of the most successful regional theatres in Britain, but by the 1970s was beginning to show its age. Substantial investment was required to restore the theatre and to bring it up to modern safety standards. The theatre's refurbishment was one of ADC's first priorities when it took over. The work required was so pressing that other major projects, such as the upgrading of the Central Library, simply had to wait. In 1982, after a closure of a little over a year, His Majesty's Theatre reopened with a seating capacity of 1,445.

In 1995, the Yggdrasil Quartet became the city's first resident string quartet on a three year contract sponsored by ADC, the SAC and the University of Aberdeen. In the same year, a new partnership between ADC and the Royal Scottish National Orchestra brought increased activity in the city by the orchestra, as it began to work closely with young people in Aberdeen, in association with the council's Musician in Residence.

Public Participation in the Arts

The ADC sought to encourage and stimulate the talents of local writers, artists, dancers and musicians, through the employment of 'artists in residence'. The council continually looked for ways to encourage people to participate in and enjoy the arts. A number of proposals were considered, such as using the councils own newspaper, Bon Accord, to stimulate local writing. The council sought to encourage the use of less traditional venues for entertainment and the arts, such as the city's parks, and the St Nicholas and Bon Accord shopping centres.

In 1983, the Aberdeen Community Arts Association was set up. It received financial support from ADC to organise a fringe programme for the Aberdeen Alternative Festival. The association and the council produced their report 'Community Arts – A Working Strategy', which stressed the importance of public participation in the arts. In 1985, an Arts Development Officer was appointed to encourage and stimulate participation in the arts. In 1994, the First Breaks Project got off the ground, when the council and the Lemon Tree teamed up to provide up-and-coming bands in Aberdeen with the opportunity to participate in workshops to improve their skills.

The council-backed 'City Moves Dance Space' was established in 1992 and was one of the few facilities of its kind in Scotland. It proved to be an immediate success, with around 250 dancers participating in a variety of classes each week. It was instrumental in taking dance to the outlying areas of the city through its outreach programme. The council also set up Aberdeen Video Access to encourage people to become involved in film-making. The 1995 Aberdeen Alternative Festival brought the two initiatives together: the Reel Moves project gave dancers and film-makers the opportunity to work together to create an unusual programme involving both video and dance. By the mid-1990s, plans to open a film and media centre in Belmont Street were well advanced. The project was supported by a partnership involving ADC, the Scottish Film Council and GEL.

Festival City

The City of Aberdeen played host to a range of local and international music, arts and sporting festivals. One of the major international festivals to receive a home in the city was the Aberdeen International Youth Festival. The annual festival brought together young talent from around the world in an eleven day celebration of the arts. In the 1980s, ADC clashed with the festival organisers over their decision to invite South African groups to participate. The city's future as the venue for the festival was briefly in doubt. The council maintained its anti-apartheid stance, which at the time involved boycotting anything South African, and the festival was saved. The threat of losing such a major international festival led the council to consider establishing alternative events in the city, and by 1995, the council was providing around £120,000 to support the festival.

In 1983, the city became host to the third largest multi-arts event after the Edinburgh Festival and Glasgow's Mayfest: the Aberdeen Alternative Festival provided a platform for music, dance, comedy and drama. Participation by local performers was also encouraged through the NATIVE community programme. During the Alternative Festival, Street Beat aimed to bring music and theatre right onto the streets of Aberdeen. Other council-funded festivals helped to bring the arts into the heart of the city. The Aberdeen Arts Carnival was established in 1984, providing a two-month programme of events, with opportunities for adults and children to become involved in a range of workshops.

The popularity of the Aberdeen Alternative Festival indicated a gap in the provision of arts facilities. Councillor David Clyne, who had been closely involved in the Alternative Festival since its inception, saw that the city lacked a permanent multi-arts venue. His vision was that such a venue would provide a focal point for a wide range of artistic activities in the city, and the success of the festival suggested that it would be popular. The St Katherine's Centre was refurbished at a cost of £1.3m and was opened as the 'Lemon Tree' by Lord Provost Wyness in January 1993. In its first year, around 500 events attracted 60,000 people to a wide range of traditional and contemporary music, dance and drama. It also provided a series of workshops where local talent could be nurtured and encouraged. Within a couple of years of its opening, the Scotland on Sunday newspaper described the Lemon Tree as 'easily the most successful multi-arts venue in the last decade'. In 1995, BBC Radio Scotland began broadcasting its weekly 'Live at the Lemon Tree' programme, and the venue became known throughout the country.

In the late 1970s, the then Aberdeen Football Club manager, Alex Ferguson, and the late Chris Anderson, discussed the idea of establishing a football coaching school in the city. Chris Anderson was then vice-chairman of Aberdeen Football Club, and he had been impressed by the community involvement in soccer which he had seen in the USA. The coaching school failed to get off the ground but it led directly to the establishment of one of Aberdeen's most successful annual festivals. The first Aberdeen International Football Festival was held in 1981, and its popularity established it as an annual event, attracting teams from throughout the UK and abroad. By the mid-1990s girls teams were also competing, including the successful Cove Rangers under-16 side: 400 players and officials took part, with over 3,000 spectators.

The festival also played a part in the early careers of some of football's greatest international names: David Roberston played and went on to be a fast and skilful full-back with Aberdeen, Rangers and Scotland; Eoin Jess played in 1984; Carlos Maldonado was 'Player of the Tournament' in 1981 (he went on to captain Venezuela in the World Cup); and Paul Gascoigne played twice for Newcastle United Youths – in the 1983 under-17 final he scored a hat trick in the victory over English side Freckleton Juniors. The festival was funded by ADC, the University of Aberdeen, and the Scottish Tourist Board.

Sport for All

In 1991, 1992 and 1993, Aberdeen was named as 'Scotland's Most Sporting City' by the Scottish Sports Council. In nationwide, one-day contests the city had the largest number of people using its sporting facilities. The figure topped 9,000 in the 1992 contest. This reflected the significant investment which the council made in its sports facilities and their popularity. The sporting life of Aberdeen received a considerable boost during the 1980s and '90s when the council began to earmark significant sums of money for the provision of new facilities and the upgrading of existing ones. Councillor Urquhart helped to increase the priority given to sport within the department's activities.

The ADC did its bit to sustain the nation's obsession with golf. It owned and managed seven golf courses. Five offered the full 18 holes, and there was one 9-hole and one 6-hole course. A golf users' group met four times a year to discuss management and user issues. Hazlehead Number One hosted the Scotland v England women's pro international, and one contestant declared the course to be as good as anything she'd encountered on the European circuit.

During the 1980s, the council considered proposals for a major redevelopment of the Queen's Links area of Aberdeen. The plans envisaged the building of a modern purpose-built leisure centre to include a sports hall, leisure pool, health suite and fitness studio. Crèche facilities and a cafeteria were also to be included. The redevelopment of the Linksfield Stadium in the mid-1980s (reopened as the Chris Anderson Stadium), provided the city with international standard athletics facilities which benefited both the city and the north east as a whole.

The city's Westburn Park was the venue for the World Bowls Championships in 1984. This followed considerable investment in upgrading the bowling greens and facilities at the park. In 1989, it became the permanent venue of the Woolwich Scottish Masters tournament.

Tennis in Aberdeen received a major boost in 1995 with the opening of a new tennis centre in Westburn Park. This time the council provided funding for the development in partnership with the Lawn Tennis Association, GEL and the SSC. Given Aberdeen's somewhat unpredictable weather, the provision of both indoor and all-weather outdoor courts proved to be an invaluable addition to tennis facilities in the city. The centre – reckoned to be one of the best of its kind – was opened by pop star Cliff Richard.

The council displayed its commitment to the development of sport within the city through the appointment of development officers to promote coaching and increase opportunities for participation in sport. In 1995, ADC was the first in Scotland to appoint a development officer for women's and girls football. This was regarded as an important factor in the growing popularity of women's football in the north east, and in the success of Cove Rangers women's team which provided a number of players for the Scottish national side.

Swimming too received a boost when, in 1995, ADC – in association with the Scottish Amateur Swimming Association and the Scottish Sports Council – launched the City of Aberdeen Swim Team. The team's head coach expressed his enthusiasm for the move adding that 'this is the first initiative of its kind in Scotland'.

1995 also saw the appointment of a development officer to raise the profile of netball in Aberdeen. The council's 'Startrack' scheme, launched in 1992 as part of a nationwide campaign to develop athletics, provided Aberdeen's budding young athletes with the opportunity to receive specialist coaching in a range of events. If further proof of the city's sporting success was needed, the search to find the winners of the council-sponsored Aberdeen Sports Person of the Year Award 1995 revealed that around 200 of the nominees had represented Scotland or Great Britain in their chosen sports in the preceding twelve months.

In order to further encourage participation in sport, the council adhered to a policy of keeping entry charges to facilities to a minimum. A similar policy was in operation for sports coaching and equipment hire. Regular users of council-run sports facilities were able to benefit from special membership rates and season ticket discounts. An 'Access to Leisure' scheme enabled people on low incomes – such as pensioners, those in receipt of benefits and disabled people – to use the city's swimming pools and sports facilities either free of charge or at reduced rates. By 1995, around 18,000 people in the city were enjoying the city's leisure facilities through the scheme.

The government's imposition of CCT made it more difficult to maintain an 'open access' policy. There was pressure to aim at activities which were guaranteed to be popular in 'the market'. The expenditure squeeze on local authorities pushed them to look at raising their charges and to promote activities which would maximise income, whether or not these were in the areas of greatest community need.

The ADC worked hard to ensure that everyone – regardless of age, sex, religion, ethnic group or disability – was able to enjoy and participate in a wide range of sporting and recreational opportunities. In 1983, it set up a sub-committee, with representatives of disabled organisations, to look at participation in music and the performing arts. It promoted participation by the disabled in sport and appointed a development officer. Sporting clubs for the disabled were given valuable support through the provision of equipment and coaching. In the same year, ADC's Leisure and Recreation Department won a 'Fit for Work' award in recognition of its policies and achievements in the employment of disabled persons.

Some of the council's initiatives were directed at specific groups of citizens. In 1992, the council decided to sponsor a programme of events, concerts and sports and arts activities for the city's senior citizens and disabled people. This became an annual event. In 1995/96, expenditure of around £220,000 was authorised from the Common Good Fund to provide a range of activities. This included

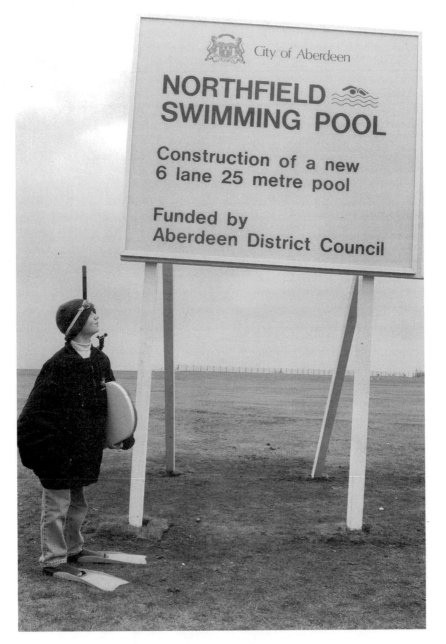

Too early for a swim!

guided bus tours of the city, tea dances, concerts, 'taster' days in a wide range of leisure activities and an extensive programme of meals and entertainment in the Beach Ballroom for 10,000 senior citizens and disabled people.

In the same year, the Women's Arts Project was launched. It sought to encourage women to participate in a wide range of arts activities. By 1995 women were also being encouraged to develop their writing skills through the council-sponsored Aberdeen Women's Fiction Project. One result of this was the publication of an anthology of women's fiction (Special Reserve) a year later.

The ADC aimed to satisfy the many and varied recreational needs of the citizen. This entailed considerable investment on the part of the council in the provision and upgrading of facilities.

Aberdonians certainly appreciated the efforts made by the district council on their behalf. When public opinion was surveyed in 1994 more than 80% thought that Aberdeen's parks, theatre, music hall and libraries were excellent and good. The corresponding figure for swimming pools was a little under 70%, for indoor sports 58% and for outdoor sports 52%. Most Aberdonians felt that ADC's efforts and investment had been worthwhile.

9: The Public Libraries

Introduction

The public library service provided by ADC came to be regarded as one of the best in Scotland. This position was achieved by good planning, investment, hard work and an ability to adapt to change. In 1975, libraries served their communities mainly by providing books which were consulted or borrowed. Two decades later libraries met community needs in a variety of ways. They provided communities with information, education, cultural and recreational resources using the best technologies available.

In the early 1990s, the service had a book stock of around 700,000 titles covering a wide and varied range of subjects and interests, an impressive range of audio, visual and arts equipment, and a host of other items ranging from children's toys to stage lighting. In 1991/92, more than 304,000 records, CDs, cassettes, talking books and videos, and over 2,000,000 books were issued. In 1994/95, the value of the stock was £3,710 for every 1,000 of the population. The service was easily accessible to all who lived, worked or studied in the city through a network of eighteen branch libraries and three mobile library units. The main services could be taken directly to those who were unable to visit their local branch because of age or disability.

The Origins of the Library Service

In Aberdeen, the first public library was established in 1884 when the directors of the Mechanics Institution in Market Street agreed to hand over their building and library to the town council for use as a public library. The service was free and open to all. The principle of free access was built in from the start. Such was the demand for the services of the public library that it soon became clear that a new purpose-built library was required and in 1892 the Central Library in Rosemount Viaduct was officially opened – the three-storey building cost £10,000. The Scottish philanthropist, Andrew Carnegie, and the Town Council each put in £1,000 with the remainder being raised by public subscription and donations. The building housed a Reading Room, Lending Library and Reference Library which were open daily, except Sundays, until 10pm.

At the opening of the Central Library in 1892, the Reverend Professor Smith in his dedication prayer asked that the library might serve:

141

...for the dispersion of ignorance and prejudice ... for the growth of understanding and sympathy among all classes of the community, for the education of children, for the equipment of men for public counsel and debate, and for the awakening of genius and invention.

The service grew as the city boundaries were extended. The incorporation of the burghs of Woodside and Old Aberdeen, and the village of Torry in 1891 created a demand for the service to be extended into new areas. However, financial constraints meant that branch libraries were out of the question. A small collection of books and other materials was made available for consultation in reading rooms around the city. The first of these was opened in 1893 in Old Aberdeen. Some of these rooms were also designated as 'delivery stations', where books ordered from the Central library stock could be delivered to the reader.

Despite the best efforts of the corporation to make the library service accessible to everyone in the city, development was severely constrained until 1920, when rates were increased to 3d. The additional resources made possible a number of new developments. In 1925, the lending library was reorganised and the public was given open access to the book stock for the first time. The city's first branch library was opened in 1929 at the corner of Union Street and Broad Street. The Sir John Anderson Branch Library was taken over by the corporation in the same year for the rapidly developing areas of Woodside and Hilton.

Branch libraries were gradually established to serve the needs of the developing areas of the city. The corporation provided three mobile libraries for outlying areas: the first of these took to the road in 1950.

The Libraries in Crisis

As early as 1951, concerns were expressed about the standards of the Scottish public library service. These were outlined in a report by the Advisory Council on Education in Scotland entitled 'Libraries, Museums and Art Galleries'. Amongst other things, the report recommended that the public library service should be grant aided, that the limit on the amount of finance which could be raised from local rates for the provision of the service be removed, and that local library authorities should be able to contribute to the costs of the Scottish Central Library. The last two recommendations were included in the Public Libraries (Scotland) Act 1955. The introduction of the rate support grant addressed the financial recommendation.

No action was taken on other recommendations made by the Advisory Council that the county and burgh library systems should be amalgamated and that central government should have responsibility for ensuring library standards through a Library Council for Scotland. South of the border the Public Libraries and Museums Act of 1964 led to a thorough and radical review of the public library service, but corresponding legislation for Scotland was postponed because of the pending discussions on local government reorganisation. In the mid-1960s, the Scottish Library Association (SLA) pressed the Scottish Office to consider the broader issues and in particular the introduction of national standards for the service. A Working Party was set up in October 1967.

The Working Party provided the opportunity that many of those who ran the public library service had been waiting for: a forum in which the service could be discussed. The report was something of an eye-opener for many library authorities in Scotland, including Aberdeen! The service provided by the libraries was reasonably good in comparison with some parts of Scotland, but nevertheless, Aberdeen City Libraries had been affected by the same malaise that had weakened the majority of national services. The main problems were inadequate funding and a lack of leadership.

As far as Aberdeen was concerned, the Working Party could not have come at a better time. The City Librarian had long recognised that the library service was in urgent need of a shot in the arm. But without the necessary statistical evidence or objective comparisons with services provided elsewhere, it was difficult to convince others about the nature and scale of the problem. The SLA was represented on the Working Party by Aberdeen's City Librarian until his retirement in 1968. The Counties of Cities Association was represented by Councillor R A Raffan of Aberdeen Town Council. With statistical information provided by the Scottish Office, the SLA and others, the working party was able to provide the most thorough and detailed assessment of the Scottish library system ever undertaken. In 1969, the Report pointed up the considerable inadequacies of the library system across Scotland and provided a blueprint for its improvement.

Aberdeen did not emerge without criticism. The report showed Aberdeen to be the third lowest in Scotland in terms of spending on books and materials per head of population. The number of qualified chartered librarians employed by the corporation was well below the recommended figure.

Significant improvements were made during the late 1960s and early '70s. In 1969, a new purpose built branch library was opened at Airyhall in the west end of the city, serving a population of around 10,000. It was a bright and modern building which proved to be a great success, with over 232,000 books borrowed in the first year alone. In 1970, borrowing figures fell compared with the previous year. This was thought to be due in the main to a lack of new material on the shelves. The problem was not confined to Airyhall, but was symptomatic of a more fundamental failing of the service city-wide. The libraries' book fund, the very lifeblood of the service, had not been significantly increased for a number of years and as a result was not keeping pace with inflation.

On the advice of the committee the library budget was increased from £16,000 (1970) to £30,000 in 1972/73. The immediate problem was resolved but the whole situation served to highlight the importance of securing adequate long-term funding for the service.

Building for the Future

Despite the unease and uncertainty created by the run up to local government reorganisation in 1975, the early 1970s saw some important developments which helped to shape the modern service. Two new branch libraries were planned for the rapidly expanding areas of Tillydrone and Linksfield.

However, the long-awaited extension to the Central Library had to wait. Plans for its extension had been produced in the 1930s, but lack of resources had prevented the plans from leaving the drawing board. By the late 1960s the matter was again under discussion. In 1963, a mezzanine floor was added which provided additional storage and office space.

By the end of the decade, the situation was critical. The building which had served the city well for almost eighty years was seriously in need of substantial renovation and extension. Lack of space was not the only problem. The building was showing its age inside and out, and public expenditure cuts again resulted in the extension being delayed. The local press reported that the Central Library had 'all the charm of a model lodging house'. However without the necessary resources there was little that the council could do.

The 1969 report was not the only factor to influence the development of the city library service. The service provided jointly by the counties of Aberdeen and Kincardine to the areas surrounding the city – which later became part of the enlarged city – had been steadily improving. New branch libraries had been built at Cults, Bridge of Don and Bucksburn. The county library service was also enhancing the service provided to readers through the introduction of records and framed prints. This provided a useful comparison for ADC's own services.

The first students to the School of Librarianship at Robert Gordon Institute of Technology enrolled in 1967. This was only the second such school to be established in Scotland and provided the opportunity for students and library staff to gain qualifications locally rather than travelling to Edinburgh to study. Librarians in the north east had been instrumental in the campaign to establish the school.

By the early 1970s, Aberdeen was establishing itself as the major servicing and administrative base for the North Sea oil and gas industry. There was an influx of new people from all parts of the world. New areas of educational, recreational, social and cultural interest and opportunity appeared, and the library service had to respond to the changing needs of the city. The influx of people also meant the opening up of new residential and business areas of the city and library services had to be extended to these areas.

The 1975 Reorganisation

In the early 1970s there was considerable unease about the future of the service, and about the possible impact of local government reform. In the run up to 1975, the City Librarian continually stressed the need for ADC to grasp the opportunity presented by reorganisation to set up a library service of the highest possible standard.

The Wheatley Commission considered whether the library service would be best administered at regional or district level. Prior to the 1974/5 reorganisation, libraries had been provided by burgh councils under the Public Libraries Acts and also by County Councils in their capacity as education authorities. In Scotland's four cities, library services were provided under local Acts.

The Wheatley Commission concluded that the service was both an educational facility and a civic amenity serving local needs and reflecting local characteristics. There was no reason why the service should be provided solely by either tier of local government. The SLA took the view that an effective library service required a minimum population of 100,000, except in remote areas. This view was endorsed by the Commission. The firm view of the corporation was that the public library service should be the responsibility of the district council. This was fully consistent with the campaign for all-purpose status for the local authorities in Scotland's four main cities.

When the government's White Paper on the reorganisation of local government was published it became clear that libraries would be a district council responsibility. This news was warmly welcomed within the library service itself where there had been real concerns that if the service became a function of the regional tier of local government, it might be swallowed up by a large semi-autonomous education department and as a result, lose some of its identity and focus.

Elsewhere in Grampian the response was mixed. Of the five districts only the City of Aberdeen had a population above the 100,000 threshold. The other four were smaller and perhaps too small to support a cost effective library service of their own. The Chief Librarians within the region met several times from 1971 onwards to consider how best to move forward. Aberdeen decided to provide its own service as did the much smaller council in Moray. Kincardine and Deeside, Banff and Buchan and Gordon districts came together to form the North East of Scotland Library Service (NESLS), a unique form of voluntary collaboration. There remained considerable co-operation between the services in inter-loan and inter-availability and a large degree of centralisation of reference and information services at the Central Library in Aberdeen.

Within the city itself, the campaign shifted to one aimed at ensuring that the public library service emerged from the whole process of reorganisation in a favourable position. There were two issues of particular concern. The first was to ensure that the new council established a separate libraries department and a committee dedicated to looking after the interests of the service. In Aberdeen the corporation had always retained a separate committee and departmental structure for the service when many authorities brought their library services under the control of more general leisure and recreation committees. The second priority was to secure a sufficiently high level of funding for the library service. In the event, both these issues were resolved satisfactorily; a separate departmental and committee structure was put in place and the annual book fund was increased.

After Reorganisation

In May 1975, the new City of Aberdeen District Council took over seventeen branch libraries. Eleven of these had previously been administered by the corporation: Airyhall, Ferryhill, Kaimhill, Mastrick, Northfield, Stockethill, Torry, Woodside, Old Aberdeen, Kincorth and the Central Library on Rosemount Viaduct. The remaining six had been provided jointly by the counties of Aberdeen and Kincardine: Bridge of Don, Cove, Culter, Cults, Dyce and Bucksburn. In addition, two mobile library units and a van were available for the provision of a service to communities on the edge of the city and to the elderly and housebound. After the Wheatley reorganisation, ADC opened new branches at Linksfield (1975), Dyce (1988) and Tillydrone (1991). Ferryhill and Cornhill were refurbished in 1994 and 1995 respectively.

Most of the 'new' areas of the city already had a long history as communities in their own right and it was quickly recognised that this could be an advantage. The branch libraries serving these areas of Aberdeen had their own local history collections and resources and they were encouraged to participate in their communities. It was recognised that the outlying branch libraries could benefit greatly from being incorporated in a larger and better financed city wide library service, whilst still retaining their individual identities. A series of public talks, publications and photographic exhibitions on local history was organised. These proved to be popular.

There appeared to be a new enthusiasm about the service from both councillors and officials following reorganisation. New faces on the committee meant new ideas were being put forward for the development of the service. Some of those ideas could be taken up given the department's increased budget. A new staff structure was established and this helped to improve morale. The City Librarian was a member of the council's Management Team and could influence the future direction of the authority as a whole. However, no amount of enthusiasm could mask the fact that the building at the very heart of the system, the Central Library, was desperately in need of substantial renovation.

The Central Library

Early in 1972, the City Architect's department drew up an ambitious plan for the transformation of the Central Library. Such was the extent of the work required that the corporation had considered whether a new purpose built building elsewhere in the city might provide a better solution. However, this proposal was rejected and attention was turned to the problem of how the building on

Rosemount Viaduct could be modernised and extended in order to provide the necessary additional space, whilst still retaining its essential character.

The plans involved the erection of a seven-storey extension to the rear of the building where the ground slopes down towards the Denburn. The proposal was once again put on ice as other priorities took precedence. The first of these was the completion of a new three storey extension to the council's headquarters at the Town House which was urgently required in order to provide additional accommodation. A second was the extensive refurbishment of His Majesty's Theatre which had recently been acquired by the council and which was in danger of being shut down if essential work did not commence immediately.

Eventually, in January 1978, work commenced on the library extension. The work was undertaken in two phases, cost £1.5m, and took four years from start to finish. Phase one of the refurbishment was completed late in 1981, and included the seven-storey extension which significantly increased the available floor space. Lifts were added, new floors constructed, and new heating and lighting systems installed. The 60% increase in floor space meant that the library stock could be displayed in a more attractive manner. Phase two, which mainly affected the Commercial and Business Library, was completed some months later. On 20 October 1982, the refurbished Central Library was officially opened by the Queen Mother.

During the four years when the refurbishment works were ongoing, the level of service offered to the city was maintained. On several occasions whole sections of the library were moved around within the building, but a full range of services was maintained. Senior staff from the libraries department were involved in the project from the start and were able to give valuable advice on how to refurbish the building in order to provide the best possible quality of service to the library user.

An Accessible Service

After 1975, the network of branch libraries in Aberdeen was strengthened to bring the service to all areas of the city. This network, supplemented by mobile library units, ensured that citizens had easy access to the public library service. Eleven branches were open to the public for more than sixty hours each week. This, by any reckoning, was an impressive figure and something in which the council took pride.

The pressure to cut opening hours, or indeed to close branches altogether was very difficult to resist. Throughout the late 1970s and '80s there was continual pressure from the Scottish Office for local authorities to cut their expenditure. In many parts of Scotland the 'easy option' of cutting opening hours was taken. This pressure reached crisis point in 1985 when guidelines issued by the Scottish Secretary effectively meant that almost £130,000 had to be cut from the Aberdeen libraries' budget in the following financial year.

This could have spelt disaster for a service which was already keeping a tight rein on spending. Closure of several branch libraries was a very real consideration but was met with a barrage of protest from all sections of the community. In a city with a reputation for having a service which was accessible to all members of the community both in terms of branch libraries and the extent of its opening hours, closures seemed totally unacceptable. Library service managers took the view that cuts to opening hours would become permanent and irreversible. The committee had little hesitation in agreeing and reaffirmed their total opposition to the Secretary of State's guidelines. From then on housekeeping had to be better than ever, but the branches stayed open and opening hours were kept to a maximum.

Accessibility however was not just about the location of a service or hours in which it was available. It was also about ensuring that all sections of the community had access. At the most basic level this meant that the public library had to supply a range of books and other materials that were of interest to men, women and children of all ages and from different cultural backgrounds. It had also to cater for the special needs and requirements of those with various disabilities. In the 1970s and 1980s there was an increased awareness of disability in general and this was reflected in the services provided in public libraries. In Aberdeen some provision had been made for library users with special needs as early as 1900 when a selection of books was made available in Braille. This was followed by the introduction of books in large print, and talking books for the blind.

A decision taken by ADC in 1975 – to provide appropriate access for the disabled to all buildings owned by the council and to which the public had access – affected the city's public libraries. Four branches already had suitable access for the disabled and over the course of the next few months, a further thirteen were converted. Wheelchair ramps and lifts were installed at the Central Library during the course of the renovations. In 1986, the Breakthrough Trust gifted a visual telephone terminal for the deaf.

Over the years, a stock of books in foreign languages was amassed to cater for and reflect the linguistic and cultural diversity within the city. The largest collections were in Urdu and Cantonese.

A Responsive Service

In 1984, the Arts and Recreation Committee of COSLA called for a report on the public library service in Scotland in order to review progress made since 1969. The report was published the following year and identified a number of changes in society which affected the public library service. These included growing levels of unemployment, the increased amount of leisure time available to individuals, new technologies, the greater need for and participation in adult learning and of course the effect of the reorganisation of Scottish local government in 1975.

The report also assessed the extent to which the recommended standards had been attained. The position in Scotland as a whole was not encouraging with a large number of authorities falling well below the recommended standards, particularly in the provision of non-fiction and reference works. Aberdeen was one of a small number of authorities which in most areas had attained and even exceeded the standards set out in 1969. In 1995, COSLA produced a further report on the public library service in Scotland, reassessing and redefining the role of the service. Aberdeen City Libraries once again emerged from the report in a favourable light, firmly established as one of the best public library services in Scotland.

A Common Vision

The importance of the library service was much better recognised after the 1975 reorganisation. In Aberdeen the vision and leadership of a succession of City Librarians helped to raise the service's profile. The COSLA report of 1986 attempted to redefine the modern role of the service: 'the purpose of the public library service is to provide for everyone in the area which it serves, a service which caters for the educational, cultural, information and leisure needs of individuals, groups, industrial and commercial concerns and any other agencies requiring assistance or information.' These objectives were restated in the 1995 report.

Developments in technology, particularly in the area of information technology played an important part in maintaining and improving the accessibility and responsiveness of the public library service. These developments had an impact on all areas of the service including library administration, reference and information services, lending services and inter-library co-operation. Every area of the public library service came to be affected by new technology in one form or another.

A number of other factors influenced the development of the library service in the 1980s and '90s. The Scottish Library and Information Council (SLIC) was established in 1991 in order to improve quality and co-ordination within the service. Two reports – the 'Charter for the Arts' from the Scottish Arts Council in 1992, and one entitled 'Libraries and the Arts' by the SLA and SLIC in 1993 – highlighted the role of public libraries in support of the arts.

Within the ADC, the report by PA Management Consultants resulted in the Libraries becoming part of the new City Arts Department and the committee becoming a sub-committee of the Arts and Recreation Committee. Whilst there was some anxiety over the library service becoming part of the large Arts and Recreation Department, the position was somewhat different to that of the early 1970s. The Libraries Department of 1989 was in considerably better shape than twenty years earlier and it had an excellent reputation both in Scotland and further afield. Students and librarians from elsewhere in the UK and other countries made visits to Aberdeen to see the service first hand. In 1991/92, twelve students, four of them from outwith the UK, had their placements with the service. The developing role of the public library service in the recreational and cultural life of the community meant that there were clear advantages in the service being amalgamated with other arts and recreation services.

Lending Services

New technology changed aspects of library management and offered new opportunities to the service. Aberdeen introduced an automated book issue and circulation system which had a dramatic impact on its operation. The need for a new system had been recognised as early as 1972, when it was proposed that it should be installed during the refurbishment of the Central Library. Financial constraints meant that the expenditure required was not approved until 1979 when work on the library was already underway.

The aim was to install a system which would improve efficiency and accuracy in the issue and return of books and other materials and better control of the library stock. The system selected was the Plessey Library Pen System. Essentially this involved each item in the libraries stock being labelled with an electronic tag or bar code and the information on each item being entered into the computer system. Readers were issued with a unique borrowers number contained in a bar code on their library ticket. In this way an up to date and accurate record could be kept of all issues and returns and a complete record of the library service's stock was readily available.

The actual task of labelling each item of stock and in re-registering readers was monumental. Young unemployed people were taken on through the Youth Opportunities Programme, and modernising the library provided them with valuable training and work experience. Planning for the installation of the system meant that a close working relationship developed between staff of the libraries and the council's computing specialists. In some respects this was an early example of the strong inter-disciplinary 'team' approach that played such an important role across the council in later years. Following its successful installation at the Central Library, the Plessey Pen Library System was extended to other library branches.

Traditionally the lending library supplied readers with a wide range of books to cater for their leisure, educational and cultural needs. Great importance has always been placed on maintaining the book stock in a clean and attractive condition, and on regularly updating the stock. This policy led to an interesting development when the committee took the decision to sell surplus books to the public. The first sale took place in 1979; they have been popular events ever since.

In the 1980s and 1990s there was a growth in the enjoyment of home-based leisure activities, and technology made many of these activities more accessible to the individual. Most citizens gained access to a range of audio and visual equipment and this led to a demand that the public libraries stock records, compact discs and video tapes. The Record Lending Service was first established at the Central Library in 1973 and extended to the branch libraries in the following years. In 1987, CDs were introduced into the stock. By 1984, video had established its popularity, and the council decided to extend the service to include video cassettes, providing they had some educational or instructional merit. After 1976, citizens were able to enjoy works of art at home by borrowing framed prints from the public library.

In 1991, an innovative Arts Equipment Lending Service was introduced. This was believed to be the first such service in the country to be provided free of charge. The scheme was introduced in order to encourage participation in arts-related activities the importance of which was increasingly recognised by local authorities. Individuals and groups were able to borrow a wide range of audio and visual equipment, musical instruments, stage lighting and a host of other items. The scheme was an immediate success with an average of around five hundred items borrowed each month.

The library service is marked by the high degree of co-operation which exists between different library authorities. Despite the large numbers of books and other materials that are available in Aberdeen, there are instances where readers request items which are not in the libraries stock. In Scotland, the National Library of Scotland Lending Service (NLSLS) has responsibility for maintaining the Scottish Union Catalogue, the Scottish Book Exchange and the Scottish Fiction Reserve. It also provided access to the rest of the UK library network. Users of the library service in Aberdeen could gain access to the wider resources of the UK library system as a whole. In 1994/95, Aberdeen generally satisfied book requests in eighteen days. The majority of Scottish library services took twenty to forty days.

Reference, Information and Local Studies Provision

Almost everyone in the community required information at some time or other on a wide variety of subjects from simple queries about community facilities or the workings of the council, to more detailed and specialised enquiries. Traditionally the reference and local history departments of the public library fulfilled this role. They provided information for educational, recreational and other purposes: printed material was still the main source of information. In the 1980s and 1990s, the impact of information technology greatly increased the range of information that could be accessed, and changed the ways in which this was best done. Developments like the Internet brought the potential to browse library holdings in Australia from the comfort of an Aberdeen library!

Nevertheless, the more 'traditional' sources of information remained the key element in the provision of the service. The Local Studies section of the public library was once described as 'the collective memory of the community'. By the 1990s, Aberdeen City Libraries had an impressive Local Studies Collection, with a large range of titles, around 15,000 photographs of local interest, and a range of local newspapers and journals some of which were stored on microfiche. The service was very popular with around 25,000 enquiries being made by the public each year, a figure only exceeded in Edinburgh and Glasgow.

Aberdeen City Libraries promoted its local studies collection through a series of talks and displays on subjects of local interest and published a series of booklets and pamphlets. The first was a history of the Anderson Library in Woodside, written by a member of staff and published in 1983 to coincide with its centenary. A similar publication – On the Viaduct, written by the same author – gave a fascinating account of the first hundred years of the Central Library on Rosemount Viaduct and was produced to mark its centenary in 1992. A number of booklets and audio cassettes were produced on subjects of historical or cultural interest. Guides to the resources of the public library service were also produced, one of the most widely used of these being 'Links in the Chain', a guide to the family history resources of Aberdeen City Libraries.

By the 1990s the public library service in the city was providing a wide range of information to all sectors of the community. New technology meant that this information could be accessed at all library points. The libraries provided information on local recreational and cultural facilities, careers information, welfare rights and a range of other information of interest to the public. An innovative database was commenced in 1985 called 'Community Contacts' which provided information on local clubs, societies and other organisations and on public services. This service was made available through new technology in all branch libraries.

The Commercial and Business Library was first established in the late 1930s in response to increasing demands for information on business, commerce and technology. It was thought to be only the second such service to be established in Scotland. The arrival of the offshore oil and gas industry led to new demands on the service. The City Libraries met this challenge by enhancing the range of services provided to include information of interest to those involved in the industry. In 1979 a modern list of holdings relevant to the business community was developed. Throughout the 1980s, the range of services was constantly reviewed and updated in response to changing needs and priorities. The installation of new communications technology such as facsimile and Prestel meant that local businesses in Aberdeen could communicate more easily with the rest of the world.

Services for Children and Young People

The first Juvenile Library in Aberdeen was opened in 1911 at the Central Library. This was the first open access department within the library and proved an immediate success. Children could join on their ninth birthday and were free to browse for books that might be of interest to them.

In 1945, when the first school visits started, it was recognised that the public

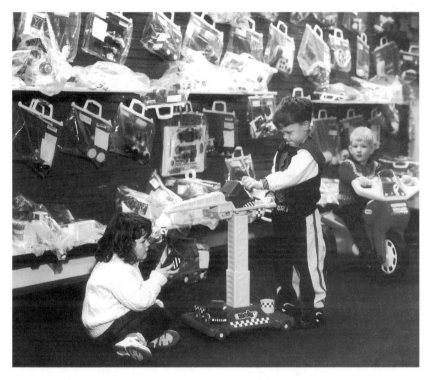

Children need councils too! The Toy Library

library could play a very important and proactive role in the educational development of children. Since then changes in the school curriculum, including a gradual movement away from direct teaching towards managed learning, and changes in the examination system, have had an impact on the way in which library services for young people are delivered. Aberdeen's public libraries provided specialist books, reference materials and study areas for children and young people, story hours, talks and displays on subjects of interest to children, and competitions. In 1991/92, over 1,600 school visits were organised. The City Libraries recognised that the particular needs of children and young people could be met by providing a range of other less 'traditional' materials, such as toys, games and magazines and by utilising audio, visual and IT formats.

A Toy Lending service was introduced first at Tillydrone in 1991 and later in other branches. The latest information technology was brought into services for young people. The libraries played their part in the development of a generation of young people who were much more familiar with new technology than most adults!

In Support of Education

The Wheatley Commission recognised the important role of the service in education. In allocating responsibility for public libraries to the districts, central government not only recognised that the service also played an important civic role, but also that the world of education extended beyond the schools and the colleges of further education which became the responsibility of the regional councils in 1975.

The establishment of the Open University opened up new and exciting opportunities for adults to enter the world of further education without leaving their own homes. This in turn created a demand for the services of the local reference library, where students could consult the book stock. Since then there has been a dramatic increase in distance learning, training opportunities, and a gradual move towards self-managed learning. The promotion of 'lifelong learning' by the UK government and the European Union in the mid-1990s promised to make the public library more important than ever.

With such strong links between education and the role of the public library, it is perhaps surprising that there was not a greater sharing of resources between the public library service and the schools library service provided by GRC. Aberdeen's neighbouring library service, NESLS, had a policy of integrating school and public library provision where appropriate. This was capable of providing certain economies in terms of sharing of resources.

With one exception this idea never really took off in the city. The exception was at Linksfield where a new branch library was opened at the Academy in 1975. The idea was that the education and public libraries authorities could share resources in terms of premises, staff, and to a certain extent, stock. This was not tried elsewhere in the city. Libraries were one service where the two-tier local government system generally made local co-ordination more difficult.

10: International Links and Community Leadership

The ADC carried out a very wide range of activities and initiatives over and above its main statutory responsibilities. It campaigned on behalf of the city and made its views known on national and international issues; it established 'twinning' and maintained links with cities in other countries; it supported charities, voluntary organisations and 'good causes' (the council also administered 125 trusts for a wide range of purposes including education, charities, and religious instruction); it honoured achievements and those responsible for them; it regulated and licensed a variety of commercial and other activities in the city; it even maintained the public clocks. In 1979, the council decided to employ an archivist to improve its records and later developed its own record store at Kittybrewster.

The council was represented in some way on most of the organisations which played a role in the governance of Aberdeen. And overall it strove to provide civic leadership.

International Links

'Twinning' with other cities formed the centrepiece of the city's international activity. There was however much more to this role. Throughout the 1975–96 period, ADC was actively involved, sometimes with NESDA and others, in promoting trade; it particularly welcomed foreign dignitaries and trade missions and, along with the other local authorities in Britain, it played an important role in the country's international policies. When the European Union passed legislation it was more likely than not that the local authorities would end up implementing it. In the 1980s and 1990s local government took greater efforts, particularly through COSLA and the professional organisations, to try to influence the EU.

The city's first 'twin' was the beautiful Bavarian city of Regensburg. The link was established in 1955 as part of the process of reconciliation with Germany after the Second World War. Many local authorities developed links of this kind. Out of these emerged broader efforts to promote better understanding and cultural links between cities and peoples. In the 1980s attention turned more to encouraging trade and economic development through twinning links.

Aberdeen city established further twinning links with Clermont-Ferrand in

France (1983), and Bulawayo in Zimbabwe (1986); Gomel in Byelarus and Stavanger in Norway were both added in 1990. These were selected from a wider range of cities which were considered as possible candidates. Some of the twins were linked with each other as well as with Aberdeen. Regensburg was already twinned with Clermont-Ferrand, which in turn was twinned with Gomel.

Each twin was chosen for some unique reason. Gomel was chosen so that ADC could help its people in the wake of the appalling nuclear disaster at Chernobyl. This followed an assessment of the area by a team from Grampian Health Board. Considerable aid was channelled to the Zimbabwean city of Bulawayo: library books, medical equipment, wheelchairs, a fire engine, a mini bus and an ambulance were amongst the donations. The common thread linking all the twinning arrangements was described by the council's International Officer as one of 'community involvement, sustainable development and mutual benefit'. Legislation in 1993 gave some further support to local authorities' international role by allowing them to work with bodies outside the UK which were engaged in carrying out local government activities. By 1993 the international work of the council was directed by the Special (International) Committee. In 1995, ADC was the winner of the prestigious Royal Mail Twin Town Awards: committee convener Councillor William Fraser accepted the award for the council.

Twinning links encouraged a very wide range of joint activities. In 1979, Regensburg celebrated its 1800th anniversary. The council helped to meet the costs of nine members of the Grampian Police Pipe Band and ten members of Fraser Ladies' Pipe Band travelling over to participate in the celebrations. In 1986, Aberdeen received a visit from the Regensburg Domspatzen Boy's Choir. In June 1995, Lord Provost Wyness led a delegation to Regensburg to join in celebrating its 750th anniversary 'Burgerfest'.

In June 1987, a delegation from Bulawayo visited the city. Aberdeen schools linked up with schools in Bulawayo, enriching the curriculum for pupils in both cities; and the Bulawayo Highlanders Football Team took part in Aberdeen's International Football Festival.

In the early 1990s, ADC helped to meet the costs of Aberdeen senior citizens' group visits to Clermont-Ferrand, Regensburg and Stavanger. In 1992, the French city took part in the Careers Fair at the Aberdeen Conference Centre and, in 1993, a delegation from the council and the city's business community went to the Clermont-Ferrand Food and Trade Fare. The Robert Gordon University also set up links with its counterpart in Clermont-Ferrand. Aberdeen YMCA was awarded a small grant to help meet the costs of a visit to Regensburg. In June 1993, ADC sent typewriters which were surplus to its requirements to Gomel. The following year a council delegation went to participate in Bulawayo's centenary celebrations, and a number of groups and organisations from the twin cities were sponsored to take part in the 'Union Street 200' celebrations.

In 1994, assistance was given to women's groups in Clermont-Ferrand and Gomel so that they could take part in the Women's Festival in Aberdeen.

Pierre Pictom and passenger David Alexander drive Chitty Chitty Bang Bang down Union Street during the 'Union Street 200' celebrations

In 1995, however, the twinning movement was marked by tragedy. During a visit to Gomel in Byelarus, two senior ADC officials were killed in a boating accident. The Lord Provost and the Mayor of Gomel both addressed the packed and very moving memorial service which was held at St Nicholas Church in Aberdeen.

Freedom of the City

The major honour which the council could bestow was the Freedom of the City, which was awarded six times between 1975 and 1996. The range of the awards provided another insight into the breadth with which ADC saw its role in providing civic leadership. Generally it was expected to be conferred on outstanding individuals. While this was the case in Aberdeen, the council also conferred the Freedom on a ship and a university!

The honour was presented in a carefully planned, intricate ceremony held in the civic splendour of the Music Hall and followed by a civic reception in the Beach Ballroom. The ceremonies followed historic traditions but also uniquely typified the characteristics of each recipient. At the end of the proceedings, the 'burgess ticket' was ceremonially tied to the person being honoured. This symbolised that the recipient now had the Freedom of the City.

In 1981, Dr Mary Esslemont became the first recipient of the honour for fifteen years. Known as 'Dr Mary', she was awarded the Freedom for a lifetime's service to medicine. She was 90 years of age when she received the award.

In 1984, the South African leader Nelson Mandela received the honour. At the time he was held prisoner on Robben Island for opposing the apartheid regime in his country. Mandela's colleague from the African National Congress, Solly Smith, accepted the award on his behalf in the Cowdray Hall, and Adelaide Tambo accepted on behalf of Nelson's wife, Winifred.

HMS *Scylla* was honoured in June 1992. The fourth HMS Scylla was commissioned in 1942 during the Second World War and was financed by money raised by the City of Aberdeen (a display in the Town House recorded the astonishing generosity of Aberdonians, which far exceeded the financial target for the subscription in just five days despite the straitened circumstances of the city in wartime). The ship saw active service until it was damaged in 1944. Its

An ADC delegation meeting Nelson Mandela after his release from prison

successor continued the close relationship with the city until its farewell visit in March 1993. The tradition of tying the 'burgess ticket' to the recipient's hat was dispensed with on this occasion.

Mikhail Gorbachev, the former reforming leader of the Soviet Union, received the award in 1993 in a high profile ceremony. As head of the Gorbachev Foundation, he was at that time campaigning internationally for peace. Thousands of Aberdonians lined the streets to watch his progress to the Music Hall where the award was made.

In 1995, the University of Aberdeen was 500 years old. The award of the Freedom of the City was made in February during the University's quincentenary celebrations, 500 years and one day after its formation. Lord Provost Wyness said that the conferral was a tribute to everyone connected with the university.

In the same year, Councillor Alex Collie MBE was similarly honoured, the Queen Mother sending a personal message of congratulations. A former lord provost, Councillor Collie had completed five decades as a local councillor, and his well-known hat seemed tailor-made for sporting the 'ticket'. The former baker described the award as 'the proudest moment in my life'.

Tourism

The ADC strongly promoted tourism throughout the 1975–96 period, some-times on its own but more often in partnership with other agencies. Many council services contributed directly to the attraction of visitors and their enjoyment of the city: the arts, leisure and recreation facilities and festivals were important; the international promotion of the city through twinning and other links contributed; the preservation of historic buildings and the planning of the city played their part. Keeping the city clean was also important, and the licensing of places of entertainment, and licensed premises and taxis played their part. In the late 1980s tourism came to be seen as a key focus for economic development.

In 1971, not long after the Scottish Tourist Board (STB) had been set up (1969), NESTA was established (this later became the Grampian Tourist Association). The association, the corporation and its neighbouring county councils, the STB, the Sports Council and the local tourist trade were all involved in promoting the city as part of the region. NESDA and the Harbour Board also played important roles. The Wheatley Commission noted that the formation of the STB and the Countryside Commission didn't appear to leave any role for local authorities in tourism. It expressed the view that perhaps there should be a role for regional councils, but it failed to make clear, specific recommendations.

The ADC, however, wanted its own unique promotion and marketing. It felt that it provided many of the attractions which brought people to the region and some of the most popular attractions in the country. These issues could easily be lost sight of in wider marketing exercises.

In the 1970s, a Director of Development and Tourism led the council's efforts. The growing level of business led to a depute being appointed in 1979. In 1979/80, tenders were sought for the production of holiday guides and accommodation guides for the city, which were produced for £9,000 and £4,000 respectively. A Tourist Information Centre was sited in ADC's St Nicholas House; an STB grant met 50% of the £69,000 cost.

In 1983, a network of Area Tourist Boards was set up across Scotland. In Aberdeen, the district Council, Scottish Tourist Board and the private sector came together under the auspices of the Aberdeen Tourist Board. Elsewhere in Grampian, the remaining district councils did likewise. At the same time, ADC recognised the value of co-operating with the other districts in the region. The result was the creation of the North East of Scotland Office of Tourism (NESCOT), which provided a focus for the marketing of Grampian's tourist activities until 1993.

Throughout the 1980s, a high level of activity continued and tourism continued to thrive. Some festivals and events, such as the Tall Ships Race in 1991, proved particularly good at attracting visitors to the city, an estimated 600,000 people turning out to see the spectacle; and ADC continued to look to new ways of encouraging tourism in Aberdeen. Many projects were jointly funded by ADC, GEL and others.

In 1993, the Grampian, Highlands and Aberdeen Tourism Marketing Company took over the task of promoting tourism for the five districts in the area. Such was the success of long term co-operation at regional level that Grampian came to be seen as a model of good practice.

Increasingly the work of service departments was assessed for its contribution to tourism. The number of visitors attracted by particular festivals and by events such as the Tall Ships Race was measured and the impact of their spending in the city was assessed: the Scottish Tourist Board published Tourism and the Arts in Scotland – A Development Strategy. The ADC identified a number of projects and proposed to GEL that they be jointly funded.

The 1994 Act which brought the reform of local government also changed the government-appointed tourist organisations, and regional bodies were put in place: the city was covered by the Aberdeen and Grampian Tourist Board. The council opposed this change, arguing that the focus on the city's needs would be weakened.

Regulating the Market

The ADC had statutory responsibilities to issue licenses to permit and control a range of activities. The best known of these roles was the licensing of the sale of alcoholic liquor. The council controlled the licensing of premises and any extensions beyond normal 'opening hours'. Less well known to the public was that it also licensed taxis and private hire cars, hot food outlets, markets, gaming clubs,

160

gaming machines, bingo halls, betting shops, second hand dealers, scrap metal merchants, street traders and window cleaners. The council was required to set up a Licensing Board and this was the body which controlled the sale of alcoholic liquor. The Board was made up of elected councillors and often had difficult decisions to make. It had a separate legal status independent of the council. The Licensing Committee took care of all the other activities which were licensed by ADC. The council's regulatory role was strengthened further in the 1980s.

The most controversial area was licensed premises in the city centre. The region's relatively high disposable incomes and the city's role as entertainment centre for the region created a lot of pressure. There was a large increase in the number of licensed premises in the city centre between 1975 and 1996. The Board had to consider whether applications might lead to over-provision, a threat to public order or safety, or whether there could be undue public nuisance. The public could object to the granting of licenses if any of these problems were felt likely, and there were other policy objectives for the city centre which had to be taken into account.

The council and the partnership were increasing housing supply with a view to increasing the resident population, so the city centre had to be an attractive and safe environment, whilst the police had to keep order and ensure that it was safe. And the transport system had to be able to cope with late night revellers making their way home. The Board was frequently criticised for allowing too many licensed premises and letting them stay open too late. The Board's critics were quick to label one street in the city centre 'Happy Valley', but actually this tag was in popular use before the accusations of over-provision. With a more restrictive policy the Board would probably have been strongly condemned for stopping people enjoying themselves! And inappropriate applications were routinely thrown out.

In many cities relationships between the taxi trade and their regulatory body were difficult. The taxi trade had an interest in restricting numbers to protect operators' incomes. Councils wanted to ensure that residents, business visitors and tourists could get taxis when they needed them, and that key facilities like railways and airports were always supplied. The trade was well-organised in the city. The main firms came together in 1980 to form the Aberdeen Licensed Taxi Trade Representatives and quickly informed the council that they were the new trade association. In 1992, a new Aberdeen Taxi Federation was formed to speak for the trade.

The council first sought to limit taxi numbers in Aberdeen to 350 and make the job full-time. This limit was too low, as the trade had warned, and it was later raised to 600. In 1984, the council's ability to set a limit was removed by the government. The number of taxis shot up to 870 and the trade protested about over-supply. The legislation was changed and councils were able to carry out surveys of the trade to determine the appropriate limit. In 1994 this was set at 850.

Relationships with the trade were improved when a consultative group was set up in 1992. This provided a forum for discussing the key issues and airing different points of view. The Licensing Committee, the ADC Taxi Inspector, the GRC Roads Department and Public Transport Unit and the Grampian Police were involved. Discussion led to the approval of a Taxi Charter setting out the standards which customers could expect.

An unusual complaint led to discussion of taxi drivers' standards of dress. A passenger complained when her driver wore a string vest. He was only trying to cope with a very hot day, but the impression that 'Rab C' might have left Govan for the Granite City was not appreciated! A dress code followed in 1994. Out went the shell suits and designer stubble and in came a clean-cut collar and tie image.

In contrast the suggestion that the city should have a fleet of easily identifiable yellow cabs like New York was thrown out by the trade. This was taking American influence too far! But the proposal did lead to the introduction of some standardisation in taxi signs.

In 1995, ADC introduced a voluntary training programme for the city's taxi drivers in order to make them more aware of the needs of disabled persons. The taxi trade quickly demonstrated their support for the scheme and took up the offer. Drivers who undertook the programme were entitled to display a specially designed logo in their cabs. The convener of the council's Licensing Committee, Councillor Allan MacLean, commenting on the enthusiasm shown by the trade, added 'Aberdeen's taxi drivers are amongst the best in the country but they are always looking at ways of improving the service to all customers.'

The responsibility for licensing sex shops passed to ADC in the early 1980s. When one opened in Chattan Place there was strong local opposition, and Councillor Gallagher, in whose ward the shop was located, protested outside the premises. The council refused a license but the shop carried on trading: the owners were subsequently prosecuted for trading without a license, and the contents of the shop were seized by the police as evidence to support the prosecution case. The level of press and public interest meant that the case had to be heard in the Advocates Hall rather than the relatively small District Court! The shop was forced to close and a subsequent application to open a similar establishment in Regent Quay rejected.

The District Court

The ADC was responsible for administering the District Court. In 1975, the District Court replaced the previous Justice of the Peace Courts, Burgh Courts and Police Courts. There was one District Court for Aberdeen. The council provided legally qualified clerks and training for the Justices of the Peace.

The District Court dealt with less serious crimes. Minor breaches of the peace, petty thefts, failure to have a television license, and some traffic offences would be heard there. The JPs who sat in the court did not have to be legally qualified, and they were often recruited from the ranks of city councillors and people of standing in the community. While the jurisdiction of the court was limited, the JPs had considerable power. In 1996 they could impose maximum penalties of 60 days in prison or a £2,500 fine!

Support for Outside Bodies

The ADC was represented by its councillors on a very wide range of outside bodies. It had a particularly long relationship with the University of Aberdeen, stretching back to the very origins of the ancient university; its representative on the University Court symbolised and helped to cement the important 'town and gown' relationship. The council also supported the formation of the RGU and formed a close relationship with it, too. Other bodies on which the council was represented included the city's further education college; a wide range of bodies for arts, leisure and recreation; the Harbour Board; the Gas Consumer Council; the Visiting Committees for Aberdeen and Peterhead prisons; the district Manpower Committee of the MSC; the SDA's Development Consultative Committee; the Chamber of Commerce and GEL; Grampian Health Board; and the North East Water Purification Board. Representation on these bodies was of much more than ceremonial importance. The presence of councillors provided links which helped partnership projects to emerge; council policies could be explained more effectively and councillors could learn at first hand how other bodies approached issues. This helped to improve decision-making. And when these bodies were changed by government – for example when GEL was created in 1991 – the presence of elected councillors could help to provide some degree of continuity.

Playing an effective role on these bodies was often difficult for councillors, adding new dimensions to their already complex role in public life. Many outside bodies dealt with highly complex and technical issues. Councillors often had to learn about new fields and issues very quickly. In many cases there was little expertise within the council on which they could rely for support. ADC put more resources into supporting councillors in the 1990s, and there was a growing awareness within the council of the importance of influencing and co-ordinating other agencies.

The council also helped outside bodies by giving grant support and by extending civic hospitality. A very wide range of organisations was helped over the 1975–96 period. These included national as well as local bodies, and ranged from prestigious cultural organisations to local self-help groups. Often the small grant was a vital resource to a local body. In 1984/85, £135 was awarded to Aberdeen Gaelic Choir and £9,600 to the Citizen's Advice Bureau. Often grants were linked to funding decisions taken by other bodies: the Aberdeen grant met 30% of the costs of the Citizen's Advice Bureau, the rest being met from other sources. In

1985, £150 was granted to help the local work of the Royal National Mission to Deep Sea Fisherman, and the 55th (Kincorth) Scouts received £240 towards the rent payable on their hut.

Local authority contributions were vital to national organisations such as Scottish Opera and the Scottish National Orchestra. In 1991/92, ADC granted £81,000 to the Scottish Arts Council. Support was given to Scotland's Blood Transfusion Service. Along with other Scottish local authorities, the council tended to support those national organisations which were recommended by COSLA.

The Common Good Fund was used as the main source of grant-giving. The fund had its origins in a grant made to the city by Robert the Bruce in 1319. In April 1976 there was £2.8m in the fund. Much of the fund's assets were in land, and the oil boom led to a rapid increase in the value of these land holdings. Careful management saw the value of the fund grow to more than £32m in the mid-1990s, and careful husbandry still allowed expenditure on a wide range of worthy causes. In 1975/76, over £3,000 was spent on entertainment for the elderly and disabled, an item which the council strove to fund every year. In the same year, £6,518 was spent on the civic car and £44 on installing lord provost's lamps. In 1979, at a cost of about £300, Grampian Television was allowed free use of the Beach ballroom as a collection centre for a Christmas toy appeal. The fund was also used to support civic hospitality and receptions. These two items cost a little over £400,000 in 1991/92.

Civic hospitality was offered to a wide range of organisations and individuals. These included local organisations whose effort and achievement was being recognised, and visiting officials or politicians from other countries. In 1993, ADC hosted a dinner as part of the celebrations for the 125th anniversary of the founding of the Trades Council. ADC also organised the celebrations for Union Street's 200th birthday. There was disagreement over the most appropriate date, but eventually one was chosen in July 1994. The £40,000 party bill was met from the Common Good Fund: an estimated 100,000 people took part in the celebrations – The Guinness Book of Records reckoned this to be the world's largest ever street party, the previous best having been at Buffalo, New York in 1991 to celebrate the birthdays of the USA and Canada, when a mere 75,000 turned up.

The following year the council worked with the Aberdeen branch of the Royal British Legion to commemorate the 50th anniversaries of the ending of the Second World War in Europe and in the Far East. The parade along Union Street included veterans of the war, ex-servicemen and women and council members. Representatives from Gomel and Regensburg attended the service of celebration at the Castlegate. There were two packed concerts of wartime music and songs in the Music Hall followed by a fireworks display.

There was always a huge volume of requests for grant assistance and civic hospitality. Simply processing them all was a massive task. The council minutes showed that, in 1984/85, the list of applicants for grants ran to nearly three pages of small type. In 1993/94, there were two pages of applications for civic hospitality and four for grant assistance. The applicants varied so much that it was very difficult to prioritise one over another. In 1993, the council reviewed its policy towards civic hospitality. It approved six categories of applicant which would be considered eligible for consideration in the future: local voluntary groups in recognition of their services to the community; local citizens who had made some major achievement or who had made a significant contribution to public service; local groups or branches of national bodies on major anniversaries; royal and other distinguished visitors and 'one off' events such as Armistice Day; major national and international conferences which brought benefit to the city; and special events, for example high profile sporting or recreational events.

Advocacy and Campaigning

The ADC was the only body elected to represent the views of Aberdeen citizens. Part of the council's role was to represent Aberdeen's views and interests not only within the north east but also throughout Scotland, in the UK, and sometimes in international forums. It took part in campaigns when it considered that this would be the best way to promote the interests of the citizens.

In 1979, the ADC endorsed a COSLA recommendation that local authority premises should not be made available to organisations promoting racialism. On a number of occasions from the late 1970s to the mid-1990s opposition was expressed to government spending cuts. Councillors Haston, Rae and Sewel were authorised to attend a demonstration organised by the STUC in Glasgow in March 1980.

In March 1985, the council declared its support for Labour's Green Paper on devolution, the first occasion when the so-called 'Tartan Tax' made its appearance. The council continued to support constitutional change for Scotland by supporting the campaign for a Scottish Assembly. In the early 1990s, Councillor Wyness represented ADC on the broadly based Scottish Constitutional Convention which was set up to bring forward consensus proposals for a Scottish Parliament.

After the Piper Alpha disaster, the council expressed its support for those who were calling for action to be taken against the oil companies involved. Backing was given to the Scottish Association for Public Transport, and Councillors Clevitt and Webster were authorised to attend the body's AGM in 1985. Throughout the life of the District Council, concern was expressed at the high level of unemployment, and efforts were made to help the unemployed. In 1985, unemployed people were offered concessions similar to those already available to pensioners and students for productions at His Majesty's Theatre. The council campaigned with others in support of the electrification of the railway line to Edinburgh. In 1991, it appeared that the RGIT might miss out on the government's extension of full university status to former polytechnic and central institutions. ADC backed the successful campaign which saw RGIT become The Robert Gordon University, Aberdeen's second university. In 1993, the council donated £138.79p to the Grampian Senior Citizen's Forum to help with the costs of hiring the Music Hall for a rally against the extension of VAT to fuel. It also opposed the changes which the government made to tourism support in 1994, which saw the city lose its Tourist Board.

The council campaigned on international issues. It supported the campaign to end apartheid in South Africa, by refusing to buy South African goods, and it fought plans to let groups from that country participate in the International Youth Festival. As previously mentioned (p. 150), it also gave the highest honour it could to Nelson Mandela and Mikhail Gorbechev by awarding them the Freedom of the City; Gorbachev gave the first Aberdeen Peace Lecture when he visited the city

The second Gorbachev Peace Lecture acknowledged the contribution made by the United Nations and marked the UN's 50th birthday. Councillor Savidge described the anniversary as 'a landmark in the UN's history'. Lord Provost Wyness, Councillor Savidge and Chief Executive Anne Mearns went to the UN building in Paris to invite the former Secretary General to deliver the lecture. Javier Perez de Cuellar expressed his honour at the invitation and delivered his lecture in 1996. The council planted commemorative roses purchased from United Nations International Children's Education Fund (UNICEF) at the Westburn Tennis Centre and the Denburn car park.

Aberdeen declared itself a 'nuclear free city'. It donated £250 to the Scottish Association of Nuclear Free Zones to help promote the main issues and it joined the international Association of Nuclear Free Authorities. The ending of the Cold War and the break-up of the Soviet Union seemed to remove the threat of a major confrontation between the 'super powers'. However, it didn't remove the threat that nuclear weapons might be used some day. The problem of 'proliferation' and the spread of nuclear capability moved up the agenda. So too did the issues of making nuclear waste relatively safe and storing it. There was plenty for the Association to do! The council expressed its opposition to the French government's decision to resume the testing of nuclear weapons in Muraroa. Councillor Savidge chaired the association in 1995.

Rewarding Citizenship

The District Council took its campaigning and advocacy role very seriously. As the democratically elected 'voice of the people' they believed that they could make a valuable contribution to the quality of life for each and every citizen. But they also recognised that many valuable contributions were made each year by the citizens themselves. These contributions did not go unnoticed. A number of annual awards were sponsored by the council. The Celebrating Age Award, for example, recognised the contribution made by an elderly person towards the welfare of other elderly citizens in the community, whilst the Marion Peterson Award was awarded to a disabled person for their contribution towards the well-being of other disabled people. The awards included a cash prize for the winners to donate to the charities of their choice. The prestigious Common Good Award was made annually to the group or citizen who contributed most to the improvement of facilities for the disabled in the city.

11: The Wider Public Sector in Aberdeen

A number of agencies provided public services besides the ADC. The GRC was a major provider of local authority services. These included the costly education, roads and social work services, water and sewerage, and police and fire. A number of non-elected bodies provided public services, notably in health care, tourism, economic development and the environment. Reforms of the 1990s established some of these as limited companies. The voluntary sector also provided a range of public services and gave citizens opportunities to contribute to society by volunteering. Most voluntary sector service delivery was in social services and was local authority funded.

Grampian Regional Council

In the Wheatley system the regions provided the upper tier and the 'strategic' services. Many of these were vital to the quality of life of Aberdonians. The city had about half of the region's population, the rest were distributed through the towns and rural areas of Kincardine and Deeside, Gordon, Banff and Buchan, and Moray. The regional council had to deliver services on an equitable basis for the whole area, so the GRC provided infrastructure through its roads, water and sewerage and transport responsibilities. It provided social work and education, two of the core services of the welfare state. It also looked after the coast and a number of harbours, and provided 'public protection' through the police force and fire brigade, though the police in particular were operationally autonomous and largely outwith the realm of local politics.

Compared with ADC, the GRC was a huge organisation. It employed more than 24,000 people and controlled a budget of nearly £520m in 1994/95. Within other regions, the GRC was viewed as a well-run organisation which achieved high standards. Its schools and community care planning were among the best in Scotland. It was an innovator in economic development, and it was well managed, winning a prestigious UK award for its quality management system.

Education

Education had the largest budget and staff of any local service. Control of education passed from the corporation to the GRC in 1975, though this did not greatly affect the day to day work of the schools. At this time the service included schools, technical colleges, adult education and a range of specialist services. It was an exciting time, particularly in the schools system. Comprehensive schooling, which became very successful in Scotland, was establishing firm roots.

A comprehensive approach to schooling was suggested to Scottish Secretary Tom Johnston by his Advisory Committee in 1947. Two decades later the Labour government legislated to introduce this approach throughout Britain. In Scotland there was strong consensus support for the comprehensive principle across the political parties. Many rural schools were effectively comprehensive before the official change in policy took place.

The corporation was enthusiastic in pushing for comprehensive reform. In the early 1960s, some time before the Scottish Office issued its 'Circular 600' to implement the reform, the issues were placed on the policy agenda for the city's schools. The removal of the Academy from its cramped city premises in Schoolhill and Belmont Street to a new and better site at Hazlehead provided the opportunity to abandon the traditional, socially-divisive post-primary selection of pupils in favour of a comprehensive approach. Hazlehead was primarily an area of private housing but only five minutes' walk away lay the council house estates of Mastrick and Summerhill. A comprehensive approach would ensure that the school served both areas. Councillor Hughes was the prime mover in this change and councillors Lamond, Middleton and Smith provided strong support.

In 1975, education became the responsibility of Grampian Regional Council. One of the most pressing tasks for the new council was to integrate and harmonise educational systems on a region-wide basis. In the Aberdeen area, this meant bringing together the education systems inherited from the corporation and the adjacent county councils. However, other pressures faced the new education authority: the recent introduction of comprehensive education and the unique pressures on the system which resulted from the relocation of the oil industry to the city.

As the majority of oil-related development during the 1970s took place outwith the city centre, in areas such as Bridge of Don and Dyce and elsewhere in the region, this meant that a degree of priority was given to capital expenditure on new educational facilities in the developing areas. In response to the closure of a number of city schools, including the secondary school at Summerhill, it was sometimes suggested that the Conservative-led regional Council was underfunding education in the city. The GRC's response was that oil-related development had simply exacerbated a nation-wide trend for falling school rolls, particularly in city centre areas, and that it had the responsibility to prioritise needs across the whole Grampian area.

The GRC inherited and built on comprehensive reform in education. It successfully introduced a wide range of reforms over the next two decades. The larger ones were driven by the Scottish Office but there were many regional innovations. Among these changes were the introduction of Standard Grade, the 5–14 curriculum, the modernisation of special needs education, and a new approach to school management. New schools were built and old ones refurbished to meet the needs of the growing population.

In the 1980s, the Parent's Charter offered parents a degree of choice over where to send their children for schooling. Between 1982 and 1996 there were 280,000 placing requests across Scotland and 90% were granted. This development led to some schools attracting pupils while schools which were perceived to be less successful lost out. In the early 1990s comparative data on school 'performance' began to be published in controversial 'league tables' by the Scottish Office. Schools were compared on issues such as examination results. This was intended to introduce a degree of competition between schools. It was believed that those lower in the tables would work hard to catch up with the best, and the tables were intended to help parents to choose between schools. Critics argued that the published data were not the most important things about schools, and that at best the tables reflected past performance. They worried that these changes would weaken the comprehensive system.

On both sides of the border the government encouraged schools to 'opt out' of the local authority systems and seek grant maintained status. This policy failed to meet its targets in England and Wales and was a flop north of the border. Only two Scottish schools, a small highland secondary and a primary near Stirling, chose this route. In 1992, legislation removed further education colleges from local authority control very much against the wishes of the local authorities.

A partnership of the regional councils and the Scottish Office developed a distinctive approach to school management. Under Devolved School Management (DSM) the school head became a manager, responsible for decisions affecting more than 80% of the school's budget. The School Board played an advisory role, in the 77% of Aberdeen's secondary schools and 52% of primaries which had one. More than 400 people took part in advisory and consultative procedures as members of school boards in the city.

Before DSM management decisions were handled in the GRC building at Woodhill House and inevitably senior staff there were not always closely in touch with what was happening in the classroom. The DSM reforms were consensually supported, and were underway, when the 1995/96 reforms passed responsibility for education to the new Aberdeen City Council. A consequence of DSM was that councils had to re-think the role which they played in education management.

Education was affected by and responded to the pressures of oil. A large population of working age meant lots of children who needed school places. New and refurbished schools were provided for the growing population centres in Bridge of Don and elsewhere. In the local areas of Aberdeen where the school age population was in decline some rationalisation of facilities took place. A French school was set up in the grounds of Aberdeen Grammar School, and American and Dutch schools appeared in Cults. The oil industry provided teachers with lots of local opportunities and material to enrich the curriculum.

In 1975, the GRC also assumed responsibility for further education colleges in the city. An acute lack of accommodation for the city's Technical College and College of Commerce proved to be a major problem which was later highlighted when the College of Commerce building in Holburn Street was declared to be structurally unsafe. A carefully managed exercise by the GRC saw the college relocate to sites in the Bridge of Don, formerly occupied by the army and Bridge of Don Academy.

In 1993/94, regional and island councils spent £2.6bn on education. This funded schools, paid for adult and community education, special needs provision, and a range of specialist services. £1.7bn was spent directly on primary and secondary schools and 75% of this went on the salaries of teachers and other staff.

The GRC had an education budget of about £250m, and employed some 5,000 teachers. Citizen's charter data showed the service cost to be £2,300 per pre-school place, £1,500 per primary pupil and £2,500 per secondary pupil. When the new.City Council resumed the education role it had responsibility for 66 infant and primary schools, twelve secondaries, and employed 2,500 teachers. There were about 35,000 children of school age in the city. The education budget for 1996/97 stood at £90m, having taken a cut of 6.8% from the level the council considered necessary because of the very tight budget provided by the Scottish Office. One of the first tasks of the city's newly appointed Director of Education was to explain the budget cuts to a packed meeting of concerned parents at St Machar Academy. Councillor Wyness convened the new Education Committee.

Social Work

The social work service was transformed by legislation in 1968. As a result this was one of the fastest growing local government services when it was passed over from the corporation to the GRC in 1975. The 1968 Act gave councils a general duty to promote the social welfare of all citizens, not simply those in the 'vulnerable' categories. This led to the evolution of a complex set of services and a highly professional social work team. Services were provided for children, adults, people with disabilities, the elderly, people with mental health problems, cases of drug/alcohol abuse, and for a host of other issues. Facilities were provided in people's homes, residential homes, prisons, and within social work and community premises. The Social Work Department provided services for the criminal justice system, these being mostly funded by the Scottish Office. In 1994/95, the GRC spent £86m net on all its social work services across the region. An estimated £28m of this was spent in the city. The Social Work Department had an estimated 2,500 staff in the city, more than 940 of whom were part-time home care workers.

Seven child care teams covered the city. They provided a comprehensive service to children and families, including child protection, counselling and supervision. Various services were provided for young children including four family centres and two pre-school day centres. Six children's homes and fostering and adoption services supported children in care. The department's home-finding team supported 65 foster carers and 38 adoptive families.

Scotland developed an innovative Children's Hearings system which aimed to keep matters involving children out of the courts. This was introduced in 1971. The Social Work Department worked closely with the volunteer children's panels and the Reporter. In 1992 there were more than 2,700 referrals to the Children's Panels in the region. During the late 1980s and 1990s more emphasis was placed on recognising and respecting children's rights. The Social Work Department was closely involved in this, but the issues had the potential to affect many aspects of local government. The 1995 Children's Act provided the new councils with the opportunity to think strategically about all of their services for children. In 1994/95, GRC spent about £18.6m on social work services for children.

A range of services helped citizens who had disabilities. Five residential projects provided more than 60 places for permanent and respite care accommodation for adults with learning difficulties. The demand for these services was very high. Three large day centres supported adults with learning difficulties and one was available for people with physical disabilities.

As society changed and there were more elderly people living longer lives, social work priorities changed. Much more attention was paid to the needs of the elderly. About 45% of the GRC budget was spent on elderly people in 1994/95. There were ten local authority residential homes in the city, one of which had a separate dementia unit. There were six day care centres, three in the north and three in the south of the city. Day care was also provided three days a week in the common rooms of sheltered housing at Dyce and Bridge of Don.

The Wheatley Report recognised that: 'People in need cannot be dealt with in the mass: they have to be considered as individuals.' Social workers were routinely involved in assessing the needs of individuals and developing appropriate responses. The Care in the Community reforms in 1993 took this focus to new levels. Following the Community Care Act, the GRC adopted a policy of enabling rather than directly providing services. Extensive partnerships were forged with the voluntary sector and the Health Services to focus on the resettlement of people from long term psychiatric and mental handicap hospitals. The independent Accounts Commission argued that the policy was seriously underfunded in Scotland, a view shared by the regional councils.

A central aim was to get individuals out of institutional care and back into the community, with adequate support. The social work departments planned community care along with the health trusts, district council housing officials and the voluntary sector. The Grampian Health Board provided strategic planning for the Health Service. The joint planning arrangements in Grampian were considered to be amongst the best in the country.

In 1994/95, the GRC Social Work Department carried out over 12,000 community care assessments and reviews. Some 10,300 received so-called 'standard' assessments, which was a bit of a misnomer because often these individuals had higher levels of need. And some 14,400 people received services.

The number of highly specialised services and groups of staff, and the existence of specialist facilities – often based in the city but serving the whole region – made social work a very difficult service to transfer to the new councils in 1996. But the changeover did present some major opportunities. Social Work and Housing became part of the same council making it possible to improve the co-ordination between them, and the new framework made it possible to think strategically about all the services, including social work, which the new City Council provided for children and young people. Similarly it became a little easier to plan a strategy for providing services for the elderly population.

In the 1995/96 changeover, the government was accused of trying to downgrade the importance of social work. The government argued that it was merely trying to give councils more flexibility. The new councils were not required to set up a special social work committee, and while they had to have a Chief Social Work Officer, they did not have to have a director for the service.

The new City Council stuck with tradition on organisational issues. It set up a Social Work Committee and appointed a director; Councillor Ironside convened the new committee.

Police and Fire

The 1975 reforms placed these protective services in regional government with some joint arrangements covering the Highlands and Islands, and Lothian and Borders. Grampian Police and the Grampian Fire Brigade serviced the city and the whole Grampian area. The police force and the fire brigade reported to the GRC's Public Protection Committee along with Consumer Protection and the Citizen's Advice Bureau. The 1996 reforms changed local government but left the police and the brigade in their existing structure. After this these services were overseen by joint boards of the three new councils in the north east.

The relationship between the police and local government was unique. The council did not and could not interfere in operational matters. The Chief Constable was not answerable to the council in the way that the main service directors were. Policing was in part a national service and in part local. This was reflected in the funding arrangements which were shared between the Scottish Office and the regional councils. Scottish Office specific grants met 51% of the costs. Good co-operation between regional forces was a part of the Scottish set up. As criminal activities became more international – the drugs trade and computer fraud, for example – mechanisms were established to support co-operation across national boundaries.

Life was varied but rarely slack for Grampian Police. In 1994/95, nearly 48,600 crimes were recorded, with a 'clear up rate' of 35%. 'Cleared up' didn't necessarily mean that someone had been arrested. In the strange world of management information in the 1990s, the Scottish Office definition meant that one or more offenders was 'apprehended, cited, warned, or traced' for the crime. Some crimes were easier to clear up than others. The clear up rates for violent crimes, housebreaking and car crime were 72%, 15% and 18% respectively. The particular mix of crimes in the north east was probably the main factor behind the apparently low overall clear up rate.

The Grampian Police budget for 1994/95 was some £24m after Police Grant. There were 1,219 officers and cadets (full time equivalent) working throughout the region, about two per 1,000 of the population. The uniformed police were supported by non-uniformed 'civilian' staff. The force's headquarters was in Queen Street, very close to the Town House. The policing of the city was co-ordinated from there and from Bucksburn. In the late 1980s and 1990s efforts were made to 'civilianise' aspects of the force's work which did not require police expertise or training, partly as a cost-cutting measure.

In the 1980s, the community became the focus of most policing. Communities were involved in a variety of initiatives like Neighbourhood Watch schemes. And much more effort was put into crime prevention and trying to combat the drugs menace. This made education and information very important. The police worked closely with the education and social work services.

The 'Police Box' scheme was started by the outgoing GRC and continued by the new City Council. The depute headteacher of Mile-End School was seconded to Grampian Police. She worked with the Police Community Involvement Department to produce the Police Box, a pack of curriculum and staff development materials. The pack had materials which were appropriate for any point of primary or secondary schools, helping children and young people to deal with issues like bullying, drugs and substance abuse. By the end of the GRC in 1996, the Police Box was in use in 280 of the region's 312 primaries and secondaries, and it was attracting interest from education authorities throughout Britain.

The fire brigade was much more a local government service, and the Firemaster a local government servant. Yet the brigade was also different from most other regional services. The professional ethos, the high requirement for physical fitness, the training to deal with and survive situations of great danger, the uniform, the almost military 'command and control' culture, and the specialised vehicles and buildings all helped to set the service apart. In 1992/93, the Grampian Fire Brigade responded to 7,424 calls. In 1994, it had 343 fire officers, and 465 retained fire-fighters (full-time equivalents). It was also encouraging women and people from the minority ethnic communities to apply to join. The 1994/95 budget for the whole region was over £14m.

The oil industry and the nature of its products raised unique issues for the brigade. There was a large and continuous demand for training in offshore survival and in fire safety. The brigade piloted offshore safety training with the RGIT in 1980, and the brigade's own training centre was opened at Portlethen in

1993. New stations were opened at Altens and Dyce to complement North Anderson Drive and the long-serving facility at King Street.

Paradoxically oil developments also reduced some fire risks. When the harbour was home to a fleet of small fishing boats, the brigade was constantly being called out to deal with generally small incidents. The oil supply ships which took over the modernised port were high tech vessels, with specialised fire fighting equipment and trained crews. Incidents were few, releasing the brigade for other activities.

In the 1980s, attention turned to fire prevention and educating the public about the risks; the brigade worked closely with the education department. Each of the stations had a fire prevention team, and officers visited schools throughout the region. The brigade and the Education Department supported a competition to find the best poster for the campaign to get smoke detectors fitted in homes. In 1992, pupils in Primary 7 were introduced to techniques for dealing safely with everyday dangers.

Fire safety work also involved inspecting buildings and certain types of buildings required fire certificates and annual inspections. In 1994/95, the brigade inspected 601 factories, 1979 offices and 609 hotels and guest houses.

Scotland had a national system of 'response times'. The brigade was expected to attend incidents within a set time of being called. In the GRC area, the brigade had to confront the problems of both urban congestion and rural isolation; in 1994/95 it achieved the main standards in more than 95% of cases, and in 93% in remote rural areas.

Non-Elected Bodies

Elected local authorities delivered key public services throughout the twentieth century, but there were always some services which were delivered by other bodies. Some issues like Children's Panels were best kept out of the political domain. The apparent proliferation of non-elected bodies became a matter of controversy in the 1990s.

It was widely believed in local government that councils were being weakened by central government policies. Some of these changes seemed to centralise control at the expense of councils; the incorporation of further education colleges, for example. In other cases the government wanted service delivery to be decentralised but decided not to make the service a local authority responsibility. Local authorities felt that they were being marginalised.

Up to the 1980s local government expected to be part of the partnership by being represented on the boards of management of non-elected bodies. This changed in the 1980s. The government favoured decision-making processes based on private sector models. The non-elected bodies were set up as executive rather than representative bodies, and they were sometimes given the legal status of limited companies. This meant that any councillor who was asked to join the board was invited as a private individual and not to represent his or her council. Sometimes, as with the local enterprise companies, the government preferred to have people from the business sector in a majority on management boards. Many councillors felt that they had been chucked out and the door had then been slammed shut! Those who found themselves on the company boards of new bodies often found it a difficult and uncomfortable experience. There were allegations that the Scottish Secretary made more appointments to non-elected bodies than the citizens were able to elect as councillors, and that the 'non-elected state' spent more public money than local authorities!

There were also changes in accountability. Members of Parliament who raised questions in Westminster were likely to be told by the Scottish Office that the object of their enquiry was an independent body and that the issue should be taken up direct. At times, MPs reported that they were unable to get the same quality of information from the non-elected bodies as they would previously have got in the parliamentary replies drafted by civil servants. Those non-elected bodies which were companies threw a 'commercial in confidence' screen round their decision-making. Some elected politicians asked whether this was appropriate when the decisions were about how to spend public money.

There seemed to be a lot of non-elected bodies, some of them adopting a high profile through their marketing campaigns. Many of them operated in areas of interest to local government and some took powers directly from local councils. The most controversial of all were the three public Water Authorities set up at the same time as the 1995/6 local government reform. The PWAs were set up to run the water and sewerage service, previously a local government responsibility. In a similar way, the Scottish Children's Reporter Administration and the new body for the valuation service simply took functions away from local councils.

Scottish Homes was the government's main housing agency. Local councils worked with it but it was often a difficult experience, particularly as the councils' housing role was tightly restricted. Scottish Natural Heritage was established, combining the Countryside Commission and the Nature Conservancy Council. The Scottish Environmental Protection Agency was formed and took away roles from district councils relating to air and water pollution.

In 1991, Scottish Enterprise (SE) took over the functions of the former Scottish Development Agency (SDA) and the Manpower Services Commission (MSC) in most of Scotland, including the north east. The local authorities had not always seen eye to eye with the SDA and the MSC but at least they felt part of their representative and advisory structures. By contrast SE was set up as a company, with a small executive board two thirds of whom were drawn from the private sector. SE was required to decentralise its operations to thirteen local enterprise companies. Grampian Enterprise Limited (GEL) was SE's arm in the north east. The local companies were also set up to be executive and had two thirds of their board drawn from the local private sector. The local authorities didn't like this arrangement and were critical of the private sector way of working.

They generally favoured a stronger local focus than was previously provided by the SDA and MSC, but felt that this would be better achieved through representative bodies in which the local authorities could be partners. After some early difficulties over planning procedures, ADC quickly established an effective relationship with GEL and the two bodies collaborated on a number of partnership ventures. They both supported the successful City Centre Partnership.

The NHS was transformed by creating an internal market with 'purchasers' and 'providers'. The local authorities had encountered this type of change in CCT, and many in local councils didn't believe that commercial principles should drive health care. Grampian Health Board provided strategic leadership and planning, and the new health system was administered by local trusts which were given a lot of managerial autonomy. Aberdeen had two: the Aberdeen Royal Hospitals NHS Trust and Grampian Healthcare. These were large organisations – the Aberdeen Royal Hospitals Trust had more than 4,000 employees. The trusts came together with ADC's Housing Department, the GRC Social Work Department, and the voluntary sector for the purpose of planning Care in the Community.

Tourism was an important industry and there was wide agreement that its importance would grow as the level of employment in the oil sector fell. In 1996 control of tourism passed to regional appointed boards. Responsibility for public funding for tourism in Aberdeen lay with the Aberdeen and Grampian Tourist Board. There were mixed feelings about this change. On the one hand it made sense to market some aspects of the north east together and avoid lots of smaller competitive tourist promotions which might just confuse the market. On the other hand Aberdeen had some of the key tourist attractions, the larger festivals, many good hotels and the airport, main regional railway station and port. The council was concerned that these unique facilities and attractions would be submerged and hidden in the wider efforts of a region-wide agency. On balance it opposed the change.

In 1996, faced with severe budgetary difficulties, many councils cut their planned contributions to the new tourist boards. In the north east there was controversy as the board and its supporters complained that the new councils were starving an essential industry of the cash needed for its promotion. It was claimed that this would lead to fewer tourists visiting and fewer jobs in the industry.

The Voluntary Sector

The voluntary sector wasn't elected either but neither was it entirely dependent on public finance for its existence. Voluntary organisations were based on volunteer efforts, fund-raising and charitable activities. When they received public money it was usually for a specific purpose. During the 1990s local authority funding was increasingly through contracts which employed the voluntary body to deliver a specific service. The service role created a tension between some councils and some voluntary bodies. At times the voluntary sector appeared as a competitor with lower costs because wages were relatively poor. In this situation the voluntary sector appeared to pose a threat to council employees.

The voluntary sector in Aberdeen was active and well-organised. In most of the service-providing organisations levels of pay were the same as in local government, which meant there was no direct threat that the council might be 'undercut.' In the city the sector was co-ordinated by the Grampian Forum of Voluntary Organisation. In Aberdeen, Voluntary Services Aberdeen (VSA) provided a number of social services, including housing, support for people with dementia, and holiday schemes for people on low incomes. ADC had a good relationship with Aberdeen's voluntary sector: when the VSA celebrated its 125th anniversary in 1995, it donated £25,000 to kick-start its fund-raising appeal. Lord Provost Wyness said: 'For the past 125 years, VSA has given a helping hand and a shoulder to lean on for so many people in this city. It is the least the council can do to show its appreciation and gratitude.'

12: Beyond 1996 – New Approaches to City Governance

In 1994 parliament passed legislation to scrap the two-tier system and replace it with a network of all-purpose councils. Unlike the Wheatley changes these reforms lacked consensus support. The opposition parties expressed the view that the shape of local government should be for a Scottish parliament to decide. Local authorities declined to co-operate with the government's plans until the legislation was approved by Westminster. There was widespread suspicion of the government's motives and widespread concern that the change had not been properly costed by the Scottish Office.

The councils on mainland Scotland were reduced in number from 62 to 29, making Scotland one of the least-governed countries anywhere in the advanced world, at least in terms of democratically elected institutions. The number of councillors was reduced to 1,161 for the whole of the country. In the north east, the GRC and the five district councils were wound up and replaced by Aberdeen City Council, Aberdeenshire Council and Moray Council.

The scope of local government was reduced. Water and sewerage services were removed to three regional non-elected boards. The Children's Reporter service was passed over to a national appointed body based in Edinburgh. The police and fire services remained in local government, but were overseen by joint boards, creating a very detached relationship with individual councils.

On 29 March 1996, Lord Provost Wyness delivered a valedictory speech to mark the last meeting of the City of Aberdeen District Council. He observed that 'it could be said to be a sad day as we leave behind twenty-one years of dedicated effort by Elected Members and Officials alike.' He continued by noting that, 'while this occasion is certainly tinged with some regret, as I look back over the years of this council I feel nothing but deep pride in what we have managed to achieve.' He wished the new Aberdeen City Council 'every success in its endeavours.'

And in many ways the much-criticised reform delivered to Aberdeen what ADC had long advocated – all-purpose local government with one fifty-member council responsible for all local authority services in the city. The change was underfunded and the cities did particularly badly out of a very tight Scottish Office budgetary settlement. The new Aberdeen City Council was scarcely up and running when the Local Government Boundary Commission proposed further

179

reducing the number of elected councillors to 43 for the next scheduled elections in 1999.

Making the change work was a very difficult challenge. There was only a sixteen-month period between the passing of the legislation in parliament and the first day of business in April 1996. The city-focused services of the GRC and the old district had to be put together. The very different organisational and political cultures of the GRC and the city district had somehow to be combined in a shape more appropriate to the new age of local government. Thousands of staff had to be 'matched' to posts and transferred with all of the human fears and anxieties raised by that kind of procedure. There was scarcely time for all the interviews! Buildings and other assets had to be transferred to the new council. Delicate negotiations were held with neighbouring authorities over specialised assets and functions which could not easily be split, and so had to be shared.

The senior officials and the councillors were simply rushed off their feet! Perhaps 1995 and early 1996 was the most challenging period ever in the history of local government. So busy were the leaders in trying to manage strategic change that sometimes day-to-day issues were overlooked and inevitably in some parts of the organisation staff morale suffered. Not every staff member ended up with the job of their preference, but the process was largely managed on time, and with no compulsory redundancies. Some appointments continued into April and May after the new City Council had fully taken over the reins.

Despite all these difficulties there was unparalleled excitement at senior levels in the Town House. The 'shadow elections' in 1995 produced a Labour administration, and the new Labour group broke with tradition by voting women into the two key leadership positions: Councillor Margaret Farquhar became lord provost, and Councillor Margaret Smith became convener of the Policy Committee, and therefore Leader of the Council. Douglas Paterson was appointed as the new Chief Executive.

This wasn't the first time that women had been prominent in the leadership of the council. The previous year Councillor Margaret Farquhar had taken over as Leader from Councillor Paine. Chief Executive Anne Mearns and her depute, the late Ann Hughes, were ADC's two most senior officials. The difference in 1996 was the decision of the Labour group to elect two women to the key political positions.

In the key area of finance 1996 could not have been more unlike 1975. In 1996, the government was determined to control and reduce public spending. In 1975, growth in public spending was believed to be good for the economy and society. In 1996 the Scottish Office grant to the new City Council was 10% less than councillors believed they needed just to maintain the existing level of service. They tried to protect education but that meant harsher cuts in other services. And the settlement was announced by the Scottish Office far too late in the day for the City Council to approach 'the cuts' with any clear strategy.

The new leadership set to the daunting task of putting all the necessary changes in place; but they also made a courageous and radical attempt to re-think some of the fundamental issues of local government and to involve the citizens in the thinking process. Wide consultations were held on the values and aspirations which the new council should have, and on how it should approach the statutory requirement to draw up a scheme of 'decentralisation'. The city had long argued for its own all-purpose council and now the leaders had the opportunity to show the benefits that the new approach could bring.

New Approaches

The two-tier system had caused some confusion where responsibilities were shared as in leisure and recreation and industrial development. And it had separated services which needed to be planned together if they were to be effective, such as housing and social work. Now all services were under one roof, overseen by one set of councillors and one management team.

This set-up seemed likely to be better understood by the public and promised to improve democratic accountability. No longer would citizens be confused over which councillor they should take up an issue with; and no longer would one tier be able to blame the other when things didn't go to plan. These were the likely benefits of a simple change of structure which could be harnessed anywhere in the country.

The new City Council wanted to go further and embrace aspects of participative democracy. The law required it to consider how best to decentralise. The feeling in the Town House was that improving access and involving citizens in decision-making was more important than thinking about the geography of service delivery or re-drawing lines on maps. The Council entered into a major consultation exercise.

At the end of this it felt able to set out key principles which would guide its operations in ways which matched the feedback received. The new City Council adopted six key principles: Quality, Partnership, Accountability, Economy, Equality and Coherence. It promised to do what it could to increase the involvement of the public and to promote a multi-agency approach to tackling issues. The council agreed a new Mission Statement which concluded: 'Aberdeen City Council will be led by its elected members, driven by its officers, supported by and supportive of its staff and accountable to its community.'

The Mission and supporting principles were to inform and co-ordinate the work of all service committees. The approach taken to access and participation led to a new Community Development Department being set up. It was to take the lead on issues which required a multi-disciplinary or corporate response. These were age-related, like children's issues, issue-focused, like crime, and area based. Councillor June Lamond convened this key committee.

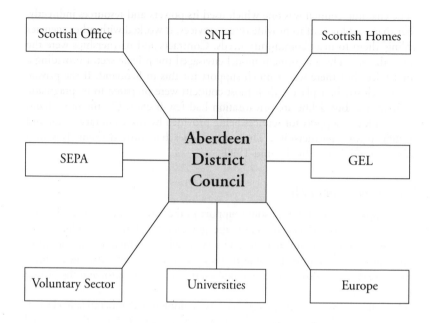

Governance – a simplified model

A Choice of Models

The new City Council was faced with competing models for designing its role. The 1980s and early 1990s seemed to breed a suspicion of 'big government' whether at local or national level. Taxpayers were believed to be reluctant to fund the costs of government, and these seemed to be international trends. Within the European Union the so-called 'convergence criteria', adopted at Maastricht as the basis for monetary union, required a tight grip on public spending. There was simply no way back to the all-powerful model of 'municipal' city councils which existed early in the twentieth century. Even Wheatley's vision of a growing local government sector seemed very unlikely.

An Enabling Council?

The Conservative government favoured councils adopting an 'enabling' role. The government's low standing in Scotland would have been enough to kill off this idea had it not been that the new approach was already clearly a part of key services like housing and community care. And some aspects of enabling enjoyed support across the political spectrum.

The enabling council was one which used its powers and resources indirectly. Rather than employ staff to provide direct services, it worked with other agencies 'enabling' them to meet community needs. Contracts and partnerships were the order of the day. The government model envisaged the private sector providing a lot of services but there wasn't much support for this in Scotland. If the private sector was clearly best-placed, then most councils were prepared to be pragmatic in their choice. But deliberate privatisation had few friends. On the other hand there was a lot of support for services being provided by the voluntary sector and by public–private partnerships. These approaches had proved themselves in a number of service areas by the mid-1990s.

A Governance Approach?

Another approach which found some support in the Town House was to develop the new council as the key player in the governance of the city. This meant examining all of the decision-making and service delivery which was important to the city and its development. Some of these were in the council's own hands. Others were dealt with by non-elected bodies, the voluntary sector and the private sector.

The council was uniquely placed because it alone was democratically elected. It had two main roles. One was to provide quality services as efficiently as it could in its areas of activity. The other was to work in a range of partnerships with the important bodies in the city, and through these to promote a common vision for Aberdeen's future development. This vision had to be negotiated. In this model the council sat at the centre of a web throughout which were distributed all of the agencies whose decisions affected the city. Many of these were local but some were national or even international bodies. The strands of the web had to be turned into strategic links by the council.

In the 1990s, local government was very critical of what it saw as the proliferation of non-elected bodies providing local services. These bodies were criticised as lacking in accountability but also because they were run by Scottish Office appointees. The governance model seemed to offer a way of trying to encourage a large number of agencies to work towards the same ends. The leadership of the City Council would confer some greater legitimacy on other bodies involved in these partnerships.

New Challenges

There were major opportunities and challenges facing many of the council's services: some of these were new. The new councils had a stronger statutory basis for their economic development role. This offered the possibility of a more equal partnership with the local enterprise companies; the City Council had a good relationship with GEL on which to build, and the NESDA tradition augured well where region-wide co-operation was desirable.

The 1995 Children's Act required councils to think more strategically. Plans for children's services were to be drawn up, and the implications for services of the relatively new agenda of children's rights had to be thought through in some detail.

The role of the Education Department was changing as schools became more autonomous. All-purpose councils had an opportunity better to link education with leisure and recreation, and to consider education's contribution to economic development.

Managerial reform was still high on the government's agenda. The Conservatives promised further CCT with almost all of the council affected in some way by 1997. The opposition Labour party hinted at abolishing CCT, but its alternative of a more powerful Accounts Commission able to intervene when it thought services weren't up to scratch wasn't very attractive either. The new City Council had to plan to cope with either scenario.

A New Environment?

The environment for the new councils seemed to be changing, and council reform was a factor in the process. Local government was no longer dominated by a few large regional councils, Strathclyde in particular. The new City Council was one of the larger councils and it had the opportunity to be a more influential player on the Scottish scene.

Once again a Scottish parliament was on the agenda. Three of Scotland's political parties wanted to see a parliament set up and that seemed from the opinion polls to be a popular choice. The most likely option was designed by the Scottish Constitutional Convention. It promised a new positive partnership between councils and the parliament. Powers would be devolved down to councils in a genuine relationship of 'subsidiary'. And the local government role would be constitutionally 'entrenched' to give it some stability. On the other hand there was concern over how remote and bureaucratic an Edinburgh-based parliament might turn out to be.

A Europe of the Regions?

The European Union was growing in importance. Some thought that as it grew Westminster's star would fade. Europe's role as lawmaker increasingly influenced local authorities and what they were expected to do. Maastricht opened education, the largest service, to more European influence. The new City Council looked likely to have to take a closer interest in Europe than the previous district council. It had the opportunity to seek influence on its own, in partnership with neighbouring councils, and through COSLA.

Europe was never a major source of funds for Aberdeen. The city's relative prosperity on the key indicators made it ineligible for most of the regional policy funds. In any case these were up for review. The enlargement of the European Union was likely to mean that the jam would be more thinly spread, and the inclusion of parts of Eastern Europe meant that there would be many areas more deserving of help than even the poorest parts of Scotland.

The new, all-purpose, council began in a mood of cautious optimism. There was some caution mainly for financial reasons. Along with most other councils, the city felt that the restructuring of 1995/96 had been underfunded by the government. It also felt that the budget settlement was too tight and didn't take account of all city's needs. There was a concern that this could undermine the quality of some services and prevent some of the potential of the new local government set up from being realised.

However the prevailing mood was one of optimism. Unitary local government had been restored to Aberdeen. This offered a lot of potential for improving public services by co-ordinating them better. The new local authority would be better placed to offer a lead to other public and private agencies in the city and that had to be good for development.

The fact that there was now only one council responsible for all local services promised to make local government simpler and easier to understand, and that might encourage more citizens to take an interest and get involved in working with their council. More citizen involvement seemed likely to benefit local democracy.

The new council offered the promise that the city would be better represented on the broader stage. Whether dealing with cities in other countries, with issues of international trade, or with other levels of government in Edinburgh or in Brussels, a single, strong local authority would now promote Aberdeen's interest.

Appendix 1

City of Aberdeen District Council Elections[1] and Candidates 1974–1995

Year of Election	Number of seats in Council	Number of candidates standing for election
1974	48	–
1977	48	113
1980	48	98
1984	50	150
1988	52	192
1992	52	166
1995[2]	50	–

[1] Its electoral dominance meant that the Labour Party governed throughout this period except for the brief Conservative–Liberal coalition in 1987/88.

[2] The election in this year was to elect members to serve on the new unitary Aberdeen City Council.

Appendix 2

Table 1: Local Authority House Completions in City of Aberdeen 1976–1985

Year	Local Authority Completions	Number of Homes Completed	Homes Completed by Local Authority, %
1976	1203	1794	67%
1977	911	1572	58%
1978	756	1782	42%
1979	430	1255	34%
1980	518	1167	45%
1981	372	1215	30.5%
1982	134	999	13%
1983	47	1033	5%
1984	117	1271	9%
1985	178	1537	12%

The total number of Local Authority houses completed in the City of Aberdeen for the period 1976–1985 was 4,666.

Table 2: Local Authority House Completions in City of Aberdeen 1986–1993

Years	Total Number of Local Authority Completions
1986–1989	433
1990–1993	262

After 1986, the method of collating housing completion statistics changed.

Appendix 3

City of Aberdeen District Council
Elected Members 1974–1996

Adam, Brian J	1988–1996	Finn, Thomas	1979–1984
Adams, Gordon	1974–1996	Forrest, Alexander J	1984–1992
Alexander, Roland	1977–1984	Fraser, William J	1974–1996
Anderson, Janetta	1977–1996	Gallagher, Richard	1974–1996
Anderson, Robert D I	1977–1980	Gordon, Stewart	1992–1996
Begg, Thomas	1975–1984	Graham, John	1988–1996
Benzie, Violet	1974–1977	Gray, Alistair	1974–1975
Bonney, Norman L	1974–1988	Greenhorn, Philip	1990–1996
Buchan, James	1985–1996	Grimes, Harold C	1974–1980
Buchan, Rita	1992–1996	Hastie, Michael C	1974–1996
Bush, Mark	1974–1978	Haston, Donald B	1977–1980
Christie, Charles B	1974–1977	Hatch, Henry W	1974–1977
Clark, Ronald	1980–1996	Havergal, Margaret E	1984–1988
Clevitt, Cecil H	1984–1996	Henry, Elizabeth H	1977–1986
Clyne, David	1980–1996	Hutcheon, Raymond	1984–1996
Collie, Alexander C	1974–1996	Irons, Maureen	1991–1996
Cooney, Neil	1983–1996	Keay, Agnes G	1974–1984
Cutler, James S	1985–1988	Keith, Douglas W M	1976–1977
Davidson, Dennis C	1980–1984	Keith, George E C	1976–1980
Dean, Katherine	1992–1996	Keith, Irene	1988–1991
Dempsey, John A	1974–1984	Kelly, Elizabeth H	1974–1991
Devine, Charles W	1974–1985	Kelman, John P	1974–1984
Donaldson, James A	1986–1986	Laing, Peter	1986–1988
Donnelly, James A	1992–1996	Lamond, June R	1974–1977
Dow, Alfred	1988–1996	Lennox, Robert S	1974–1980
Dunnett, Nigel G M	1974–1976	Lindsay, Nigel B	1977–1988
Durward, Douglas P	1984–1990	Logan, John	1986–1996
Ewen, John	1974–1990	Lovell, Howard G	1974–1980
Farquhar, Margaret E	1974–1996	Low, James McK	1980–1987
Farquhar, William	1974–1984	Ludbrook, Anne	1985–1989
Fenwick, Barry	1984–1996	MacDonald, Pamela	1992–1996

Mackintosh, Janette M	1974–1976	Rutherford, Brian	1992–1996
MacLean, Allan P	1980–1996	Rutherford, Olive	1986–1996
MacRae, Alan	1988–1992	Savidge, Malcolm K	1980–1996
Magee, Frank	1974–1984	Selbie, Harold	1974–1980
Massie, Charles	1987–1996	Sewel, John B	1974–1984
Massie, Edward S	1984–1996	Sharp, Alice H	1988–1990
McAllister, Margaret	1985–1988	Sheehan, Michael	1984–1988
McCallum, Forbes	1977–1988	Shirran, Anne	1986–1992
McRobb, Alistair	1986–1992	Sim, John	1984–1988
Mearns, Benjamin M	1982–1991	Slater, Ronald	1984–1985
Milne, Nanette	1988–1996	Smith, John F	1974–1977
Milne, Ramsay G	1980–1996	Smith, Margaret E	1988–1996
Morris, Gordon	1977–1980	Stevely, Anne	1988–1996
Morrison, Bernard S	1974–1984	Stevenson, A L	1976–1984
Munro, Kenneth McK	1974–1977	Stewart, John	1974–1977
Mutch, Freda	1974–1988	Stott, Susan	1981–1981
Ness, Sylvia	1992–1996	Third, Gordon	1988–1996
Nikodem, Catherine F	1984–1986	Thomson, Douglas	1974–1982
Paine, Thomas	1980–1996	Thomson, Roy H	1974–1988
Park, George M	1974–1984	Traynor, William	1992–1996
Paterson, Alexander C	1974–1980	Tulloch, William J C	1974–1984
Paul, Neville G	1974–1980	Twine, Frederick E	1974–1980
Pearce, Dorothy	1992–1996	Urquhart, George	1981–1996
Rae, Henry E	1974–1996	Walley, David B	1984–1986
Rattray, Brian	1984–1996	Walls, Andrew F	1974–1984
Ray, Robert D	1992–1996	Watmough, Kenneth	1974–1984
Reid, Scott R	1992–1996	Webster, Ronald	1984–1988
Reith, Shauna	1988–1996	Whyte, George A	1974–1984
Reynolds, John	1986–1996	Whyte, William J	1974–1984
Ritchie, Derek W	1992–1996	Wilson, Margaret F	1974–1980
Robb, John A	1974–1977	Wisely, Jillian	1984–1992
Robertson, Graham	1980–1984	Wood, John	1988–1992
Robertson, Robert A	1980–1988	Woodward Nutt, Peter J	1980–1985
Rose, George	1974–1980	Wyness, James	1980–1996